Neither Here nor There

D1725054

Neither Here nor There
The Many Voices of Liminality

edited by
Timothy Carson

foreword by
Barbara Brown Taylor

Ⓛ
The Lutterworth Press

The Lutterworth Press
P.O. Box 60
Cambridge
CB1 2NT
United Kingdom

www.lutterworth.com
publishing@lutterworth.com

PB ISBN: 978 0 7188 9543 3
PDF ISBN: 978 0 7188 4787 6
ePub ISBN: 978 0 7188 4788 3
Kindle ISBN: 978 0 7188 4789 0

British Library Cataloguing in Publication Data
A record is available from the British Library

First published by The Lutterworth Press, 2019

Jesus, on whom be peace, said
This world is a bridge.
Pass over it but do not build your dwelling there.

Inscribed in Persian on Buland Darwaza,
the main gateway to the palace at Fatehpur Sikri, south of Delhi, India,
by the Moghul emperor Akbar I in 1601.

Table of Contents

Contributors

Joshua Boettiger is a rabbi who serves Emek Shalom in Ashland, Oregon, U.S., and is a teacher of Mussar (Jewish Ethics) and Meditation. He is a graduate of the Reconstructionist Rabbinical College in Philadelphia, is a Rabbis Without Borders Fellow, and is currently studying towards an MFA in Poetry. Rabbi Boettiger has an abiding interest in sacred spaces and continues to work as a builder of ritual structures – from sukkahs and chuppahs to prayer/meditation spaces. He has published work in *Parabola*, *Zeek* and the *San Pedro River Review*.

Timothy Carson, D.Min., is the editor of *Neither Here nor There: The Many Voices of Liminality*. He is a pastor and writer, the author of several books including *Your Calling as a Christian, The Square Root of God, Six Doors to the Seventh Dimension* and *Liminal Reality and Transformational Power*. Liminality was the subject of his doctoral work, and he has continued his study and writing on transitional states ever since. An avid musician, world traveler and motorcyclist, he is also the Curator of TheLiminalityProject.org.

Colleen Warner Colaner, Ph.D., is an associate professor in the Department of Communication and co-director of the Institute of Family Diversity and Communication at the University of Missouri, U.S. Her research explores how communication creates and sustains personal, social, and family identities in diverse family structures. A major focus of her research is communication in adoptive families and she presently leads the Communication in Open Adoption Relationships Project (COARP), examining how adoptive and foster parents communicate with and about birth parents.

Nicole Conner, M.A., was raised by parents deeply affected by the horrors of World War II. As a child, she moved to South Africa, where she observed the corrosive effect of apartheid on its people. She relocated to Australia, where she served for many years as a pastor on the staff of a mega church in Melbourne. After finding herself sidelined by fundamentalist groups for her affirming views and voice for the LGBTIQA community, she left those forms of organized religion. She now continues her life and work differently, as a storyteller, an advocate, and healer in the mystery of "betwixt and between." She is currently pursuing a Masters degree in Narrative Therapy at Melbourne University.

Kristine A. Culp, Ph.D., teaches theology at the Divinity School and is the dean of the Disciples Divinity House of the University of Chicago, Chicago, Illinois, U.S. She is the author of *Vulnerability and Glory: A Theological Account* and editor of *The Responsibility of the Church for Society and Other Essays by H. Richard Niebuhr*. She serves on the Faith and Order Commission of the World Council of Churches. She was one of thirty-five scholars in the Enhancing Life Project, funded by the John Templeton Foundation, and is writing a book on "aliveness" or the glory of living things, as part of the project.

Jacob Davis is a writer and student who has lived in the Tennessee prison system since 1998 and is serving a life sentence with possibility of parole, which in Tennessee is 51 years. He is a founding member of No Exceptions Prison Collective, and the interfaith community, Harriet Tubman House. His work has been published in Contemporary Justice Review, The Huffington Post, LEAVEN (published quarterly by Pepperdine University, Malibu, CA), by Tenx9 Nashville Storytelling, and Scalawag magazine.

Dianne Dentice, Ph.D., teaches classes in race and ethnic relations, gender, social problems and social psychology at Stephen F. Austin State University in Nacogdoches, Texas, U.S. From January 2005 until December 2012, she conducted extensive field research among white supremacist groups in Texas, Arkansas, Louisiana, and Mississippi. Her current work explores the Christian Identity movement and other home-grown racist religions. She has also published on transgender workplace rights issues in both civilian and military life.

Michelle Dietert, Ph.D., teaches gender, sexuality, and sociological theory at Texas A&M University, Central Texas. Her published research has highlighted topics regarding the transgender population, including workplace discrimination, early socialization, the experiences of transgender veterans and active duty personnel, and religious extremism against the LGBTQ community.

John Eliastam, Ph.D. After completing studies in theology John served as the pastor of a congregation in Cape Town, SA. He later earned his doctorate from the University of Pretoria where he presently serves as a research associate in the Department of Practical Theology. For the past ten years John has worked as a consultant with organizations and communities focusing on transformation, inclusion, and social cohesion. Since 2015 he has been a part of an interdisciplinary research project on the African social value of *ubuntu*.

Elena Huegel, M.A., is a teacher, storyteller, and artist, who facilitates group-learning processes in peace and environmental education at the Institute for Intercultural Studies and Research in Chiapas, Mexico. Having served in Latin America for over twenty years, Elena coordinates the Roots in the Ruins: Hope in Trauma program in central and southern Mexico, as well as in Puerto Rico, Chile, Argentina, Paraguay, and Nicaragua. Her self-identified mission is to walk alongside others on the path to healing and transformation with God, others, ourselves, and all of God's creation.

Debra Jarvis, M.Div., lives in Seattle, Oregon, U.S., and is ordained in the United Church of Christ. She has worked as a hospice and hospital chaplain, and pastoral consultant, training volunteers to work with persons with AIDS and MS. She is the author of several books, the most recent of which is *It's Not About the Hair: And Other Certainties of Life & Cancer*. She is host and producer of the podcast, "*The Final Say: Conversations with Those Facing Life's End.*" You can find Debra on her TEDMEd talk.

Kenneth J. Krushel serves as a professor at the New School in New York City, U.S. He was founding chairman and CEO of College Enterprise and CEO of Proteus. He has held senior leadership and strategy positions with several entertainment and telecommunication companies, including NBC, USA Networks, American Cablesystems, King World Productions, Paramount Communications, Warner Bros., MGM, Television New Zealand, and Sega Corporation. He is on the board of *Parabola*, a quarterly magazine on philosophy, religion. and cultural traditions, and of School Year Abroad, the pre-eminent high school international study program.

Jill Cameron Michel, M.Div., serves as senior pastor of the First Christian Church (Disciples of Christ) in Coralville, Iowa, U.S. She has served congregations for twenty-five years and, during her Joplin, Missouri tenure, a deadly category five tornado raged through the center of the city. In the three years following, her congregation housed hundreds of disaster recovery volunteers. Jill is a contributor to *Help and Hope: Disaster Preparedness and Response Tools for Congregations* and she was a founder of the Joplin Interfaith Coalition.

Pádraig Ó Tuama, M.Th., is a poet and theologian, who brings interest in conflict and religion to his work. Since 2014, he has been the leader of the Corrymeela Community, Northern Ireland's oldest peace and reconciliation organization, bringing 10,000 people a year through programs and engagements of peace and reconciliation. Featured on Krista Tippett's On Being project, Ó Tuama's work has drawn attention from broadcasters, poets, theologians, and politicians for an attention to human encounter at the heart of public life.

Adam Pryor, Ph.D., is an assistant professor of religion at Bethany College in Lindsborg, Kansas, U.S. He is the author of *The God Who Lives* and *Body of Christ Incarnate for You*, and his research broadly focuses on issues related to emergence theory, religion and science, and phenomenologies of the body. He is currently working on the phenomenological implications of astrobiology for religious reflection and what it means to "live" in the cosmos.

Timothy Robinson, Ph.D., is the Alberta and Harold Lunger Associate Professor of Spirituality at Brite Divinity School at Texas Christian University, Fort Worth, Texas. Some of his previous published works include *Spirit and Nature: The Study of Christian Spirituality in a Time of Ecological Urgency*, edited with Ray Maria McNamara, and several articles on spirituality, liturgy, and ecology. His research and teaching interests include the history of Christian spirituality and mysticism, ecojustice, and the life and work of Howard Thurman.

Barbara Brown Taylor is a *New York Times* best-selling author, teacher, and Episcopal priest. Her first memoir, *Leaving Church*, won an Author of the Year award from the Georgia Writers Association. Her last book, *Learning to Walk in the Dark*, was featured on the cover of *TIME* magazine. She has served on the faculties of Piedmont College, Columbia Theological Seminary, Candler School of Theology at Emory University, McAfee School of Theology at Mercer University, and the Certificate in Theological Studies program at Arrendale State Prison for Women in Alto, Georgia. Her new book, *Holy Envy*, is forthcoming from HarperOne in March 2019.

Kate Hendricks Thomas, Ph.D., is an assistant professor of public health at Charleston Southern University, Charleston, South Carolina, U.S. She focuses her research on evidence-based mental fitness and peak performance, and is the author of two books – *Brave, Strong, True: The Modern Warrior's Battle for Balance* and *Bulletproofing the Psyche*. She is also a former Marine Corps Military Police Officer with experience leading teams in law enforcement, training, and combat commands. Her present research focuses on program evaluation and neurological enhancements made possible through somatic practice.

Michelle Trebilcock, Ph.D., lives in Melbourne, Australia, where she serves as a priest and chaplain in an Anglican welfare agency. Her doctoral work explored love as a hermeneutical principle in the context of liminality, and she continues this passion in works of love, spirituality, and society. Her daily rhythms are shaped by the private practices of meditation and yoga but she also joins with the community to dance, celebrate the Eucharist, offer hospitality, and attention.

Acknowledgments

Not every publishing company would embrace such a large project based on liminality, but Lutterworth Press enthusiastically did just that. I cannot thank them enough. This adds another volume to their new and growing collection of liminal studies.

Our many authors bring a splendid combination of personal expertise, experience, and unique insight. Their multiple perspectives illuminate our exploration of liminality in exciting ways, adding to the depth and application of liminality as a descriptive and interpretive model. I thank them for their passion, creativity, and devotion to their craft. They have been, each one, wonderful collaborative partners. As I worked with these many contributions, I strove to stay true to their original intents even as I pursued the larger objectives of the entire project.

I am appreciative of the fine, tireless copy-editing of Nancy Miller. Her eye to the nuts and bolts of the text was a sharp one, and she gathered together our many writers into the same literary universe.

As always, I have received ample encouragement and the gift of time from those who love and care for me most, and that, beyond any quantitative measure, makes the biggest qualitative difference. As always, thank you.

Foreword

Barbara Brown Taylor

My favorite ginger cat has been missing for six days now. I have checked all of his hideouts: the crawl space in the basement, the rafters in the garage, the hayloft in the barn. Someone pulled him out of a rain pipe in town and brought him to me for safekeeping, and I named him Rosie because I thought he was a girl. After the vet said he was a boy, I changed his name to Roosevelt, but by then he answered to Rosie so the name stuck.

He is a quirky cat, who waggles his head like a bobblehead doll when I greet him in the morning. When I walk the quarter mile to the garden, he walks with me all the way. He still prefers to eat what he can catch instead of the kibble from the grocery store, which means that I never know what I will have to pry from the back-porch floor when I sweep on Saturdays: the hollow corpse of a blue-tailed skink, the severed head of a velvet-gray vole, the feet and wings of a baby wren. Rosie is not a barbarian. He just knows that he has to eat to live.

"How long since you saw Rosie?" I leave this note on a pad next to the stove for my husband Ed to find when he wakes up. When I come back later to make a second cup of tea, I see his response: "Two days. Coyote?"

In the last couple of weeks we have lost six chickens and a guinea hen to something that moves so fast we cannot tell if it is a gray fox or a coyote. This happens every year during whelping season. There are hungry babies in a burrow somewhere whose mother has grown bold to feed them. Ed wants to shoot her, whatever she is. I plead with him to wait a while. As sad as I am about losing the chickens, they are my tithe to the divine economy of the farm. Everything has to eat to live.

After Rosie goes missing I realize that my pledge is based on a one-sided bargain: you may have some of my chickens, but not my cat. You may advance this far, but no farther. The problem is that the coyote never agreed to my terms. We share a liminal space together: half wild, half tame. My control over it is all in my head. If I want to hear the wild turkeys in the woods; if I want to see a great blue heron fishing in the spring pond; if I want to watch summer lightning break the night sky over Mount Yonah without a single house light on the horizon: my bargaining days are over. I can take it or leave it.

I cannot imagine leaving it.

* * *

You are holding a wondrous book in your hands, full of startling stories about people who accept the risks of engaging liminal space. Plenty of them did not consent to go there. Some were catapulted there by war, illness, abuse, or natural disaster. Others found themselves there due to poverty, gender, apartheid, or immigration. The authors of the stories constitute an exception, since most of them chose to go places they did not have to. They willingly entered the passageway between here and there, between structure and chaos, both to serve as witnesses of transformation and to offer what aid they could to those still in its throes.

As different as their stories are, they share certain convictions. Being in community is better than being alone. Rites of passage help, even if you have to make them up. Things generally get darker before they get lighter. The only way through is through. There are no guarantees. This last truth is the one that separates this book from anything you will find on the self-help shelf. To engage liminal space is to live in faith, not certainty. Maybe you will come through with all your parts intact and maybe you will not. You may emerge with a shiny new name or with a painful lifelong limp. Who knows? Maybe you will come through with both.

The only thing missing from this book, as far as I can tell, is a testimony to the liminal passages of an ordinary day in the country. It just so happens that this is the only thing I can add, since I have never fought in a war, survived an earthquake, or been diagnosed with something that could kill me. I am a white, educated, cisgender woman who has never so much as broken a bone. I live in the country because I could afford to move here, though it meant leaving the city where all of my skills were honed and most of my friends still live.

The first night Ed and I spent in the singlewide trailer on our new farm, a pickup truck full of men with guns arrived after dark to ask whether they could hunt raccoons on our land. After they left, I went to the sink for a drink of water, but when I turned the handle, the faucet just sighed.

"We have to dig a well first," Ed said. That was how much I had to learn.

For the purposes of this book, what I most had to learn was how to live in a place that is not quite wild and not quite tame, governed by elemental realities that are easier to ignore inside the city limits. In the country, a week of heavy rain can rot an entire year's potato crop. A coyote can eat my favorite cat. At the same time, this is where I have learned that the difference between wild and tame is not as clear-cut as I once thought. Neither is the difference between night and day, light and dark, weal and woe. The "between" turns out to be more interesting than what is on either side of it. In most ways that matter, it is the truest part.

*　*　*

I moved here because of something Ed said one night during a walk around our urban neighborhood. We lived at the corner of a busy street where the weight of city buses made our house jump on its foundations every time one passed. If we walked in one direction, we came to a city park named for a battle where more than 4,000 soldiers died during the Civil War. I tried not to think about their bones underfoot while Ed and I talked about all the things married people talk about: chores, children, work, vacation plans. We looked for the moon but could not find it in the light-polluted sky. Plus, neither of us knew what we were looking for. Was the moon waxing or waning? Was it coming up early or late?

"I'm going to die sooner than I have to if we don't leave this place," Ed said. So, we left that place, making an even trade of our quarter-acre city lot for ninety acres in the country. We lived in the singlewide while we built a house. We added two horses and a bunch of chickens. Ed tilled two acres of bottomland for an organic vegetable farm. We have been here for two and a half decades now and he is still alive.

But he can tell his own story. My story goes like this: when I lived in the city, I lived on a human scale. The buildings all around me were designed and built by humans. Humans lived and worked inside them. When we left one building, we got into cars or buses to go to other, sometimes wonderful, buildings, filling the roads with traffic that lasted for hours. When it got hot inside our cars or buildings, we turned on the air-conditioning. When it got cold, we turned up the heat. Torrential rain might slow us down on our ways from one kind of roof to another, but it did not rot anything. Light snow, on the other hand, could keep us inside for days. When we looked out of our windows, it was easy to decide whether it was light or dark outside. When it was light, we could see things. When it was dark, we could not. That was when we pulled down the shades in our place so no one could see inside. We turned on the lights so the darkness did not slow us down until we were good and ready to call it a night.

I worked in a downtown church where the human scale could get pretty intense, so the words "wild" and "tame" meant something to me even in the city. As did other paired opposites, such as "light" and "dark," though in retrospect their meaning was entirely metaphorical. I did not run into them on a physical level until I moved to the country, which was how I discovered how much "between" there really was. My Jack Russell terrier was tame until she smelled something wild in the woods. Then she was gone like a shot, deaf to the sound of my voice, until she limped home hours later with a mud-caked muzzle and bloody tooth marks in one ear.

Then there was the difference between day and night. Since I had to feed the horses every night, I soon learned how deceptive the view from my kitchen window was. Standing under the five spotlights in the ceiling and the four in the oven hood, I would look outside and decide it was dark. Then I would walk outside and discover it was light. Determined to learn how long this transition really took, I hauled an air mattress out onto the front lawn one evening and resolved to stay put until three stars appeared in the night sky.

This required far more time than I had allotted.

According to the U.S. Naval Observatory, every day ends with three different twilights. Civil twilight begins a little before dark, when it is time to use the headlights on the car. Nautical twilight comes next, when a sailor can navigate by the brightest stars. Astronomical twilight arrives when even the faintest stars are visible overhead. By this time the warm grass under my air mattress has become wet with dew. I have not only gained a visceral understanding of how long it takes for light to become dark; I have also been walloped with an acute sense of my own size. The trees are alive with cicadas. The sky is alive with stars. The scale of what is going on all around me is so beyond-human that by the time astronomical twilight arrives I have already spent quite a while thinking about mortality, infinity, deity, and the origins of the universe.

I know this can happen in the city. It happened to me once on the roof of a tall building, with fireworks going off overhead. It happened more than once in different intensive care units, holding the hands of people I loved. It even happened in church, though not as often as I hoped. In all of those places and more, the human order opened to the more-than-human order in redeeming ways that reminded me of my true size. But here is a strange thing: when this happened in city places, my questions were mostly about justice: why this person and not that one? Why these people and not those?

After a few years in the county, I gave up on finding satisfying answers to such questions.

I learned that I could raise a chick from an egg, keeping it warm and fed until it was three months old, then watch a hawk take it away on the first day I let it loose in the yard. I could count the blossoms on the peach tree, looking forward to the first full harvest in years, then stare at the thermometer as the temperature dropped below freezing during a late frost, so there was nothing left in the morning but dead buds. Of course, I also raised plenty of chicks that lived to lay eggs of their own and learned to make wild blackberry cobbler in place of the peach. I just gave up needing to know why things happened the way they did. My questions about justice became questions about agency instead: what good can I do here and what is beyond my control? When can I change things and when is there nothing to do but witness?

There is a story in the Bible about a man named Job. Even God agreed that he was without sin, but that did not prevent terrible things from happening to him. His livestock were stolen. His children were killed. His body erupted with sores. Job said all the right things at first. Then his grief overcame his reverence and he started yelling at God to tell him why. Why have you made me your target? Why did I not die at birth? Why do the wicked grow mighty in power? Why do you hide your face? This went on for a very long time without a single word from God. When God finally spoke to Job out of the whirlwind, it was not to give him any answers but to ask him a bunch of questions in return. Where were you when I laid the foundations of the Earth? Can you bind the chains of the Pleiades or loose the cords of Orion? Do you know when the mountain goats give birth? Is it by your wisdom that the hawk soars, and spreads its wings toward the south?

Make of that what you will, but I think God destabilizes Job's questions about divine justice with questions about human agency, especially in those liminal places where few humans go: the recesses of the deep, the waterskins of the heavens, the dens of young lions, the rocks where eagles make their nests. In one of the most acerbic verses of all, God reminds Job that rain falls even "on a land where no one lives, on the desert, which is empty of human life." Job is not at the center of God's universe, in other words. God has a lot on His plate. Counterintuitively, this revelation calms Job right down. God has taken the time to show him his place in the family of things, and while it is not as central a place as he had hoped – nor has God answered a single one of his questions – it is enough to turn Job's outrage to praise. He has heard of God before, but now he has survived a direct encounter. He has seen enough of God to remember his true size, which has turned out to be much more comforting than it may sound. It is a great help to know what you can manage and what you cannot. It is a great help to know that you are not God.

Thanks to Ed's long-ago premonition of doom, I live in a place rich with the liquid boundaries between death and life, dark and light, wild and tame. There is so much "between" in them that it is no longer possible to think of them as opposed realities but as constant companions on a great wheel that keeps turning, giving as much as it takes. My community here includes cats and coyotes, chickens and hawks, raccoons and raccoon hunters. Our rites of passage include the ones from sunrise to sunset and winter to spring, along with the one from the nest to the grave. I can ignore these liminal gifts as easily as anyone but, like the other authors in this book, I am convinced that they deserve my best attention, both for myself and for the life of the world. In all the ways that matter, they are the truest parts.

Introduction
Timothy Carson

The original emergence of liminal studies took place in the halls of anthropology. The 1909 publication of Arnold van Gennep's *Rites of Passage*[1] was the original big bang from which many ensuing manifestations came. No one person has advanced this exploration more than anthropologist Victor Turner. At the annual meeting of the American Ethnological Society in Pittsburgh, March 1964, Turner presented a paper which both built on and extended beyond the previous work of van Gennep.[2] His careful descriptions of structure and positions, geography, caste, emotional condition, social turmoil, and disaster expanded the scope and application of liminality. With the publication of Turner's well-known and cited work, *The Ritual Process: Structure and Anti-Structure,*[3] the doorway opened to a much broader multidisciplinary exploration of comparative liminality.

The most intentional effort at interdisciplinary study of liminality of its time was the Jerusalem Seminar on Comparative Liminality, which was held for many years at the Hebrew University of Jerusalem under the direction of S.N. Eisenstadt and Victor Turner. These seminars of the 1980s pushed ever more directly into the ways that liminality manifests itself in contemporary culture, especially under the auspices of increasingly industrial, technological, urban, individualized, mobile, pluralistic, rapidly-moving societies. Of special interest were interior affective states which mirrored the external passages between different structures and domains.

1. Arnold van Gennep, *Rites of Passage* (London: Routledge & Kegan Paul, 1960).
2. Victor Turner, "Betwixt and Between: The Liminal Period in Rites of Passage," in *The Forest of Symbols* (Ithaca: Cornell University Press, 1967), 93-111.
3. Victor Turner, *The Ritual Process: Structure and Anti-Structure* (New York: Aldine Publishing Company, 1969).

Since that time many of the social sciences have borrowed liberally from the insights of liminality. Sociology, psychology, psychotherapies, education, history, literature, and religion have all related liminality to the driving themes, concerns, and questions of their own disciplines. A good example in the Jungian Chiron clinical series is the anthology *Liminality and Transitional Phenomena*.[4] This collection features Jungian analysts who relate liminality to their already existing analytical themes as they reframe their practices with new liminal insights.

With the arrival of the 100th anniversary of van Gennep's *Rites of Passage,* the journal *International Political Anthropology* published a special edition dedicated to the issue of liminality.[5] Out of that effort grew the anthology *Breaking Boundaries: Varieties of Liminality*,[6] which contains expansions of the earlier journal articles as well as newly written chapters. Its focus is primarily on social, political, and international dimensions. The fact that the study of liminality remains relevant a century after the publication of van Gennep's seminal book is a testimony to its staying power.

The most recent anthology addressing liminal themes is *Landscapes of Liminality: Between Space and Place*.[7] The genesis of the project was a 2014 conference at Trinity College, Dublin that resulted in a published anthology two years later. The guiding focus of the anthology is the description of the liminal domain which is found beyond the structure of place, abiding in the undefined reality of open space. In addition to expanding the discussion of spatial studies, this eclectic collection of essays explores liminality through the lens of literature, culture, sociology, and the arts.

In the world of theological studies, liminality has provided a new hermeneutic, a new interpretive key for analyzing and presenting texts, narratives, theological constructs, and the ways that that transformation takes place. From Biblical studies to liturgy to pastoral care to spiritual formation, the rites of passage and unique qualities of the liminal domain have risen to a place of new prominence among many academics and clergy. When revered emeritus professor of theology at Princeton Theological Seminary Sang Hyun Lee released his long-awaited theological summa in the winter of his life, it was entitled *From a Liminal Place: An Asian American Theology*.[8]

---

4. Nathan Schwartz-Salant and Murray Stein, eds, *Liminality and Transitional Phenomena* (Wilmette, IL: Chiron Publications, 1991).

5. *International Political Anthropology* 2, no. 1 (2009).

6. Agnes Horvath, Bjorn Thomassen, and Harald Wydra, eds, *Breaking Boundaries: Varieties of Liminality* (New York and Oxford: Berghahn Books, 2015).

7. Dara Downey, Ian Kinane, and Elizabeth Parker, eds, *Landscapes of Liminality: Between Space and Place* (London: Rowman & Littlefield International, 2016).

8. Sang Hyun Lee, *From a Liminal Place: An Asian American Theology* (Minneapolis: Fortress Press, 2010).

For Lee, liminal categories provided an additional dimension that helped more completely express what was most important to him.

As important as the original contributions of anthropology in liminality have been for these many disciplines, it may be more accurate to say that they didn't simply borrow; they were awakened to what was already there. Human experience is full of passage and liminal dimension. From the *Odyssey* to *Hamlet*, classical literature has always depended on plot lines with deep liminal elements. The great religious traditions frequently include overarching narratives of passage, transition, and transformation. Personal experience often includes many liminal passages. These passages have always been there, and we now understand that more completely. Liminality is always characterized by crossing a definitive threshold and passing into and often through an undifferentiated yet potentially transforming time and space. To know this is to be aware of it when it happens, and having that awareness may bring help and guidance to others passing through parallel territory.

This anthology is the next project within the growing tradition of liminal studies. We have gathered many of the voices of liminality under one cover, those writers who work, teach, research, and live in close proximity to liminal thresholds and boundaries. Their curiosity and explorations provide the substance of a continuing conversation within the field of liminality.

In the following chapters, you will discover many facets of the liminal domain. Some of the authors focus on the interior passages of the spirit. Others are primarily preoccupied with the way social experience and transition shapes communities into what they are. The primary concern of some of our authors is the collision of cultures and communities and the negotiation of conflict. Many of our writers describe the ways in which liminal reality shapes, forms, and transforms human life through and with faith. Several chapters examine liminality as the result of disaster, war, and great social upheaval. The focus of some of our authors is the creative intersection between cultures and religious traditions. The intersection of religion and science creates its own kind of liminal space, one that often reinvigorates both of those worlds. And no anthology on liminality would be complete without universal elements such as mythical narrative, symbolism, the natural world, human sexuality, and mystical experience, aspects our authors do not neglect.

In the closing chapters of the Biblical book of Job, one of the great masterpieces of sacred literature devoted to the question of suffering, the impatient Job poses existential questions out of the confines of his liminal experience of loss. In his despair, he cross-examines God, demanding an explanation for his dire circumstances. Against a backdrop of deafening silence, a voice spins out of the whirlwind: "Where were you when I created the foundations of the world?" At that, Job is struck silent. The only possible answer is that at the moment of creation, he was nowhere, he was nothing. The story ends that way, without a rational answer. No answer is the answer. Job asks for an explanation and he receives mystery instead.

This collection of the many voices of liminality represents, in one way or another, the questions and the answers circling inside that whirlwind.

I

Neither Here nor There

Timothy Carson

When I was a young man, I traveled with a scuba diving club to a nearby lake to participate in a deep dive. This kind of dive was of a technical nature, not typical or even suggested for a sport diver. It was carefully supervised and an experienced master diver accompanied each team. In retrospect, I believe I was too inexperienced to be doing such a thing. I discovered later that diving in a group of three is itself poor practice because there is not a one-on-one accountability to a buddy.

My two diving partners, older and more experienced than I, were better and more adequately equipped. They both had double tanks, while I had a single, giving them twice the volume of air that I had. That shouldn't have been much of a problem as we were not planning to stay on the bottom for more than five minutes. To stay longer at that depth would require several decompression stops on the way up to avoid getting the bends. A one-tank deep dive was a round trip to the bottom without lingering there. That would be the plan. But plans are often foiled.

We dove on the high side of a dam where the water was deepest and most accessible. This was an inland, manmade lake, so the underwater slope we traversed on the way down was covered with various debris, tree stumps, wire, and other obstacles. My last memory was passing through that mire as the temperature became bitterly cold and the light dimmed.

I woke up on the bottom sitting very still in a small circle of divers, our dive lights illuminating our faces in the pitch-black darkness. The water was so cold I couldn't feel the regulator in my mouth. The reason we lost consciousness is that we had all succumbed to nitrogen narcosis, the effect of nitrogen on the body and brain when it is under great pressure. It has indeed a narcotic effect. I had no idea how long we had been sitting there, drifting in the narcosis fog. The water was perfectly clear so that meant we had been there long enough for the plume of silt to settle. I looked at the depth gauge strapped to my wrist. We were at 180 feet on the bottom. I quickly reached down to my side and grasped my air pressure gauge. Pulling it up to my facemask I read the numbers slowly: 200 pounds. At 180 feet that pressure is next to nothing. I was suddenly, shockingly awake.

I shook my buddies to awaken them and they came out of their groggy slumbers, pulling themselves together. Since they had double tanks their situation was much less urgent than mine. I gave the universal signal to ascend and pulled their elbows upward. We lifted off the bottom and began the ascent to the surface.

Somewhere in that upward journey I became separated from the other two. I don't know how it happened except that, in the fog of narcosis, great depth, and a mighty adrenalin surge, I was probably swimming faster than they were. When I realized that I was on my own I fled to the surface.

During the ascent, my light went out. I was disoriented, kicking in the jet-black darkness and not sure what direction I was heading. By that time, I was literally sucking the air out of my tank, one slow inhalation at a time. I clearly remember hearing myself think, "This might be it."

It is a strange thing to be suspended somewhere between the bottom and the surface, thrashing in the darkness, coordinates absent, suddenly and wildly alone in your own consciousness. It is quiet, very quiet. Anything could happen. You act but also watch and wait. Time stands still or seems to move in slow motion.

The first sign that I was heading in the right direction was the darkness giving way to deep, dark green and then to lighter green. I passed through a thermocline where the temperature changes and silt sprawled out like a paper umbrella. With less water pressure my vest started to inflate and pulled me upward with great acceleration. I broke the surface into blinding sunlight and abundant air. I gasped, "Thank you God."

After I swam to shore I turned and watched the bubble stream on the surface where my partners were beneath. One diver broke the surface. But only one. The other didn't come up. He never did. The water patrol dragged for his body and never found it. Whatever happened in those critical moments, he somehow sank back down to the depths, like a burial at sea, his final resting place a watery tomb.

I really don't know why I made it and the other diver did not. I could refer to the obvious, that I was younger, in good shape, and an excellent swimmer. I could turn to the benefits of practice and training and recall all of those times when I was a boy and swam the full length of an Olympic-style pool underwater, holding my breath. I could argue that, because I was loaded with less gear, I was more streamlined, less encumbered, and more able successfully to flee to the surface. Maybe I had had a good sleep the night before and maybe the other guy went on a drinking expedition. Whatever the conjecture, we will, in the end, never know for certain. I survived and he did not. Three went down and two came back up. And I was left to tell the story.

Was this experience stored in my unconscious and later connected in powerful ways to my discovery of liminality? Or was it other experiences, perhaps less dramatic but equally powerful in their own way? Was it a particular loss and attending grief, the physical relocation, growing up, from one city to another, a mysterious experience I could only name as sacred, a conglomerate of predictable but nevertheless stirring rituals in my early religious development, or several disasters that I shared with so many others? All of these experiences became living exemplars of what has come to be named liminality.

Origins of a Discipline

At the beginning of the twentieth century, anthropologist Arnold van Gennep was drawn to the broad patterns of regeneration he observed within communal systems, an array of cultural transitions mediated by rites and rituals. From those he came to understand a particular genre of social transition he named "the rites of passage." This descriptive phrase became the title of his landmark book first published in 1909.[1]

Van Gennep concluded that the energy in any system eventually dissipates and must be renewed at crucial intervals. This renewal is accomplished in the social milieu by various rites of passage. These rites not only foster transition but protect the social structure from undue disturbance. Developmental transitions include such rites of passage as pregnancy, childbirth, childhood, departure from childhood, puberty, marriage, and death. Territorial transitions also require certain rituals as one moves from one geographic area to another, moving between actual and symbolic worlds. Rites of passage mediate the movement between tribes and castes. They are especially important in providing passage in times of crisis such as illness, war, and death. The rites of passage act to mediate virtually all of the most important occasions of life.

The term "liminal" derives from the Latin, *limins*, and refers to the threshold passageway between two separate places. The liminal state is therefore a transitional one, the result of crossing a threshold between location, status, position, mental state, social condition, war and peace, or illness and death.

---

1. Gennep, *The Rites of Passage.*

The structure of the rites of passage falls into a tripartite form:

Pre-liminal – the known and assumed structure of life;
Liminal – the ambiguous transitional period;
Post-liminal – the new adjusted and transformed state of being.

Whereas much liminality is related to predictable passages of development and maturation, other forms are more directly tied to recurring seasons; an entirely different class of liminality is the result of involuntary crisis. Some rites of passage involve the individual over and against the structure of society, while other liminality is social and includes entire groups, even nations.

Each transition requires rituals, ceremonies, and leadership to assist in the passage. When a person or group crosses a new threshold or boundary, they are separated from the previous world and ushered into the unknown. As they pass out of the liminal time and space, they cross into a new time and space and are incorporated into a new world. Van Gennep came to believe that regardless of form or content, rites of passage are most often universal, varying only in regard to detail:

> For groups as well as for individuals, life itself means to separate and
> to be reunited, to change form and condition, to die and be reborn.
> It is to act and to cease, to wait and rest, and to begin acting again,
> but in a different way . . . and there are always new thresholds to
> cross: the thresholds of summer and winter, of a season or a year, of
> a month or a night; the thresholds of birth, adolescence, maturity,
> and old age; the threshold of death and that of the afterlife – for
> those who believe in it.[2]

At the annual meeting of the American Ethnological Society in Pittsburgh, March 1964, anthropologist Victor Turner presented a paper which built on and extended the work of van Gennep. Since society is a "structure of positions," reasoned Turner, liminality is an "interstructural situation."[3]

The person who moves through the rites of passage is a transitional being, a liminal person, and as such takes on a new identity and is defined by a whole new set of symbols. The condition is one of ambiguity, paradox and confusion of all the customary categories. Citing the work of Mary Douglas, Turner described one of the central characteristics of the liminal person as being ritual uncleanliness. Liminal persons are dangerous by virtue of their undefined transitional status. They are considered to be

---

2. Ibid., 189-90.
3. Turner, "Betwixt and Between," 93-111.

polluting to those who have not been initiated into the same state of being. Rites and rituals of passage create and mediate transition and order for those passing through or near the perceived danger and impurity.[4]

In Turner's well-known and often cited work, *The Ritual Process: Structure and Anti-Structure*, he continued to develop his analysis of the liminal person.[5] Life within community is to be understood as a dialectical process moving between structure and anti-structure with individuals transitioning between those poles. The attributes of the liminal person stand in opposition to the established structure. The liminal person takes up symbolic and transitional status that includes a kind of stripping away of the self, gender neutrality, anonymity, and submission to the process itself.

To describe the special bond between those who share the same liminal passage, Turner coined the word "communitas." Those who share the liminal passage develop a community of the in-between, a connection that transcends any former distinctions between status and station created by social structure. This unique community formed within anti-structure continues even after the liminal period has concluded. Communitas is found among numerous people and groups who have passed through the same intense, shared experience.

Turner also coined another term within the liminal lexicon: "liminoid." This shade of liminality reflects an experience of separation from structure without rootedness in community, rituals of transformation, or adequate ritual leadership. In many cases liminoid experience is contrived, artificial and does not necessarily include the critical aspect of transition from one state of being to another. It also may be more characteristic of complex, industrial, technological, rapid communication, and virtually driven societies.[6]

Universal Liminal Experience

All of these phenomena, though not named in the same way, existed before anthropologists studied them with their cross-cultural analysis. The ideas, rituals, and narratives were present in world literature, mythology, religions, and philosophy. They were practiced by small cohesive agrarian tribes as well as large and sophisticated pre-industrial societies. Their stories and rites varied according to context but held remarkable and universal parallels.

---

4. Mary Douglas, *Purity and Danger* (New York: Frederick A. Praeger, 1966).
5. Turner, *The Ritual Process* (1969), 96-104.
6. Victor Turner, "Liminality, Kabbalah, and the Media," *Religion* 15 (1985), 205-17.

From the mythic-symbolic perspective, the rites of passage are passages of death and rebirth leading to another form of existence. Time and space yield to great discontinuities and the liminal domain becomes the container of transformation. As such, liminal persons may discover revelatory knowledge and new awareness in that liminal time and space. Sacred time and space are characterized by the experience of darkness, death, awe, and descent to the womb of initiation and transformation. Forms of ecstasy are commonly experienced through the passages.[7]

The experience of liminality is feeling a loss of steady and familiar landmarks, the kind of security that accompanied past structure, even as the future has not yet materialized. With everything in flux, angst becomes the predominant mood. Very often action seems fruitless because some transitions cannot be hurried. One has entered an incubation period in which time shifts. The liminal person does not necessarily know that transformation is occurring at the time it is happening. Does a caterpillar have any idea that a metamorphosis is about to take place as it enters the cocoon?

* * *

The narratives of the Hebrew and Christian scriptures often present divine activity and revelation as unfolding within the womb of liminal transformation. Noah huddled in his ark surrounded by pairs of opposites and passed through forty days of transition between the old and new worlds (Genesis 6-8); Jacob's dream floated somewhere between earth and heaven (Genesis 28:12-19); Moses trod on holy, separated ground on the way to divine encounter (Exodus 3:5); Isaiah was filled with awe in the temple of holiness (Isaiah 6:1-6); Jesus was tested in the wilderness (Matthew 4:1-11); and the tomb of death was transformed into a path of light (Matthew 28:1-10).

According to Dante, he was thirty-five in the year 1300, the date the great journey of his *Commedia* began. It was then that he crossed the threshold to the larger journey, the famed dark wood. Generations of readers have been captivated by such an entrance into the shadows of life, stumbling in the dark, suffering the necessary losses and discovering the next hope:

> Midway through life's journey
> I woke to find myself in a darkened wood,
> Where the right road was wholly lost and gone.[8]

7. Mircea Eliade, *Rites and Symbols of Initiation* (New York: Harper & Row, 1958), 62.

8. Dorothy Sayers, *The Comedy of Dante Alighieri: Cantica 1, Hell* (London and Baltimore: Penguin Books, 1949), 121.

That, of course, was only the first of the thresholds he would cross. Within the liminal passage there were multiple thresholds of consciousness to traverse, truths to face, and sublime beauty to receive. The dark wood was a threshold beyond which the process continued and concluded.

African American Spirituals often embodied hopes of passage – earthly and eternal. As slaves participated in dangerous passages toward freedom, their songs simultaneously described two hopes. "Swing Low, Sweet Chariot" expressed the longing to be delivered to the free north by way of the Underground Railroad as well as deliverance from this world of woe. "Wade in the Water" reflected two Biblical images: the Exodus from bondage to liberation, and crossing the river of death into the ultimate peace of paradise. Hope for deliverance emerged from the liminal experience of bondage and captivity.

On 20 January 1912, when Rainer Maria Rilke was thirty-seven, while on a walk by Duino Castle near Trieste, he claimed he heard the words that would eventually become the opening line of his first elegy: "Who, if I cried out, would hear me among the angels' hierarchies?" From that initial encounter came the outpouring of several elegies at once. But that was only the beginning of his midlife liminal journey. His metamorphosis was filled with an extended season of emptiness and disorientation. The completion of his midlife passage took a full ten years, ending with another explosion of creativity in January of 1922, the month in which he finished all ten *Duino Elegies*.[9]

Once upon a time, a cargo ship that carried a family's entire future sank mid-journey, and the only ones who eventually survived were a boy and a Bengal tiger. Yann Martel's *Life of Pi* is the quintessential fictional story of the liminal passage and the dramatic transformations that may take place because of it. Is the story real, and in what sense? Or is it a fanciful rendition? What is true or more true, and why? Adrift at sea, surrounded by all elemental forms and forces, life and death at stake, a new and transformed person emerges as a result. The meaning of the story can only be relayed in mythic terms.[10]

A virus slowly passed through a population and eventually rendered all who were infected as blind, overcome with a great whiteness that blocked all seeing. In José Saramago's provocative and award-winning work of fiction *Blindness*,[11] a community of the blind is quarantined in a prison under conditions of great deprivation. Within this community of the blind, the prisoners slowly devolve to their basest natures. But one

---

9. Rainer Maria Rilke, *Duino Elegies* (New York: W.W. Norton & Co., 1978).
10. Yann Martel, *Life of Pi* (New York: Harcourt, 2001).
11. José Saramago, *Blindness* (New York: Harcourt, 1997).

character is somehow immune to the virus, continues to see, and becomes a strong guide for the others. As the virus spreads, the gates of the prison are eventually opened to reveal that the entire city has gone blind. What does it mean to pass through a time of collective blindness? What can be known, trusted or revealed? And where is hope? These are the questions that arise within the liminal domain.

When Temporary Becomes Permanent

In most cases the liminality that is embodied by rites of passage is temporary in nature, even if that means for an extended period of time. There are, however, more permanent forms of liminality and they come in both voluntary and involuntary varieties, by choice or condition.

A familiar voluntary form of permanent liminality is found in the highly developed monastic traditions of separation and communal life. Within these communities, certain aspects of liminality are maintained for indefinite periods. An accompanying communitas is created through the practices of self-discipline, humility and obedience to authority, sexual abstinence, homogeneity, equality, holding of all possessions in common, elimination of status levels, and the minimizing of gender distinctions.[12] This communal form of permanent liminality is often expressed in a form of social anti-structure; it positions itself over and against social norms and prevailing culture, often removing itself from the mainstream into a separate location and lifestyle.

Other forms of voluntary permanent liminality include communities of intentional isolation. The most obvious American example is that of the Amish. Communities of Amish heritage choose to separate from the world for the sake of ritual purity, clear identity, and a chosen way of life. The various forms of Amish communities express that separation by degree, but their practices of communal farming, shared religious experience, common dress, prescribed mores, and clear rules of belonging mark them as a community of voluntary permanent liminality.

Few eras in the history of this planet have witnessed so many utopian experiments as in the United States during the middle decades of the nineteenth century. Scores of people on both sides of the Atlantic believed that a way of life was transpiring in the wilderness of America that had only been dreamed of before. They came by the thousands carrying similar and dramatically contrasting visions of what life in community could and should be. They came with deep religious millennialism. They came with enlightened humanist yearnings. They came escaping old confining ways

---

12. Turner, *The Ritual Process* (1969), 107.

of love and the spirit-destroying routines of industrialization. They came abstaining from sex as well as proclaiming free love. They came as scientists, artists, philosophers, and communities of spiritual ecstasy like the Shakers, who danced the truth in their tightly regulated society.

However different the Shakers were from their secular counterparts, the Owenites in New Harmony, Indiana, or the free-love Fourierists or the high-minded Oneida Community in New York state, they all shared several common convictions: they believed that a new day had arrived and they were to be central players in it. They believed that the old conventions of the societies of their past needed to be replaced by something superior. They believed that male and female roles should be equalized and transformed. And they believed in theory, if not always in practice, that they should share all material things equally and in common.[13]

They chose to establish a permanent form of liminal existence over and against the prevailing structure of the world from which they had departed. They would live in-between all the time, a form of voluntary, permanent social liminality. That was their goal, whether their project realized a long tenure or not.

As a dramatic contrast, permanent liminality has also been expressed in itinerancy, in wandering. Rootlessness is also a social revolt against the dominant culture. Well-known religious figures, east and west, have often engaged in itinerancy to express their non-attachment to the world and what it values. Jesus and his movement demonstrated an itinerant radicalism that stressed non-attachment resulting in spiritual freedom. Others such as the Greco-Roman Cynics and the Jewish Maskilim, an order of mendicant kabbalists, wandered through the societies from which they kept a sanctified distance. Wandering and rootlessness were their distinctive liminal characteristics.

The itinerant appears first and foremost in the guise of the stranger. The stranger is the one who emerges from beyond our structure while moving near our thresholds and boundaries. The identity of the itinerant stranger is at once dangerous, fascinating and ambiguous.

In ethical monotheism, the stranger is to be protected and revered because we all can become strangers, aliens, and refugees. We are to treat the stranger with kindness and special respect. In the Christian tradition, the stranger is to be revered and welcomed as one would Christ. This is the origin of the mandate of monastic houses to extend hospitality. The stranger also carries a charmed status, bringing an unusual presence to the community from beyond. And in some religious

13. Chris Jennings, *Paradise Now: The Story of American Utopianism* (New York: Random House, 2016), 377.

traditions attaining the non-attachment of the stranger is the ultimate goal; to be in but not of this world, to know oneself as transient and in perpetual passage.

In contrast to voluntary permanent liminality is its opposite, the involuntary form. Life thrusts some into liminal domains not because they choose to go but rather because it is forced upon them or chosen for them. The sudden death of a loved one, the loss of a treasured career, the forced move from one's home due to calamity, forced slavery, and prison are all involuntary forms of liminality. And some of them become permanent.

During World War II Japanese Americans were rounded up by the thousands and quarantined in internment camps. Their captors considered them security risks in a time of war. American-born Japanese children lived behind barbed wire in the country of their birth. Within these boundaries, they experienced a form of suspended animation, an unreal world of the in-between. The impact of this involuntary liminality on their individual psyches and family life was very often disastrous:

> My own family, after three years of mess hall living, collapsed as an integrated unit. Whatever dignity or feeling of filial strength we may have known before December 1941 was lost and we did not recover it until many years after the war.[14]

The Inward Passage

Many of these external liminal passages are also accompanied by interior parallels; the subjective perception of the event or experience by those who pass through them makes liminality what it is.

Whether communal tragedies are caused by random circumstance or human malevolence, they still disorient all those who are touched by them. When people escape a stadium concert bombing or an apartment building fire, they are thrust beyond a world of safety and structure into an unknown and unsafe world. As the moorings are stripped away, something in the psyche shifts. This is the inner reflection of the outer experience. Trauma is the combined reaction and response to outer crisis.

The immediate survivors of a large communal chaos event, however, are not the only ones thrust into the liminal domain. Instantaneous media coverage allows for millions of eyes and brains to share in events transpiring in great, repeating detail. When a shooter recently opened up with automatic rifle fire from a Las Vegas hotel room, spraying the crowds attending a concert below, those images and sounds were broadcast immediately around the world,

---

14. Jeanne Wakatsuki Houston and James D. Houston, *Farewell to Manzanar* (New York: Ember, 1973), 37.

over and over. Citizen journalists recorded and broadcast the moment on their smart phones. This phenomenon explains why social liminality may rapidly unfold beyond the immediate geography of a particular event; the dire situation of one locale is shared by another.

But internal passages are not only precipitated by external events. Great transformations also occur inside the house of consciousness, often quite independent of outer circumstance. That is confirmed by all manner of spiritual, emotional, and perceptual transitions fostered by unfolding religious life, psychotherapeutic shifts, and social reorientation. In all of these transformations, whether deeply personal or socially shared, rites of passage and liminal sojourns are ubiquitous.

Jan and Murray Stein, for instance, believe that many current psychotherapies replace earlier ritual patterns of passage. They provide counterparts to separation, liminality, and reintegration, and contain sacred space and ritual leadership.[15] Spiritual directors have become highly cognizant of the existence of intrapsychic liminal boundaries in the experience of transcendence.[16] Brain researchers have identified parallel neurological phenomena which are directly related to shared ritual, meditation, prayer, and trance states.[17] And all manner of disciplines, from the social sciences to education, recognize that one of the most important internal transitional factors of any system is the internal liminal one, the ways in which our minds cross from one known reality through ambiguity to new states of awareness.

The inward apprehension of outer experience and outer expression of inward transformation are integrally connected. When people enter into liminal experience they discover both dimensions in play, often in equal measure.

In a cursory reading, it is easy to believe that Helen Macdonald's book, *H is for Hawk*,[18] is really about the rigors and tradition of training a goshawk. After all, she spends pages and pages describing exactly that in intricate detail. We are ushered into the sleepless world of the mew, the locale of training, instinct, and identification. We observe the simplest rituals and the most complex unfolding relationship.

---

15. Jan and Murray Stein, "Psychotherapy, Initiation and the Midlife Transition," in *Betwixt and Between*, ed. Louise Cams Mahdi (La Salle, IL: Open Court Pub. Co., 1987), 289.

16. Kenneth Stifler, Joanne Greer, William Sneck, and Robert Dovenmuehle, "An Empirical Investigation of the Discriminability of Reported Mystical Experiences among Religious Contemplatives, Psychotic Inpatients, and Normal Adults," *Journal for the Scientific Study of Religion* 32, no. 4 (1993), 366-72.

17. Eugene d'Aquili and Andrew Newberg, "Liminality, Trance, and Unitary States in Ritual and Meditation," *Studia Liturgica* 23, no. 1 (1993), 2-34.

18. Helen Macdonald, *H is for Hawk* (New York: Grove Press, 2016).

What we may not realize, not until much later in the book, is what is really at work. The author's father has died and this ritual with the hawk runs parallel to the vigil of grief. She has been abiding in the physical liminal territory where hawks and falconers become one, but she has also been traversing the deep inner recesses where one's most important loves and losses are sorted out. She has lost and lost deeply. Her life shall never be the same again. She struggles toward an unimaginable future without him.

Finally, in a terrible and truthful epiphany, a conjunction of planets, the two dimensions collapse together and become one, the hawk and her father, the ritual of training and the vigil of great loss:

> Gos was still out there in the forest, the dark forest to which all things lost must go. I'd wanted to slip across the borders to this world into that wood and bring back the hawk. Some part of me that was very small and old had known this, some part of me that didn't work according to the everyday rules of the world but with the logic of myths and dreams. And that part of me had hoped, too, that somewhere in that other world was my father. His death had been so sudden. There had been no time to prepare for it, no sense in it happening at all. He could only be lost. He was out there, still, somewhere out there in that tangled wood with all the rest of the lost and dead. I know now what those dreams in the spring had meant, the ones of a hawk slipping through a rent in the air into another world. I'd wanted to fly with the hawk to find my father; find him and bring him home.[19]

This is the story of the liminal domain and the liminal persons who traverse it. We may travel voluntarily or have that netherworld thrust upon us. The passage may be solitary or taken up in the company of a great number of souls. We may experience passage to the next stage of life, another place, or a new status among our own, but the crossing of that threshold always holds a great challenge and opportunity for transformation, one built into the fabric of existence itself.

---

19. Ibid., 220.

2

The Place Between

Pádraig Ó Tuama

I open at the close.

> J.K. Rowling, *Harry Potter and the Deathly Hallows*

He demands a closeness
We all have earned a lightness
Carry my joy on the left
Carry my pain on the right

> Björk, "Who Is It"

I am the wind which breathes upon the sea,
I am the wave of the ocean,
I am the murmur of the billows.

> Amergin Glúingel, *The Song of Amergin*

* * *

I always dream about my friends after they have died.

I got used to this. When I was sixteen I hitchhiked from Cork to Dublin with a girl called Mags. She was a year older than me, wore oxblood boots, and a dress over her ripped jeans. We got a lift from Cork to Dublin after forty-five minutes of trying. The truck driver let us buy him two cups of tea in a café and he asked us whether we would mind if he unloaded his truck in Portarlington on the way. We got to Dublin and walked to our friend's house. Mags died a year later, knocked over by a drunk driver. I didn't know her very well. But for months she wandered into my dreams, always wearing yellow, always with her hair down, always clear and truthful and brave, just like she had always been.

When my grandmother died, she appeared in the dreams of my auntie. My aunt had not been able to sleep. When she finally did, her dead mother showed up, dancing, with a baby in her arms, crooning a song. "What are you doing?" my auntie asked. "Waltzing with a baby," my grandmother replied, as if that were the most natural thing to do for the living and the dead.

Which, I suppose, it is.

When my friend Cathal took his own life, I was twenty-four. We had been friends since I ran into the middle of a fight to pull him out. It wasn't an act of heroism. I didn't have many friends myself, so dragging him along the ground over to where I had been standing was more a confirmation of just how unpopular he had become, rather than a welcome into a circle of courage. Anyway, we were friends then. We walked for hours in the dark roads around our village, him smoking cigarettes, me talking about poetry. We lied to our parents, bought a tent, slept in woods, shivered, lied to each other, never asked each other how we were, and dreamt of leaving. When he died, I was in Australia. Too far to get a plane to a funeral I didn't want to go to.

I got a phone call late one night – wrong night of the week – from my mother saying he was dead. I said, "Thanks." I remember crying at the stupidest times: in the shower, taking a piss, washing up.

A few nights later, he arrived, fully himself, in a dream. I'd forgotten the way of dead friends. This was a new grief and I wasn't sure what the rules were.

Anyway.

More of that later.

* * *

I hate much of what's written about Celtic spirituality. Dreamscapes of ancestors who lived at one with the earth are drawn without any question about how they ate, where they shat, how they grieved or fought. It is all well and good to think about the thin places where the living and the dead interacted, but what about the winter?

I heard a retreat leader – a visitor who spoke not a word of Irish – speak about a valley in Wicklow once. Wicklow is known as the garden of Ireland. It has heathers that are purple and green and yellow and moss brown. "Look at the inherent spirituality of the valley," he said. Jesus, Mary and Joseph, I thought. Landscapes don't have spirituality; this one had heather, or, in Irish *fraoch*. It comes from a word meaning rage, or fury, or fierceness. *Fraoch* is gorgeous on the eye, tough for eating. I wondered about people – from thousands of years back – from that valley. It must have been admired for generations, beauty in the eyes of the ancestral beholders. But what animals would thrive in such thick bracken? What could a mammal eat from there without ripping its tongue? What farmers farmed there? What invaders claimed there? Where is the blood spilt? Who has wept there? Who ran away from there? What is the story that the landscape has held?

If we are to speak about spirituality, we must speak about breathing and dying. Spirit, from *spirare*, meaning to breathe. To be spiritual is to breathe, to be unspiritual is to die; it is the most concrete thing we can think of. After you die, you die.

* * *

And then you show up in dreams, but we know that already.

* * *

Landscaped spiritualities usually arose from a desire of people not to die. They discerned movements in seasons and invented gods to pray to – to keep the weather clement, to keep the seasons in season, to keep the living alive. The longest day of the year; the shortest day of the year; the days in between those days; the day when flowers flower, when the moon seems fullest, when the sun hits the spot it hit that year that everything was perfect, or so we heard; the swell on the sea that year of destruction; the smell of thyme in the air that year the babies died. We take those, we remember the living and the dead, we turn them into prayers, and the gods of war listen.

* * *

Ray Davey was a Presbyterian minister from Belfast, born in Belfast in early 1915, back when the land was still just called Ireland, and the tinder-dry politics of Europe had just sparked into war the prior year. One hundred years later and some people still don't understand why World War I began. Maybe people just like a fight. Ray grew up in World War I and, in World War II, he went as a volunteer padré with the YMCA to a respite camp in North Africa. There, he was captured and held in many prisoner of war camps. He writes about the inhumanity and the humanity he saw in those camps. He saw men whose bodies gave up on them. They became bedmen, unable to move. He made a rota – oh, lifesaving Presbyterian rotas! – and kept men alive with time and company.

The last camp he was kept in was outside Dresden. His liberation came with the annihilation of that city. Some cheered. He wondered how to be glad.

"When your enemy falls, do not rejoice," someone wrote once. Whoever wrote that must have known rejoicing, either because their enemy fell or they were the enemy of someone, and they fell, and they saw their opponent's joy. Ray wasn't sure what to do. He was free now. Or soon to be. But twenty-five thousand people were dead in Dresden.

1, 2, 3, 4, 5, 6, 7, 8, 9, 10, 11, 12, 13, 14, 15, 16, 17, . . .

It takes a long time to count to 25,000. It takes approximately 240 times longer to count to 6,000,000. What terrible places we find ourselves in.

* * *

Ray came back to an Ireland still in the first quarter century of its partition, and saw that enemies were still stirring there: some loved the border, some hated it. Some were spoiling for a fight and rejoiced at the possibility of fallen enemies. He became chaplain of Queen's University in Belfast and began groups where the living could encounter each other before they knocked the living daylights out of each other. These experiments in community were with students who didn't know each other, they were on the edges of religion. I met a man who was about to go to Queen's as a seventeen year-old. His mathematics teacher summoned him to her bedroom – she lived in a little flat on the top floor of the school. "There are three things to stay away from at university," she said to him in her bedroom, "dances, girls, and Ray Davey." He was in his eighties when he told me this, and he laughed as he remembered the delight he took in avoiding each clause of her advice.

Ray made little communities of people wherever he went: prisoner of war camps; chaplaincies; summer trips; Sunday evenings at his house. In 1965 he heard of a place for sale fifty miles north of Belfast, a few fields with a rickety house and a view over the sea across to Scotland. The civil rights movement was in full swing. Some believed that marching would work. Others itched for blood. There was talk of strikes and bombs and guns and military command. What was needed, he thought, was a place for encounter between the living, so that enemies don't need to come back in dreams. He raised the money in three weeks and bought the house with the view on the fields called Corrymeela. The Corrymeela Community was named by the land and began its mission to transform division through human encounter.

* * *

Some naive idiot said it meant "Hill of Harmony."

* * *

They were wrong. It means "Lumpy Crossing Place."

Corrymeela became known as a place of reconciliation. Not because it is easy, but because it is not. It is an argument, an accusation, a list of words coming from your mouth in the presence of the other that is worse than saying nothing, but saying nothing is killing you so you have to say something. It is the meeting of people who feel like they are barely living, and that their circumstances are squeezing the breath out from them, so they need the release of language in the presence of their enemy.

It is not an end. It is just barely the beginning.

I lead Corrymeela now. I arrived exhausted fifteen years ago and found myself breathing — for the first thing it felt like — because I could say that I was gay and human and full of faith and fear. And it was not that nobody cared. It was the opposite. They did. It was not that I was welcome regardless of those things. Those things were regarded.

Regard: from the French, meaning a steady gaze or esteemed.

To lead a place of reconciliation is to think of the stories that have been disregarded, that have been discarded, cast away, considered peripheral, or ignorable, and to know that people who have lived fragmented lives need to have their edges re-enlivened. Stories of hatred and stories of survival, stories of hope and stories of dreams where dignity is a reality. Reconciling involves making mistakes while trying to do good. Sometimes bad mistakes.

Even if we cannot make dreams true, we can regard each other. Because one thing is true: we are perfectly capable of making nightmares real. Just look around. Regard.

* * *

While I have met plenty of the dead in my dreams, I have never asked them what it is like to be dead. I do not know why. I am more concerned with me when they turn up than I am with curiosity. Maybe the next time a dead friend visits, I shall remember to ask, but I doubt it. All of that goes to say that I know nothing of death. Some of us do, because we have come close, or because we have died a little, or because we are hanging on by a thread.

But there are things that feel like death: invasion, exile, survival, compromise, separation.

To move towards each other in some reconciling project is a rejection of other options. It is the rejection of a solitary path. Reconciling involves others, sometimes even those we have been estranged by. It means to connect again. Partly, the word is naive because people who have hurt people are already connected by terrible events. Perhaps reconciliation is the introduction of some new agency to a connection that has had a taste of death. It involves feeling, maybe not for the person on the other side, but perhaps for yourself. And that which feels, lives. It is a threshold between the way things could have been, and the way things are. You do not step through that threshold once. You step through it every time you breathe.

Remember: Spirituality.

* * *

This week, I phoned someone to say sorry. I had written a poem that I thought was loving, but he had taken it differently. I had sent it to him, hoping to make his day.

It didn't.

Right now, I am feeling like there will be the relationship before and after that damned poem. Maybe not, but some wars begin over something as small as words on a bit of paper: ignorable by some, and inflammatory to others. Maybe all of this will be forgotten. Maybe it has caused a small bit of death in a space that was breathing. Maybe death was there all along waiting for a page on which to be written. And I wrote it: rhyming, in quatrains, with assonance and rhythm.

Forgiving, if it means anything, must be true. It cannot undo what was done. It can only help us through a threshold. It must tell its story of death. Again, and again.

* * *

Again, and again and.

* * *

This can feel like an almost unbearable compromise. Welcome to a practice of peace. It is messy. It is not easy. It is fragile and thin and breakable. It is a verb, not an achievement. It needs to be conjugated regularly. It is the experience of having been torn. And, having been torn, staying with that new shape and finding dignity in language, in protest, in lamentation, in justice, in re-ordering, in catharsis.

It's not a landscape; it's staying alive.

* * *

When my friend came to visit me in my dream, I was unprepared. I knew people died – I had seen enough dead bodies at funerals – but friends do not die. Not like that. Well, they did, and they do. He turned up two nights after that phone call with my mother, and in my dream, I was trying to put something right. "What's this? An apology?" he asked, laughing the way he always did, eyes disappearing and face crinkling with laugh lines.

Such dreams do not bring friends back. Apologies do not change anything except the story we tell. It is not great. It is not even good. But it might be good enough.

* * *

There are some things we say when we are in pain that make the pain more bearable. Sometimes those are things we regret. Sometimes those are things we will never regret. When Jesus of Nazareth was being executed slowly by the state authorities, he was held in place by nails and shortened breath and a body and language.

He spoke of forgiveness; he extended kindness to people he believed did not understand their actions; he spoke to one man beside him, but not the other; he spoke to his mother; he prayed; he shouted; he begged; he tried to keep up; he gave up.

Christianity is built on the actions and language and story of this character. His words at death indicate a way of living. He was like lots of us, trying anything that would work to keep alive. It is a fine practice, and he is remembered for it.

Many try to force us towards resurrection, but I have not seen any true resurrection without a true giving up. Jesus went, some stories say, to the places of the dead. Where is that then? Is it here? Certainly, some people think that the twentieth century — with all its wars — is evidence that, even if there is no hell, we are perfectly capable of making one all by ourselves. That night, did he visit anyone in their sabbath dreams? Was he cooking fish? Was he showing bloody hands and saying the same kinds of things he had always said? Was he angry? Or was he still surprising people with his survival?

Many of us spend time in the Saturday between crucifixion and resurrection. Some of us live there permanently, in our lives, in our country's life, in our sexed and disempowered lives. We have the torture of the past at our back and some kind of horizon hoped for at our front. It is a threshold, with hints of one and the other always tapping us. It is both exhausting and exhilarating to be on the cusp of breakthrough and the cliff edge of destruction. It is utterly physical. There is nothing abstract about it.

* * *

Years ago, a boy from Britain was kidnapped and brought to Ireland. We know him as Patrick. In his confessing, he spoke of the tangible. Under the guard of his kidnappers, he said up to one hundred prayers a day. That poor boy. How awful to have nothing to count except days of captivity, sheep and prayers. Kidnapping is not an abstract state, it is entirely physical: your body is captured. It is here, in a state of living that is barely living, that Patrick defined what many of us dream about. Finding language that praises the surface while ploughing the depths.

I arise today
through the strength of heaven:
Light of sun,
Radiance of moon,

Splendour of fire,
Speed of lightning,
Swiftness of wind,
Depth of sea,
Stability of earth,
Firmness of rock.[1]

* * *

I've heard some people describe liminality in the language of Celtic spirituality: a thin place, a narrow place, a place where the living and the dead commune, where heaven and earth all regard each other.

Hell too, I hope. Otherwise what's the point?

"Narrow" in Irish is *caol,* meaning narrow, slender, subtle, or tenuous. In Irish, to speak of the "narrowness of the hand" means the wrist, or the "narrowness of the leg" the ankle. It is a place of mobility or action, a place easily twisted and when twisted, it hurts. Lots of us live in this narrow place, easily open to twisting. Our past and our future each have a hold of us in the present and we wonder how we shall manage. How do any of us survive this fragile place? Liminality, if it means anything, must be as truthful as forgiving, as confessing, as breathing, as surviving.

* * *

For some reason, my computer keeps autocorrecting the word surviving to surfing.

* * *

Last year, my friend Lynn was surfing the waves near Corrymeela. The crossing between Ireland and Scotland is only fourteen miles at its closest. The waves are not always huge, but the current is vicious. A pod of dolphins had moved into the bay. She caught a wave at the same time a dolphin did and for a few seconds they surfed together, buoyed up by the current and the tide. I swam that frigid water too. One Easter Sunday morning, my friend Ross said he was going for a swim and invited me. I said I did not have shorts with me and he laughed and produced a spare pair. Damn, I thought, I should have told a better lie. It was biting, bracing, bitterly cold. It was physical, and I shook when I came out, body covered in silt and salt and little dead things that the surf had surfaced.

---

1. More information about the Corrymeela Community can be sourced at www. corrymeela.org.
2. St Patrick, "The Deer's Cry" (St Patrick's Breastplate), in *The Deer's Cry: A Treasury of Irish Religious Verse*, ed. Patrick Murray (Blackrock, Co. Dublin: Four Courts Press, 1986).

The source of the word surf is uncertain. Some people think it refers to a coastal region of India. Others think it might be onomatopoeic, the sound of water on a shore: a place of exhilaration and exhaustion, a place where land meets sea and creates something else: a noise, an invitation, a threat, a promise, a place to swim or drown in, a place of horizons, waves, tides and crashing. A place of sound and salt; a space where stones are ground into sand; where whales come to die; where people delight in splashing; a place on the living earth controlled by the movements of a moon where nothing lives; an in-between place for the living and the dying.

3
Where Heaven Caresses the Earth
Elena Huegel

The elemental truths fit on the wing of a hummingbird.

José Martí[1]

* * *

A shimmering green flash is here and gone. The hummingbirds greet us with rhythmic clicks, zooming around our heads as we begin the week-long course called "Roots in the Ruins: Hope in Trauma," which was developed in Chile after the devastating 2010 earthquake and tsunami. We gather at the Shalom Center, in the foothills of the Andes Mountains, to pause and enter into this sacred space by sharing our histories, singing together, creating art, learning from each other and reconfiguring the pieces of our trauma into a new pattern of iridescent beauty. The shimmering hummingbirds invite us into a holy covenant, a commitment to healing our relationships with God, ourselves, others, and all of creation.

During the Roots in the Ruins course, we walk a labyrinth from our traumatic experiences, through depressive or aggressive reactions, to the place where we can break free, tell our stories, seek justice, restore our dignity, and reconnect in healthy, life-giving ways. In the center of the labyrinth is the *espacio liminal* or liminal space:

> the threshold in time and space where change occurs. It is the place of transformation, the ephemeral scene after "that which has been" and just before "what will be." It is a sacred space, "holy ground," where in our vulnerability and uncertainty the Spirit of God gives us new perspectives and inspires us with vision. . . . Liminal space

---

1. "Who Was Jose Marti?" http://www.unesco.org/new/en/social-and-human-sciences/
events/prizes-and-celebrations/unesco-prizes/jose-marti-prize/jose-marti/..

is fleeting, and often we don't realize we have been there until afterwards when we discover that we have been changed. It is a place of synergy, where all things reconnect for a moment.[2]

This week, as we leave the valley and brave the labyrinth in the ancient forests of the Andes, we reach the liminal space where we stretch deeply inwards, past our traumas and towards our healing, before returning to the path where we will continue on the quest towards a richer and fuller life. At first just one, and then a dozen hummingbirds, swarm around us, messengers celebrating the renewal of hopes and dreams in the midst of ruins and ashes.

One of the women on the course has recently suffered the loss of her newborn baby. She wrestles with the paradox of death at the beginning of life, of despair at the end of dreams, of questions responding to answers. With her soul laid bare, I take her by the hand and lead her under the blooming tree where the hummingbirds come and go. We stand in silence, and she weeps. I leave her there under the care of the hummingbirds to attend to the rest of the participants. Eventually, she returns to the group. She tells us that the hummingbirds have taken her grief and brought back from God a tiny message of peace, just big enough to be carried on diminutive wings. "Rest in me, in the mystery of the unanswerable, in the hope of things not yet known or seen, but that will be abundantly good," the hummingbirds seem to say in buzzing whispers.

Participants in the course from Paraguay explain that, in their Guaraní culture, the hummingbird represents the place where heaven caresses the earth, and its flight is a reminder of the existence of the land without evils, here with us now and yet beyond our limited perception of time and space. Hummingbirds, or the *mainumby* as they are called in Guaraní, invite us to search for and believe in the land without evils, the place where we will live into *py'aguapy*, literally, "tranquil stomachs," which is the Guaraní metaphor for peace. The first place we feel the lack of peace, the Guaraní say, is in the pit of our stomachs. When one's stomach is at ease, one experiences peace. That peace, however, is not complete until everyone in the community enjoys a tranquil stomach with enough food, a sense of their own dignity as well as the dignity of others, and a vision of hope and renewal in the present and the future. For the Guaraní, peace comes with equality – everyone's stomach at ease, and justice – enough food and opportunities for everyone both locally and beyond the boundaries of a particular community. The hummingbird, the liminality messenger, calls us to seek individual and community peace with equality, dignity and justice in our quest for the land without evils.

2. Beverly Prestwood-Taylor and Elena Huegel. Unpublished materials in Spanish, "*Manual de Retoños en Las Ruinas: Esperanza en el Trauma, nivel 1 (curso básico),*" 33, trans. Elena Huegel (Chile: Centro Shalom, 2013, *revisión* 2017).

As more people participate in the Roots in the Ruins: Hope in Trauma course, we receive requests to share what we have learned in other countries beyond Chile: Argentina, Paraguay, Mexico, Puerto Rico, and Nicaragua. In Chiapas, a southern state of Mexico, I met Elena, my *tocaya*, the term in Spanish we affectionately use for someone who has our same name. She belongs to the Tseltal-Tzotzil people, and her Mayan ancestors have lived in the Chiapan highlands of Mexico, near the Guatemalan border, for thousands of years. We have something else in common besides our names: we both love and identify with hummingbirds, the tiny birds native only to the Americas and incapable of surviving in cages that limit their freedom. On the very first morning when I arrived in San Cristóbal de las Casas in Chiapas, a familiar humming greeted me on my way from the bunkhouse to the bathroom. I veered off course, hunting through the flowers, my eyes flicking back and forth, hoping to catch a glimpse of the sound-maker. It was there in an instant, then gone, the sound fading quickly. A week later when I found a house to rent, I recognized the same sound in the neighbor's flowering bushes over the back wall; hummingbirds welcomed me to this city and to a new home.

Because of our hummingbird connection, Elena asked me to join her in a hummingbird art project. I painted a hummingbird with flowers encircled by the sun and the moon. She then transferred the design onto a cloth and embroidered it in the style which she had learned from her mother and grandmother and is unique to her particular Mayan village. As we worked together, she introduced me to her Mayan spirituality and to the Tseltal language, with which her people describe "mother earth" and the story of the existence of the "true men and women." She tells me that the hummingbirds are the ancestors, the grandmothers and grandfathers, coming to reassure us and to infuse us with strength and hope. A legend of the Mayan people recounts how the hummingbird received the task of carrying wishes and thoughts between the gods and people. "Hummingbirds are here to remind us to enjoy and protect our freedom, to be true to ourselves, to all that is good and life-giving," my *tocaya* explained to me one day. "When I see a hummingbird pause on a branch, I remember that I, too, must stop, rest, breathe, and tell myself to simply be in the middle of all my doing." Our common art project unfolds into a deeper friendship, and Elena invites me into the traditional liminal space of the Mayan altar.

Mayan altars are always created in community. They are made of transient gifts from nature: flowers, water, soil, seashells, or beeswax candles. Early one morning I join Elena and three other co-workers – an American woman, a Tzotzil woman, and a Tseltal man – in preparing a Mayan altar with fresh cut flowers arranged in yellow, white, red, and lilac pie pieces completing a circle on the floor. When everything is ready, the *ocote*, a piece of the resinous heart wood of the Montezuma pine, is lit and the pungent spice smell, along with the deep melodious moan of the conk shell, calls to us. We gather around the altar holding candles to represent the four cardinal directions. Christians, those with Mayan spirituality, those who profess no faith, Tseltales, Tzotziles, Europeans, Mexicans, Americans, Canadians, and Lebanese are drawn into the sacred space by the smell, the smoke, the candles, and the flowers. We pray for our personal and collective awakening to peace in the midst of political crisis and government-sponsored violence. We pray for courage as the diversity of the environment disappears around us. We pray for justice in communities devastated by migration, alcoholism, and drug trafficking. We pray for the people of all nations to have the courage and perseverance, the wisdom and strength to stand in dignity, just as the Mayan have stood again and again over the centuries, bending but not breaking under oppression, remaining resilient and resistant. With each prayer we turn – east, west, north, south.

On this morning around the Mayan altar and across from my new friend, Elena, I resist opening my heart to the liminal space because of the smell. Thousands of miles away, the pine plantations owned by powerful lumber companies are burning like blue matchsticks and covering Chile in a heavy gray blanket. Homes, churches, native forests catch on fire. A blaze near the Shalom Center threatens the place where that first group gathered on the Roots in the Ruins course. As with the many other situations mentioned in the prayers, there is so little I can do. Finally, when we turn to the south, I give in: I feel the trembling of the hummingbirds, lizards, condors, foxes, and ancient trees as they fear the fire and the ravages of humanity. Here, in the pine and oak highlands of Chiapas, surrounded by people in a place where "Mercy and truth have met together; righteousness and peace have kissed" (Psalms 85:10), I fight off insidious despair and breathe deeply, filling my lungs with the smell of commitment, imagination, and joy which abounds in the midst of the struggle for *shalom*. "For God has not given us the spirit of fear, but of power, and love, and self-control" (2 Timothy 1:7). I dare to step toward the altar, light my candle and enter the circle of liminality. I weep as the fear, helplessness, shame, anger, and horror of my pain and trauma surface and then waft away on the breath of breeze, soft as the wind from a hummingbird wing.

Back at the Shalom Center, the hot South American summer, the fire-threatening season, has ended, and the April rains mark the beginning of fall. The hummingbirds prepare to leave the Andes Mountains traveling north towards warmer weather. I write to my spiritual companion, who lives in Massachusetts, "The hummingbirds have left. I will miss them through the long winter." But two weeks later, she writes back: "The first hummingbirds have arrived!" Spring comes to Massachusetts as fall comes to Chile and the hummingbirds remind us both to pause between the seasons. The two-week silence is the waiting room for the burst of new life in the north and the bedding down for winter in the south. The hummingbirds invite us, twice a year, into an "in-between time" to reflect and prepare for a new season in our lives. The hummers in Massachusetts are not the same ones that live in Chile, but some species of these tiny birds travel thousands of miles in transcontinental migrations across North, Central and South America. All through the southern winter, my friend entertains me with the exploits of hummingbirds defending or attacking the feeder outside her window, until one day in October she writes saying good-bye to the brilliant fall foliage around the pond and to the hummingbirds flying south. We enter the liminal space, the pause marked by tiny birds that live their lives in rhythm with the earth's rotation. Two weeks later, I spot a green flash at the Shalom Center. The hummingbirds are back!

Except for last year, that is. The hummingbirds did not leave the Shalom Center in April; the winter cold never arrived. One heavy snowfall in June blanketed the still leafy tree branches that bent and broke under the weight. Hundreds of downed trees and branches littered the forest after the snow melted a couple of days later, another chaotic clue to the confusion coming from climate change. The Massachusetts hummingbirds arrived in the northern spring while I watched and waited, and still the Shalom Center hummingbirds did not leave. There was no seasonal pause, no invitation into the waiting time, no sense of expectation, no practice of hope. Forces far beyond the forest in Chile and the pond side in Massachusetts are depriving us of our liminal space. The hummingbirds find food, water and warm shelter out of season, a sign pointing to that which has gone wrong. Climate change is not just about shifting weather patterns; it lays bare our greed and deep-seated terror of entering into a space where we must face what we have done individually and collectively, who we are and what we dream of being and becoming, how we live and what we expect out of life on this planet.

The hummingbirds bring me new insight and wisdom again, now in the desert plateau outside San Luis Potosí in central Mexico. We are preparing for another Roots in the Ruins course. Outside, under the trees, I pray with my co-facilitator, Mercedes, as we prepare to accompany the next group through the liminality labyrinth in hopes of reaching healing and wholeness. These very same trees were planted by my father thirty years ago when the dry, rock-strewn landscape lacked anything green for miles around. Today, I count ten different bird calls among the trees and spot a pair of hawks in the tallest branches. Just as Mercedes tells me how nervous she is about facilitating for the first time, she spies a tiny hummingbird nest. And she confides in me: "When I was a young girl, I found a hummingbird nest, with two tiny eggs in it, that had fallen out of a tree. I didn't touch it but called my father. He gave me a piece of cloth and taught me how to gently pick up the nest. We observed the silver, shimmering-soft lining of the nest, and he explained that some hummingbirds line their nests with spider webs. Then my father brought out a ladder, and, while he held the ladder up, balancing it where there was no wall or tree trunk to lean on, he encouraged me to climb, one hand gently holding the nest and the other clutching the rungs. I was terrified, but I trusted my father. In that moment I learned that, whenever I am shaking with fear, there are special people I can trust who are there to hold me up even as I reach out to help another in need."

As she tells her story, her countenance and her whole body changes. She sits up straighter, joy spreads across her face, and she laughs. "I am ready now!" she exclaims, and we link arms as we walk towards the area prepared for the course. The delicate strands of trust, faith, and love have been woven into a physical, emotional, relational, and spiritual space where the new participants can break out of their shells and learn to fly. We have woven our own hummingbird nest; a safe space, a place of liminality, that has been created to welcome each participant at the threshold of freedom and abundant life.

My father, who grew up in the Anahuac valley of Mexico City, recently shared a special word in Nahuatl, the language of the Aztec people. The word is *nepantla*, which means the "between times" or the "land between lands." It is a word that perfectly describes my own flight of the hummingbird, liminal life. This present time and space are *nepantla*, a reflection of the interval between the earthly life of Jesus with his invitation into the kingdom of God and the fullness of the peace, hope, and joy which is yet to come.

The blog *Nepantlera: Exploring Boundaries, Edges and Borders* offers this description of the Nahuatl word, *nepantla*:

> These edges, boundaries and borders are dynamic places of transformation. While they are unstable, unpredictable and precarious, they are also places of greater diversity and therefore greater potential for creativity, innovation and productivity. These liminal spaces provide "dynamic spaces for transformation, community and social action." Or as the beloved Chicana author and cultural pioneer, Gloria Anzaldúa puts it, "*nepantleras* facilitate passages between two worlds."[3]

3. *Nepantlera:* Exploring Boundaries, Edges and Borders, Blog description, reviewed and trans. by Elena Huegel, on 5 October 2017, https://bettebooth.wordpress.com/about/.

I have had my own challenges growing up as the daughter of missionaries in Mexico. I balanced two languages, two cultures, two histories, and two countries often antagonistic to each other. Every time I crossed the border between the United States and Mexico, I would be reminded of the political, economic, and social tensions between my two countries. Since my father is a Mexican citizen and my mother is a citizen of the United States, we would often suffer harassment on both sides of the border. The American officials would strip our car, go through all of our belongings, and send their dogs to sniff us for drugs or firearms. The Mexican officials would quickly glance at us and then find some excuse to demand a bribe. Crossing the border was not the only source of fear during my childhood and adolescence. In Mexico, there is a deeply ingrained cultural conflict that sets the pride and courage of the original peoples against the supposed beauty and intellectual superiority of the European settlers. Parents will often tell their male children, "better the race, my son," which means that they are to marry fair or blond women. Blond and fair-skinned women are thought to be easy, loose, and desirable sexual targets. This myth, along with the ever-present power play of "machismo," made growing up in Mexico as a blond and blue-eyed young woman scary and confusing. Then, when I would visit the United States, I was told that Mexicans were inferior and no more than "greasers," "wetbacks," or "illegals." I remember feeling stubbornly defiant when one of my great aunts in Texas pointed her finger at me and declared, "You are an American so had you better start living and speaking like one." I did not respond, but rebelliously thought to myself, "Only the outside of me is from the United States; on the inside, I am Mexican!"

While struggling to understand my bi-cultural identity, I found in my family a *nepantlera*, a safe space in which to navigate between worlds. My parents challenged me to be creative, explore my interests, and develop the gifts offered by my multifaceted heritage. I discovered my first hummingbirds as a small child in the gardens of the Theological Community in Mexico City where I was encouraged to nourish my love for nature while caring for others by cooperating, respecting, and sharing in the many social and spiritual activities with people from all over Latin America. Tucked gently away in my soul and mind is the gift of seeing the world from the borderlands, the in-between spaces, the *nepantlera* of "either/or" and "neither/nor," with thousands of beautifully colored hues and nuances of language and culture. With the hummingbirds in the *nepantlera*, the liminal space, at the heart of the intercultural labyrinth, I found my quest to weave together the torn edges of our relationships in "the healing of the nations" (Revelation 22:2).

As I travel up, down and across the Americas, I am always on the lookout for glimpses of wisdom hidden in hummingbird stories. It never ceases to amaze me how many people have had a hummingbird moment that changed the direction of their lives. In preparing the Roots in the Ruins materials, I wrote a series of stories to help the children of Chile heal their relationship with nature after the earthquake and tsunami. The tales invited the children to open their souls to the beauty, well-being, and grounding attained by reconnecting with nature, even as the aftershocks rumbled and shook their sense of security. I distilled my own intercultural perspective with these hummingbird encounters, dreams and experiences into a story:

Among all the birds created by God, there was one that was the smallest. This bird was excitable and hyperactive, with an insatiable appetite. Instead of singing, it clicked like the static electricity from a wool sweater. Since its wings buzzed and it drank nectar from the flowers like the bees, the other birds decided that it wasn't a bird at all but an insect and they threw it out of the aviary kingdom. The hummingbird, confused, flew away wondering who she was and for what purpose she had been created.

At the same time, a grumpy old man who did not get along with anyone fell sick and died. Since he had never learned to be kind, he did not know how to find the way of goodness, that path marked by the first ray of daybreak that leads to heaven. This lost soul wandered around the world, afraid and lonely, until he hid in a brilliant red flower growing in a garden.

The hummingbird, hungry as usual, flew to the very same flower and discovered, much to her surprise, the soul of the old man curled up inside.

"Who are you and what are you doing here?" the hummingbird asked.

"Humpf!" grumbled the soul of the old man. "I was not a good person in my life and I haven't found the way to heaven. I am afraid I will never get there, so I have taken refuge in this flower."

"I have never been to heaven, but I am sure I can chase the first ray of dawn if I fly fast enough. If you want, I can try to take you," answered the hummingbird.

The very next morning, right before the first ray of sunlight peeked into the garden, the hummingbird arrived at the flower. A soul is a very light and fragile thing, so the hummingbird lifted it carefully in her beak and launched herself into the air. Her small wings beat with such speed that they seemed to disappear. Just at the moment when the first sunray was joined by others to announce the breaking of the day, the hummingbird flew through the gates of heaven, crashing into the chest of the angel in charge of guarding the entrance.

"What do we have here?" asked the angel.

The soul of the old man responded before the hummingbird could say a word. "I am a lost soul being transported to heaven with the hope of being let in even though I don't deserve it."

"All who wish it can find rest in this place," answered the angel, pointing the way deeper into heaven. The soul jumped out of the hummingbird's beak and disappeared into the brilliance of beyond.

"And you, small one," continued the angel, "must go back to earth. I have a message I want to send which you can deliver for me. It is a message in a package fit for your size. Please leave this bit of peace on earth so that those who find it can take comfort in it."

From that morning on, the hummingbird was very busy finding more lost souls hidden in the flowers, taking them to heaven, and returning to the world with pinches of peace, love, hope and joy.

One dawn, when she arrived in heaven with another lost soul, the angel wasn't there to meet her. God was waiting at the gates of heaven.

"I have come to congratulate you and thank you for your excellent work, small one," said God.

The hummingbird, taking advantage of the fact that she was face to face with the Creator of all things, answered with a timid and trembling voice. "God, may I ask you a question? The other birds threw me out of their kingdom because they said I look, fly and sound like an insect. It is true that I don't behave like a bird at all, but I have feathers and my heart beats like theirs do. What am I? If I don't sing or eat worms but am excitable and impulsive, what was I created for?"

"You, my small one, are unique. I gave you the form of a bird, but you on your own have discovered your true purpose. You bring souls who have not known goodness to me and you take pieces of heaven to be enjoyed in the midst of suffering on earth. You are the messenger between heaven and earth."

So it was that the hummingbird discovered she was special, created by the hand of God, to fulfill a task that required her special abilities. Even today, if you find a hummingbird in the garden, you will observe how it flicks speedily from flower to flower, searching for lost souls, and when it finds one, it disappears on the path towards heaven. Then, when it suddenly reappears, your soul will give a little leap of hope, peace and love. In that moment, pause, breathe deep, and receive a heavenly caress that just might change your life forever. [4]

---

4. This story was adapted from a legend told by the Guaraní people of Paraguay that says that the souls of people live in the flowers until a hummingbird arrives to take them to heaven. The Guaraní believe that the hummingbird's flight indicates the places where heaven caresses the earth, and, when we see one of these tiny birds, we should remember that the hope and joy of heaven are never far away from us even in the midst of the challenges we face while living on earth. I wrote this story for the Roots in the Ruins: Hope in Trauma program as I worked with children in South America, and it appears in the materials called "*Con Esperanza y Valiente: Imágenes de la Naturaleza para la Sanidad de Traumas y el Desarrollo de la Resiliencia en Niños y Niñas*," ("With Hope and Bravery: Images from Nature for the Healing of Trauma and Development of Resilience in Children"), trans. Elena Huegel (Chile: Centro Shalom, Chile, 2014), 57-59.

4

Pilgrims, Thresholds, and the *Camino*

Kristine A. Culp

Pilgrimage is an ancient, global, popular, and often ambiguous phenomenon: pilgrims circulating the Kaaba in Mecca; standing before the Wailing Wall in Jerusalem; journeying to the banks of the holy Ganges; landing in Plymouth Harbor; seeking the Virgin of Guadalupe, or of Lourdes, Fatima, Medjugorje; walking arm in arm across the Edmund Pettus Bridge to march from Selma to Montgomery, Alabama; moving with a sea of pink pussyhats to stand in solidarity with women around the world.

In pilgrimage, an extended and often difficult journey becomes a process of separating from the given, everyday world. Pilgrimage entails stepping away from daily routines and expectations and moving with special deliberateness toward a place where one might be changed. In marches that are part of social movements, one journeys with others to bring about change and to move together as the wider world is being changed. Movement away from the given world and toward a distant goal can create a wide threshold of transition and transformation.

The Phenomenon of Pilgrimage

Anthropologists Victor and Edith Turner characterize pilgrimage as "the great liminal experience of the religious life."[1] Their 1978 book, *Image and Pilgrimage in Christian Culture*, places pilgrimage as an anti-type to obligatory structure. Generally, individuals choose to go on pilgrimage. Pilgrimage's voluntary nature contrasts with the rites de passage that Arnold van Gennep studied and with "the ritual process" in preindustrial societies that Victor Turner himself wrote about, both of which are

---

1. Victor Turner and Edith L.B. Turner, *Image and Pilgrimage in Christian Culture: Anthropological Perspectives* (New York: Columbia University Press, 1978), 7.

undergone and socially obligatory rather than chosen and representing a release from social processes. Yet, salient comparisons of symbols and processes can be made:

> Pilgrimage has some of the liminal phase attributes in passage rites: release from mundane structure; homogenization of status; simplicity of dress and behavior; communitas, both on the journey, and as a characteristic of the goal, which is itself a source of communitas, healing, and renewal; ordeal; reflection on the meaning of religious and cultural core-values; ritualized enactment of correspondences between a religious paradigm and shared human experiences; movement from a mundane center to a sacred periphery which suddenly, transiently, becomes central for the individual, an *axis mundi* of his faith; movement in general (as against stasis), symbolizing the uncapturability and temporal transience of communitas; individuality posed against the institutionalized milieu; and so forth.[2]

The Turners accent the voluntary, de-centered, bottom-up nature of most Christian pilgrimage. In a way that seems recognizable, retrospectively, as a 1970s sort of way, they celebrate the antistructural quality of communitas that potentially arises on a pilgrimage and as its goal. Communitas is "antistructural and liberating," "anti-clerical," and rooted in the world of ordinary folk rather than that of the elite. It is "a relational quality of full unmediated communication, even communion, between definite and determinate identities which arises spontaneously in all kinds of groups, situations, and circumstances." "Communitas breaks into society at the interstices of structure, in liminality; at the edges of structure, in marginality; and from beneath structure, in inferiority."[3]

A Very Brief History of Pilgrimage in Ancient and Medieval Christianity

The Bible relates several accounts of the people of God in the form of itineraries: the flight from Egypt and the sojourn in the wilderness, the pilgrims' ascent to the holy city sung in the psalms, the life of Jesus, the travels and ministry of Paul. One of the earliest Christian pilgrims, Egeria, traveled to the Middle East in 382. Her diary recounts how she traced the lives and actions of prophets, Jesus, apostles, and

---

2. Ibid., 253-54, see also 34-35.
3. Ibid., 250-51.

martyrs through Palestine, venerating the places where they had lived, taught, and died. She read aloud passages from Scripture, the *Acts of the Christian Martyrs,* and Eusebius's *Ecclesiastical History* as she traveled, joining those ancient texts with physical places through imagination and emotion to produce deeper understanding and mystical adoration of God. Egeria's itinerary and practices offered both a literal and a mystical way of *imitatio dei.*[4] Through the seventh century, Jerusalem pilgrims took pinches of dust from the "actual footprints" as souvenirs.[5] An interest in physical artifacts, relics, of Christ's passion and of martyrs, grew from there.[6]

In medieval times, the great Christian pilgrimages – to Jerusalem, Rome, Canterbury in England, and Santiago de Compostela in northwest Spain – required months and even years of travel. Pilgrims made arduous journeys to central places of remembrance, adoration, and penance, stopping at cathedrals and abbeys along the route to venerate lesser saints and their relics. Pilgrims also sought miracles and healing, relief from guilt, consecration, an opportunity to pray and draw near to the life and power of Christ and the saints, plus a measure of adventure and a glimpse of a broader existence. Pilgrimages became profoundly social, cultural, economic, and political events, as well as solitary and religious ones. They brought people together from far-flung places to worship, form bonds, seek release, and be changed. They created systems of global cultural, economic, and artistic exchange. They often also served highly ambiguous religio-political aims, notably the Crusades and the Reconquista.[7]

According to the twelfth-century "sermon," *Veneranda Dies,* which was to be read on one of the feast days of Saint James (Santiago), manifold benefits were bestowed on people who made pilgrimages to Compostela:

---

4. "If mysticism is an interior pilgrimage, [physical] pilgrimage is exteriorized mysticism," Victor and Edith Turner observe pithily, ibid., 7. Historically considered, ancient itineraries and ancient pilgrims' practices become interiorized as templates for mysticism, see ibid., 33.

5. Jonathan Sumption, *Pilgrimage: An Image of Mediaeval Religion* (Totowa, NJ: Rowman & Littlefield, 1975), 91.

6. William Melczer, "Introduction," in *The Pilgrim's Guide to Santiago de Compostela,* trans. with introduction, commentaries, and notes by William Melczer (New York: Italica Press, 1993), 2.

7. For example, Saint James (Santiago) and Isidore of Seville were among a half-dozen saints who were featured along the medieval Camino de Santiago recast as *matamoros* ("Moorslayers"), placed on horseback, equipped with swords, and conscripted, as it were, as warring apparitions waging apocryphal battles.

Many poor people, in fact, have gone there who, with God's grace, afterwards were made happy, many weak were made healthy, many dissenters agreeable, many perverse pious, many lustful chaste, many worldly later monks, many misers generous, many usurers later bestowing their goods, many haughty later gentle, many deceitful later truthful, many taking the belongings of others later giving their own clothes to the poor, many perjurers later law-abiders, many declaring falsehood later asserting the truth, many dishonest later just.[8]

The preacher portrays Santiago de Compostela as a threshold of transition from "what was" to the graced *potentiality* of "what may be."[9] Perhaps above all other spiritual benefits, the great pilgrimages offered the possibility of cleansing from sin and starting spiritual life anew. The reigning theology pictured people as living in a world that drew them inexorably toward sin, and so, "the prospect of . . . starting his spiritual life anew, stood before [the medieval pilgrim] like a mirage, irresistibly attractive."[10]

The Pilgrim Way to Santiago de Compostela

In 950, nearly two hundred monks, the first recorded group of pilgrims to Santiago de Compostela, departed from Le Puy, a large town in what is now south-central France, under the leadership of the bishop of Le Puy. Over the centuries, Le Puy became the starting point for the *Via Podiensis*, one of several established routes to Santiago de Compostela. The 1,600 km route leads through Conques and Moissac, both monastic centers with significant sanctuaries, crosses the Garonne River to St-Jean-Pied-de-Port, where it joins with two other pilgrim routes through the Pyrénées, and then continues across most of northern Spain, almost to the Atlantic Ocean, as part of the *Camino de Santiago*.[11]

---

8. *Veneranda Dies* Sermon, in *The Miracles of Saint James: Translations from the Liber Sancti Jacobi*, trans. and introduction by Thomas F. Coffey, Linda Kay Davidson, and Maryjane Dunn (New York: Italica Press, 1996), 20.

9. See Turner and Turner, *Image and Pilgrimage*, 3: "It has become clear to us that liminality is not only *transition* but also *potentiality*, not only 'going to be' but also 'what may be,' a formulable domain in which all that is not manifest in the normal day-to-day operation of social structures . . . can be studied objectively, despite the often bizarre and metaphorical character of its contents."

10. Sumption, *Pilgrimage*, 128.

11. Some of the following is revised and adapted from Kristine A. Culp, "Pilgrimage: Journey Toward the Holy," cover story and photos in collaboration with Kay Bessler Northcutt, *The Disciple* 137, no. 1 (January/February 1999), 2-7.

Contemporary travelers describe Le Puy's setting as "theatrical;" Turner and Turner characterize it as "liminal."[12] According to one travel guide, the landscape "erupts in a chaos of volcanic acne." The eleventh-century Chapelle Saint-Michel d'Aiguilhe looks over the town from atop a 260-foot pinnacle of lava. Equally prominent on the horizon is "a colossal 16-meter [52-foot] statue of the Virgin and child in brick-red;" erected in 1860, it was "cast from guns captured at Sebastapol and colored to match the tiled roofs below." The immense eleventh-century Notre-Dame-de-l'Annonciation, or Le Puy cathedral, set high on the same hill as the rust-red Virgin, features rounded Romanesque arches whose striped patterns reveal a Spanish Arabic (Moorish) influence (and an example of the cross-cultural connection) of the route to Santiago. The cathedral shelters a Black Madonna and incorporates remains of a Druid megalith. Le Puy was an ancient site of Celtic worship and then a center of Marian devotion long before it became a starting point for the pilgrimage to Santiago.

From Le Puy the *Via Podiensis* stretches across the Aubrac plateau, a desolate, rocky terrain with "granite villages hunkered down out of the weather," as one guide puts it. Here and elsewhere, the route is marked by crosses. Far more cows than people populate the plateau today. There is little modernization, little tourism. The landscape has a bleak beauty, and crossing it by foot requires days of rugged walking. This isolated stretch of the *Via Podiensis* seems to interpret itself as the way of the cross.

In the middle of this austere plateau, the village of Aubrac is not much more than a crossroads. In the twelfth century, a hospice there sheltered hundreds of pilgrims each night. Pilgrims may have been imitating Christ's way of the cross, but they were taking it up with fellow pilgrims and sufferers. Like Egeria before them, pilgrims on this *via* adopt a stylized pattern for their journey: they move step by step, day by day, across the challenging terrain. Refocussing attention through prayer and confession, they disconnect from whence they came and from whom they were. They engage the communion of sinners and saints who walk with them, literally on the pilgrim road and spiritually through the ages.

Beyond Aubrac, the trail descends to the Lot River valley, where desolation gives way to lush vegetation and riverside villages. Crossing wooded ridges and streams, travelers emerge from a narrow gorge, as if

---

12. See Turner and Turner, *Image and Pilgrimage*, 200ff.: "In Le Puy we have a magnificent instance of how archaic pilgrimage centers graft new pilgrimages onto old. . . . Le Puy suggests an *axis mundi*, perched as it is on a huge lump of volcanic rock rising, like the hub of a wheel, in the center of a prosperous plain surrounded by mountains."

having reached rainbow's end, to find the shimmering village of Conques clinging to the side of the valley. The village's silvery-yellow stone buildings, clad with steep fish-scale roofs, are built in descending terraces around a glorious, elegantly proportioned abbey church. In the golden church, a bejeweled golden effigy of Sainte-Foy (Saint Faith) holds the treasure that pilgrims seek to venerate, the precious relic of her skull. *La Majesté de Sainte-Foy*, as the reliquary is called, is an enormous head borne by a disproportionately small body seated on a throne. She wears a martyr's crown. Medieval pilgrims encountered her in the sanctuary, not in the glass case that surrounds her today. They may have felt compelled to seek her recognition or favor, winning it from the awe and judgment that they felt before her.[13]

It is not only Sainte-Foy's piercing gaze that chastens pilgrims. They can only enter the sanctuary to see her by passing under a vivid depiction of the Last Judgment sculpted over the church's doorway. The tympanum portrays an enthroned Christ whose outstretched arms lead the blessed through the gates of heaven to eternal peace, while the damned are directed to the jaws of Leviathan (a shaggy demon shoves them through) to eternal terror. An inscription translates, "O sinners if you do not change your lives, know that a harsh judgment awaits you."[14]

Below the figure of Christ, souls are weighed while a demon tries, unsuccessfully, to tip the scales. The blessed are arranged in orderly fashion at Christ's right hand: Mary first, then Peter, followed by the hermit Dadon who founded the abbey in the eighth century, an abbot leading Charlemagne and other members of the Carolingian royal family, the three martyrs who died with Sainte-Foy, the monk Avariscius who secured her relics for the abbey by means of "holy theft," and others.[15] The damned are types from medieval life: a knight, an adulterous woman, a poacher, a forger. They represent the seven deadly sins plus a few more: gossip, power, fornication, and heresy.[16] A horde of demons administer ingeniously

---

13. In the early eleventh century, Bernard, master of the episcopal school at Angers, commented on the effects of a similar effigy of Saint-Gerald at nearby Aurillac. He wrote that it "reproduced with such art the features of the human face that the peasants who looked on it felt themselves pierced by a penetrating gaze and sometimes thought that they glimpsed in the rays from his eyes the indication of a favor more indulgent to their wishes." As quoted by Andreas Petzold, *Romanesque Art* (New York: Harry N. Abrams, 1995), 118.

14. Ibid., 74.

15. On "holy theft," see Patrick J. Geary, *Furta Sacra: Thefts of Relics in the Central Middle Ages*, rev. ed. (Princeton, NJ: Princeton University Press, 1990).

16. Delia Evans, *Blue Guide Midi-Pyrénées: Albi, Toulouse, Conques, Moissac* (New York: W.W. Norton, 1995), 178-79.

suitable punishments: for example, one demon tumbles a prideful knight from his mount with a pitchfork; a pair of demons, one sporting the head of a hare, roast the poacher on a spit.[17]

Would medieval pilgrims have attempted to place themselves within this scene of Christ's glory and judgment? Or would they have stood back to delight in its artistry and animation, as contemporary visitors do? Perhaps they dismissed it as a moralizing tale from the monks. Perhaps they placed themselves among the blessed and found assurance. Perhaps they recognized their own sins and sought the favor of Sainte-Foy all the more ardently.

Scenes of Christ's glory and rule were a regular feature of the cathedrals and monastic churches that were built or reconstructed in the eleventh and twelfth centuries along the four French routes to Compostela. At Saint-Trophîme in Arles, the elect, clothed, advance across the left face of the church toward Christ; an angel receives their souls, depicted as naked children, and drops them into the laps of Abraham, Isaac, and Jacob, where the souls – still child-sized but clothed once again – perch. Christ sits in glory, surrounded by the symbols of the four evangelists, a host of angels above, and the twelve apostles below. On Christ's left, an angel guards the gates of heaven where a group of sinners (prelates, men, and women) are refused admission. The damned – naked, chained together, and led by a demon – retreat across the right face of the church with flames licking their heels. These portals were the sculpted counterpart to the words preached in *Veneranda Dies,* "The road is, in fact, narrow that leads man to life, and the road is wide and spacious that leads to death."[18]

Any doubts about where pilgrims belonged in the divine panorama of judgment, salvation, and glory are answered in the tympanum at Autun.[19] Christ's outstretched arms gesture toward the peaceful and orderly blessed to his right; behind them is the heavenly city of Jerusalem. To his left are the contorted and damned, the scale of judgment, and the yawning mouth of hell. Across the lintel, the dead step out of their tombs, naked. Some writhe, while the calm demeanor of others – including two wearing nothing but pilgrim pouches decorated with symbols of Jerusalem and Santiago – marks them as among the blessed. Autun's tympanum and the preacher say, "The pilgrim road is the best way, but the most narrow." What did the road offer? A way to train their feet and their souls to follow Christ? A way to alter their eternal destiny? Had they been told or did they believe, as Luther and Calvin protested, that they must work their own salvation through penance and pilgrimage?

---

17. Petzold, *Romanesque Art,* 74-75.
18. *Veneranda Dies,* 23.
19. See Linda Seidel, *Legends in Limestone: Lazarus, Gislebertus, and the Cathedral of Autun* (Chicago: University of Chicago Press, 1999).

Viewed from a post-Reformation perspective, the scenes seem to convey an unambiguous either/or, right hand/left hand, salvation/damnation choice that is to be made once and for all by the individual who stands at the doorway to the cathedral. However, the scenes do not necessarily suggest a once-and-for-all event of justification, of a sinner simultaneously justified. Rather, the carved tympanum and surrounding portal portray Christ's glory as a just judgment that orders earth and heaven; all who would cross the threshold below symbolically enter that order, surrounded by the portrayed communion of the blessed and the damned through time. Like the preacher of *Veneranda Dies*, these scenes of Christ's judgment and glory challenged, implored, and threatened those who looked upon them not to take their salvation for granted, but to take heed of the final ordering of the world to come in Christ. Walking to Santiago de Compostela, following the way of the cross, pilgrims made their penance real down to their toes, and they joined literally and symbolically with a communion of fellow pilgrims through time.

No doubt medieval fears were real – people knew the ravages of disease and hunger, of unceasing labor, and of guilt more intimately than they knew restoration, release, or redemption. In fact, a few hundred years later, Martin Luther himself shared the diagnosis of a fearful and frightening world. Luther protested against a highly controlled system of penance – which by then had centralized and incorporated the practice of pilgrimage and the veneration of relics – that he saw as exacerbating rather than relieving the dire situation. He denounced the theological and ecclesiastical system that had come to control and propagate these practices as presumptions upon the grace and sovereignty of God and as inadequate to human need. John Calvin shared Luther's protest against the prevailing institution, but he retained the image of the Christian life as a pilgrim journey on a road that could be perilous and difficult to follow.

When I drove along the *Via Podiensis* twenty years ago, I saw more cyclists training (for the Tour de France?) than pilgrims walking. Frankly, the motivations and rewards of the cyclists' dedication were more accessible and appealing than the pilgrims' asceticism. Yet, cyclists and pilgrims may share more than the same roadway, or so Victor and Edith Turner thought. They argued that "flow" – the intense "selfless" concentration and resulting sense of enjoyment and well-being that athletes, artists, and others may achieve in rigorously framed, goal-directed activities – can also help explain the experience and enduring appeal of pilgrimage. Engaging Mihaly Csikszentmihalyi's (then just emerging) work on flow, they venture that:

> pilgrimage as a cultural form, and particular pilgrimages as historical institutions . . . provide eminently satisfactory frames for the flow

experience, in both the journey to and the exercises at the pilgrimage center. Asceticism has its joys – the joys of flow. And flow can serve to reinforce the symbols and values with which its frames are associated.[20]

The experience of flow involves not only a sense of intrinsic reward, but also a sense of effortlessness that comes from balancing challenge and skills. It involves a transformation of the experience of time and space as well as a falling away of self-preoccupation and an opportunity to merge with more encompassing passions and purposes. The ability of pilgrimage to provide "eminently satisfactory frames for the flow experience" can help to explain the power of pilgrimages for personal and socio-cultural integration and reorientation. This power to effect change can be for good and, in the case of particular pilgrimages' historical associations with reactionary and populist movements, for ill.

Lourdes and the Ambiguity of Pilgrimage

Millions go on pilgrimage today, aided by global transportation networks. Lourdes, France, is among the most visited sites of Christian pilgrimage. It has been praised, dismissed, denounced, reformed, despised, and beloved. It is still ardently sought: each year three to six million people go to Lourdes, a small city below a rocky outcrop in the Pyrénées mountains. In 1858, an impoverished, asthmatic, fourteen year-old named Bernadette Soubirous experienced a series of eighteen visitations in a riverside grotto on the outskirts of town. The small female being who appeared to her revealed a spring, requested a procession and a chapel, and eventually explained, "I am the Immaculate Conception." Today's pilgrims to Lourdes seek healing from the spring's waters and the Virgin's beneficence, and they find more tourist accommodations than in any French city except Paris.[21]

---

20. To their notions of communitas and liminality, Turner and Turner joined Mihaly Csikszentmihalyi's then emerging work on "flow," see *Image and Pilgrimage*, 136-39, 254-55. Csikszentmihalyi's work has subsequently been developed theoretically as "positive psychology," and made famous in best-selling books, popular works, and a 2004 TEDTalk, "Flow: The Secret of Happiness," that has had several million viewers. His best-selling book, *Flow: The Psychology of Optimal Experience* (New York: Harper Perennial, 1990), has been translated into twenty languages. In it he defines flow as: "A state in which people are so involved in an activity that nothing else seems to matter; the experience is so enjoyable that people will continue to do it even at great cost, for the sheer sake of doing it."

21. The discussion of Lourdes is adapted and revised from Kristine A. Culp, "'A World Split Open?' Experience and Feminist Theologies," in *The Experience of God: A Postmodern Response*, ed. Kevin Hart and Barbara Wall (New York: Fordham University Press, 2005), 47-67.

A popular image portrays Bernadette Soubirous kneeling in ecstasy in the grotto. "Her appeal was non-verbal and non-literate," historian Ruth Harris explains, "not unlike the apparitions themselves, in which her bodily comportment was more important than language." The image of her kneeling, her comportment, and her limited but insistent messages to the priests, conveyed a picture of simplicity and goodness. Bernadette herself was effectively hidden, says Harris, "behind the enormity of her encounter."[22] She kept the content of her visions partly hidden, thus resisting pressures for access from photographers, pilgrims, priests, and the Pope himself. In addition, she literally removed herself from public view, entering a cloistered order nearby and later moving to the motherhouse across the country. She died in 1879 at the age of thirty-five, ill from asthma and tuberculosis.

Bernadette became an icon of an ecstatic, all-encompassing encounter with divinity, and of a world saturated by the divine in a time when that worldview was challenged forcefully. Harris argues that: "Bernadette's enigmatic figure perhaps partly explains the sanctuary's capacity to attract so many people of divergent spiritual inclinations, for on her frail form could be projected the many different longings of different eras."[23] Many interests, organizations, and ideologies attempted to delimit a proper interpretation and response to what Bernadette underwent in the grotto. Meanwhile, innumerable pilgrims themselves interpreted and responded to what Lourdes offered and represented to them.

Harris traces the rise of the phenomenon of Lourdes in her study, *Lourdes: Body and Spirit in the Secular Age*. As the ecclesiastical and civil powers certified Bernadette's experiences, built the shrine, and organized pilgrimages, authority shifted from her experience to their dogmas, organizations, and agendas. The shrine at Lourdes came to bolster Pope Pius IX's promulgation of the dogma of the Immaculate Conception (decreed just four years earlier), his stand against modernism, and, relatedly, the tenet of papal infallibility. Later, the promotion of national pilgrimages to Lourdes became entwined with a French anti-Republican, anti-humanist agenda of restoring both the Bourbon monarchy and so-called "traditional Catholic values." These interests also reinforced a gender-stratified social order and promoted a feminized piety.

Lourdes offered a model and an occasion for women and men "to encounter Mary and Jesus sometimes without mediation, to use the imaginative resources that their religious universe afforded without

22. Ruth Harris, *Lourdes: Body and Spirit in the Secular Age* (London: Allen Lane, 1999), 162. See also Turner and Turner, 226-30.
23. Harris, *Lourdes*, 366.

recourse to hierarchy."[24] At Lourdes, "the sick and dying, usually relegated to the unseen margins of society, took center stage." Privileged women and women religious who organized to aid the suffering found measures of autonomy and religious freedom that were unusual in their day. For the suffering masses, indeed for many of the millions who still come every year, Lourdes offered possibilities of healing and wholeness, a new vision of body and spirit, changed social relations, and revitalized pieties. Yet, away from Lourdes, these temporary inversions of poor and rich, weak and strong, women and men, laity and hierarchy, often served to reinforce social hierarchies.[25]

To the modern world, Lourdes became an icon of anti-modernity, of belief in miracles and the supernatural. Few modern persons have denounced religion as illusion more forcefully than the French novelist, and later defender of Dreyfus, Emile Zola. "Lourdes grew up in spite of all opposition, just as the Christian religion did, because suffering humanity in its despair must cling to something, must have some hope: and, on the other hand, because humanity thirsts after illusions," Zola wrote. "In a word, it is the story of the foundation of all religions."[26]

When Pope Leo XIII broke with his predecessor's intransigence toward the modern world, the Assumptionist order, promoter of the national pilgrimages, did not. Instead, the order moved farther to the right, and its fears of "degeneracy" found expression in the virulent anti-Jewishness of the Dreyfus Affair. The order was expelled from France in 1900 for plotting against the Republic. The Lourdes establishment itself was reshaped under the provisions of the 1905 French Law on the Separation of the Churches and the State. However, it was not purged of anti-Jewishness. In 1940, "Lourdes came to symbolize the partnership between the Catholic Church and the new Vichy regime, which reasserted the phantom of conspiratorial links between Jews, freemasons, and republicans."[27]

Yet the story of Lourdes as more than a tale about naive experience was reengineered into a propaganda machine for the extreme right. Even while the odious collaborations with the Vichy regime were emerging, a Jewish novelist from Vienna, Franz Werfel, found refuge in Lourdes as he was fleeing to the United States. In his book about his experience, *The Song of Bernadette*, later made into a Hollywood movie, he explained that the

---

24. Ibid., 356.

25. Ibid., 286-87.

26. Emile Zola, *Lourdes*, trans. by Ernest A. Vizetelly, reprint ed. (Amherst, NY: Prometheus Books, 2000), x. See Harris's discussion of Zola's novel in *Lourdes*, chapter 10, esp. 331-39.

27. Ibid., 365.

shrine enabled him to "magnify the divine mystery and the holiness of man – careless of a period which has turned away with scorn and rage and indifference from these ultimate values of our mortal lot."[28]

Victor and Edith Turner called what Werfel experienced "communitas." They reported a similar experience of solidarity:

> In Lourdes there is a sense of living communitas, whether in the great singing processions by torchlight or in the agreeable little cafes of the back streets, where tourists and pilgrims gaily sip their wine and coffee. Something of Bernadette has tinctured the entire social milieu – a cheerful simplicity, a great depth of communion.[29]

Pilgrims and Tourists

I encountered my first Lourdes pilgrim at Paris Orly airport in 1995. There, boarding the same flight to Chicago, was a tall, pleasant-looking woman toting a large, perhaps five-liter, plastic jug marked "Lourdes Water." (Curiously, the label wasn't in French. Perhaps more curious now is to imagine carrying more than three ounces of any liquid onto a plane.) I didn't speak with her. I didn't learn what she was seeking at Lourdes or whether she had found it. Had she found healing? Consolation? Regeneration?

I had gone to France a little restless myself, hoping for many of the things that tourists seek: good food, a change of routine, and a change of scenery, to see grand things and to place my work in proper proportion. I had sought a sense of a broader world – broader aesthetically, culturally, geographically, and historically. If only I could have returned with containers full of baguettes, *vin rouge*, and that brilliant mustard color that covers the fields of Burgundy.

Two years later, I went to Lourdes – not as a pilgrim, but as a tourist. I had anticipated, with a mixture of curiosity and dread, a kitschy spectacle. The gauntlet of shops on the way to the shrine did not disappoint. There was the Immaculate Conception souvenir shop, the Rosary Palace, and a bonanza of plastic water bottles available in the Virgin's likeness and supposedly approved for delivery by the French post office. A late nineteenth-century "Romanesque-Byzantine" basilica featured an awkward tympanum of Jesus standing on his mother's lap and holding, with her, an enormous rosary. Pilgrims drank from, washed in, and filled every manner of container at the holy water faucets nearby.

A man with a flag marched past leading a proud but wearied band of pilgrims. They each seemed worn by a lifetime of hard work and harsh

28. Franz Werfel, *The Song of Bernadette* (London: Hamish Hamilton, 1942), 6, as quoted in Harris, 366.

29. Turner and Turner, *Image and Pilgrimage*, 230.

conditions, not only by a long journey. They headed toward the ugly basilica and disappeared. I followed them. Along the promenade, a larger-than-life statue, clad in white with a blue sash, proclaimed that she was the Immaculate Conception. A fence surrounding her gathered bouquets from her admirers; how they loved her! Toward the shrine, the crowd thickened as wimple-wearing attendants steered the wheelchair-bound into its midst. I was touched and slightly alarmed by these pilgrims, some proud and beaming, others weak and wobbly.

Warily, I crossed into the basilica under Mary, Jesus, and the giant rosary. As I circled the aisles, the superfluity of images, rituals, and processions overwhelmed me. Did I ever feel Protestant. Individuals begged for healing, scrounged for a miracle, perhaps willing to secure it at the price of deception. The walls started to close in. In the streets and in the basilica, I had seen the pleading faces of those who had already waited in other places for healing and consolation. There was desperation under the spectacle of Lourdes.

And yet, even as these pilgrims sought favor and miracles, they bore the undeniable dignity of fellow souls. Their suffering was real; they deserved sympathy, not disdain. Lourdes was too overwhelming, too unrelenting, and its pilgrims were too earnest to allow an ironic, bemused distance. It demanded consent at the same time that its pilgrims deserved their dignity. I threw away my mailable Marian holy water bottle there and then. I fled the shrine without ever entering Bernadette's grotto.

"Marian icons excite the greatest devotion from iconophiles, and the greatest hostility and hate from iconophobes," Victor and Edith Turner observed.[30]

At Lourdes, the Virgin garners bouquets and prayers from her admirers and bears holy water for them. I suspect her admirers of some romanticism and anti-modernism, and I suspect the Turners themselves, at certain moments in their study, of their own brand of 1970s-tinged romanticism. I suspect myself of a certain Protestant iconophobia. Nevertheless, iconophily alone cannot account for the lasting power of pilgrimage any more than iconophobia adequately accounts for what I experienced that day.

I've thought about and written about that visit to Lourdes many times since. I came to view my experience as something other than mere revolt against the expressions of piety that I saw that day. I connected it with the kind of felt resistance to encroachments upon God and fellow creatures that can be found at the heart of Judaism, Christianity, and Islam. A deeply felt resistance has been a wellspring of Protestant piety and theology, together with a sense of relying on God's mercy and of finding life's fullness in

30. Ibid., 235.

glorifying and enjoying God.[31] The experience at Lourdes did not come out of the blue, and it was hardly my first encounter with ambiguous Christian ideas and practices. I arrived with Protestant, feminist, and liberationist sensibilities and a well-exercised hermeneutic of suspicion.

In addition, my attention had also been focussed by my own somewhat disciplined tourist itinerary and practices. It had been drawn to the luminous soaring spaces of Romanesque cathedrals and abbey churches, and shaped by habits of exploring closely on foot and of attuning sight, sound, touch, and taste to unknown spaces. Lourdes placed me in the middle of the palpable suffering and sincere need of its pilgrims, and also in the midst of a complexly ambiguous religious institution. I may have come to Lourdes as a tourist, but, like the medieval pilgrims and the modern-day cyclists who may share aspects of common roadway after all, I found myself in an in-between situation where self and time and space seemed to fall away. It was a threshold where I was vulnerable to being changed – even if it was not in a direction that the Lourdes establishment had tried to foster.

Ultimately, the purpose of pilgrimage is to bring the pilgrim, transformed in the journey, back home again. Some religious pilgrimages are liminal – obliging, unifying, and incorporative, sometimes problematically so. Others may be better comprehended with the term Victor Turner coined, "liminoid." Pilgrimage takes individuals out of the everyday places and mundane temporality of their lives. It places them in a framework and attunes their attention through participatory and ascetic practices that create a more spacious threshold of change. Victor Turner and Edith Turner thought communitas could arise in all kinds of situations and circumstances. They were nonsectarian about it, as it were, explaining communitas as "an essential and generic human bond," which cannot be comprehended adequately in the contrast between sacred and secular spheres. Tourism is liminoid at best; however, as the Turners observed, like art, literature, and other modern pursuits,[32] even tourist travel may become an occasion when communitas is experienced and travelers return home having been changed.

---

31. See Kristine A. Culp, *Vulnerability and Glory: A Theological Account* (Louisville, KY: Westminster John Knox Press, 2010), especially chapter 7, "Always Reforming, Always Resisting."

32. Turner and Turner, *Image and Pilgrimage*, 232-37.

5

Ye Shall Be Changed

Joshua Boettiger

In a twinkling of an eye, when the last trumpet blows
The dead will arise and burst out of your clothes
And ye shall be changed

        Bob Dylan, "Ye Shall Be Changed"

* * *

The liminal dimension undergirds all human experience. In some sense, there is nothing that is not liminal. We live our lives (and perhaps find sanity) by fashioning fixed structures of meaning and identity; selves and narratives that are generally static and contained. But that is not life, as much as it is the mask we put onto life. Meanwhile, the liminal waits for us.

Carl Jung chose to write his autobiography, *Memory Dreams and Reflections*,[1] as a succession of liminal occurrences – moments when his unconscious life dramatically broke through into his conscious one. I put down the book at its conclusion still not knowing any of what would commonly be referred to as the basic facts of his life. But Jung's brilliant choice of structure challenges us to think about how we narrate who we are. All of us to some degree can look back and identify a similar chain of moments when our lives were interrupted by the intrusion of a disorienting rupture; threshold moments when we found ourselves fundamentally between poles of knowing. Many factors play into when and how such portals into the liminal make themselves known.

Sometimes our inherited religious traditions make it seem as if there is only one true liminal threshold to endure; the one at which we are on the precipice

---

1. C.G. Jung and Aniela Jaffe, *C.G. Jung: Memories, Dreams, Reflections* (London: Routledge, 1963).

of an absolute enlightenment, or redemption. Yet our lives consist of many enlightenments and redemptions, small and large, harrowing odysseys, and trials by fire. The "last trumpet" that Dylan writes of (referencing a Biblical image heralding the Messiah's return) is always blowing. It's just that we are able to hear it only when a particular set of circumstances, inner and outer, align. It is easy to forget that the dead are perpetually arising and wanting to burst out of our clothes. How do we deal with this reality? How does the liminal press upon us in a daily way? How does Judaism or any religious tradition invite, block, legislate, and dance with the liminal?

As part of the Jewish morning liturgy, we pray, "Every day God renews the work of creation." We assert our faith that creation was not just a one-time thing, but rather is something ongoing and dynamic. On one hand, this awareness of the world being re-created over and over brings with it a mind-bending state of gratitude and astonishment for our continually being nourished and sustained. On the other hand, this awareness threatens our imagining that our self and world are complete and that our work here is more about maintenance. To say we are in the process of becoming is not just a saccharine, new-age truism. If creation is ongoing and literally being wrought each moment, then the ground underfoot that I thought was solid is less solid (if it exists at all). If each day is new, then each day I am also someone new, who I was not before. Each morning God picks up the lump of clay that is our body and breathes life into it again. There is promise in this, and also awe and trembling. When we enter (or are entered) into any liminal state, everything is at risk. Our strategies break down.

Ellen Bryant Voight's title poem from her collection *Headwaters* is both an *ars poetica* and, as I read it, a kind of response to the challenge of entering the re-created world each day, in a way that is both responsible and authentic.

> I made a large mistake I left my house I went into the world it was not
> the most perilous hostile part but I couldn't tell among the people there
>
> who needed what no tracks in the snow no boot pointed toward me
>   or away
> no snow as in my dooryard only the many currents of self-doubt I clung
>
> to my own life raft I had room on it for only me you're not surprised
> it grew smaller and smaller or maybe I grew larger and heavier
>
> but don't you think I'm doing better in this regard I try to do better[2]

If the liminal exists underneath each moment as a kind of vortex and destabilizing force, then one task of religious practice is to help us find ways

---

2. Ellen Bryant Voight, *Headwaters* (New York: W.W. Norton, 2013).

whereby we can appropriately be in relationship to the liminal. In many ways this is the function of *halacha*, Jewish law, which literally means "walking." *Halacha* gives us guidelines for moving through the world. As has been pointed out earlier in this collection, the liminal both feeds and threatens established religious order. It is the juice that gave rise to religion in the first place, but because it is not in the business of sustaining ordered societies, it can undermine the very structures it helped create. I realize I am speaking about liminality as a kind of misunderstood monster who dwells on the outskirts of town. But perhaps in the realm of metaphor, that is as good a personification as any. . . .

One way the Torah could be described is as our ancestors' early record of encountering the Holy.[3] In the presence of the Holy, the self is de-centered. When we encounter the Holy we are left with this sense that who we think we are is not necessarily the case. My Mussar teacher Ira Stone once said, whether or not you believe in God is not a Jewish question; a Jewish question is, how true are you to your experience of holiness as you encounter it in the world? If the liminal is defined as the place between, the thin space where the normative boundaries of the small self dissolve somewhat, then the Holy can only be encountered through a liminal gate. The self encountering the Holy is not a static entity. The initiate is someone different and so the "I" itself is in flux. The stories in the Torah that describe these encounters with the Holy often involve the collective, or a representative of the collective, experiencing an initiation, where the self is changed. The story of the transformation of the self becomes a metaphor and archetype for the transformation of selves to come, of the tribe, and of the greater tribe of all beings.

Seen in this light, all of the core tales in the Torah are stories of the negotiation of the liminal state – the anticipation of entering the liminal zone, the experience itself (to whatever degree it can be brought back and put into language), and the meaning made after the fact.

In a liminal experience, just as we are between selves, so we are often between languages. The way we might have perceived, understood or processed something has profoundly shifted. True liminal texts describe this tension by narrating in a fractured, incomplete/confusing manner. The medium becomes the message. On a collective level, witness the Israelites coming through the birth canal of the Sea of Reeds. The text describes a scene of total chaos – the darkness, the clouds, the wind shifting, the presence of God first behind the people, then in front of them. No one seems to know exactly what's going on.

In a similar fashion, the people's experience on Mount Sinai, getting ready to receive the Torah, describes a discombobulation and sense of synesthesia:

---

3. Alan Lew, *Be Still and Get Going: A Jewish Meditation Practice for Real Life* (New York: Little Brown & Co., 2005).

The dawn of the third day broke amid thunder and lightning that filled the air. Heavy clouds hung over the mountain, and the steadily growing sound of the Shofar made the people shake and tremble with fear. Moses led the children of Israel out of the camp and placed them at the foot of Mount Sinai, which was all covered by smoke and was quaking, for God had descended upon it in fire.[4]

The text itself breaks down and is no longer a reliable narrator – though in its unreliability, perhaps it proves its trustworthiness. At the shore of the sea, and at Sinai, there is a felt experience of not having the bandwidth to understand what is happening that is communicated to the generations that follow. Recounting the epiphany on Mount Sinai, Deuteronomy (4:12) reminds the people, "You heard the sound of words, but saw no form – only a voice." The description of what happens in the communal/collective liminal experiences at the Sea and on Mount Sinai is dislocating and topsy-turvy by design. The nature of a liminal encounter is that the very way we understand ourselves has changed, and so any pat attempt to describe will not be reflective. The initiate has been transformed, and the old language cannot hold.

One thinks of Paul Celan, trying to write in German (as a German Jew) after the indescribable horror of the Sho'ah. Celan, in trying to somehow fashion a new German, held that one who went on to write as if it were business as usual, as if the very tools of the language had not themselves committed a terrible atrocity, would be perpetuating the culture that produced the barbarism of the twentieth century. When Celan received the Literature Prize of Bremen in 1958, his first time back in Germany since World War II, he said in his speech:

> It, the language remained, not lost, yes in spite of everything. But it had to pass through its own answerlessness, pass through frightful muting, pass through the thousand darknesses of deathbringing speech. It passed through and gave back no words for that which happened; yet it passed through this happening. Passed through and could come to light again, "enriched" by all this.[5]

The old language does not work anymore, and/or we must make the old language new by smashing it up against the liminal, by making ruptures in the original text that yield new insights. This is one way of naming the overarching project of rabbinic Judaism in how it approached Biblical Hebrew, the Holy tongue, the language of the original openings. Marc

---

4. Exodus 19:16-18.
5. John Felstiner, *Paul Celan: Poet, Survivor, Jew* (New Haven, CT: Yale University Press, 1995).

Alain Ouaknin extrapolates on the verse in Exodus, which commands the people to keep the staves of the ark always in place, as being an eternal commandment to keep the Word moving, not to let it ever be sedentary or relegated to a monolithic interpretation.[6]

There is this lovely category in Jewish ritual vocabulary called *shomrim* – guardians/keepers who are entrusted with watching over a liminal person, someone who is about to undergo an initiatory experience. *Shomrim* guard couples the night before their wedding, baby boys the night before their bris/naming ceremony, and so on. Some of the traditional language frames it in this way – the evil forces in the world will be awakened to do whatever they can to disrupt a ritual of such holiness. So, the night before the ritual, when the person has left their old state but has not yet entered into their new state, our guard must be up.

> You enter the night,
> as a thread enters the needle,
> through an opening
> propitious or bloody,
> through the most luminous breach.
> Being both thread and needle,
> you enter the night
> as you enter yourself.
>
> Edmond Jabes[7]

In the more individual examples of liminal experience the Torah records, all the accounts happen at night, and Jacob is our spiritual ancestor most at home in the dark of night. While there are a few nighttime threshold moments that Jacob endures, his encounter with the mysterious being with whom he grapples throughout the night[8] feels most germane within this larger unpacking of liminality. First of all, Jacob has this encounter the night before his reunion with Esau, connecting to this pattern/trope of the night before a ritual or convocation being the most dangerous and propitious. Secondly, Jacob only receives his blessing after he has had his hip socket wrenched; after he has been wounded. Jewish tradition locates this in the sciatic nerve, which the people of Israel are forever after bidden to avoid eating. This is not just a dietary prohibition. As George Savran understands it, "Israel refrains from eating the sciatic nerve as a way of continuing the 'limp,' the state of vulnerability to

---

6. Marc-Alain Ouaknin, *The Burnt Book: Reading the Talmud* (Princeton, NJ: Princeton University Press, 1998).

7. Edmond Jabes, "The Commentary of Reb Zam," in *The Book of Questions, Volume 1*, trans. Rosemarie Waldrop (Hanover, NH: Wesleyan University Press, 1991).

8. Genesis 32:22-32.

YHWH reflected by Jacob's new name, Israel."[9] To the liminal mind, wound and blessing are inextricably entwined, to the degree that it might not qualify as a liminal experience were there not an injury or scar that serves to both remind the initiate of the encounter and to underscore the danger that he or she had to pass through. The dietary restriction is a way that future members of the clan can continue to connect to the archetypal experience. Our ancestors, as in any wisdom or lineage tradition, are archetypes of transitional beings. We enter them and they enter us. It is a kind of possession, though we do not use this language most of the time.

Thirdly, the wound/blessing is given in the form of a name change, from Jacob to Israel. However, going forward in the Torah, this character is referred to as both Jacob and Israel, with no discernible pattern as to when either name is used. We have a longing that the undergone initiation will transform us once and for all, but often this is not the case. In some ways, this is why the collective liminal moment is returned to again and again in sacred text. We read of Jacob's initiation and map it onto our own narrow passage experiences, and we puzzle both about how we have been changed, and also about why we have *not* been. One of the reasons we are bewitched and haunted by these stories is that we do not understand them. We do not understand what changes took place or what these changes awoke or how we are commanded as a result of them. Sometimes we imagine that a brush with the liminal will spit us out, relatively intact, just new and improved; we imagine that the change we experience will be lasting and total. However, the Torah tells us otherwise.

Israel will always be regressing back into Jacob. The Israelites, whom we imagine after the crossing at the sea passed in some absolute sense from slavery into freedom, will in reality spend the next generation (and then some) trying to shake the dregs of slavery from their system. The Promised Land remains on the horizon. They (we) will constantly regress and re-emerge. We tend to want to either avoid the liminal or have the liminal change us once and for all. Often, however, neither is an option. We have to learn a practice for being in relationship to these destabilizing, malleable realities as our lives unfold.

Once we get used to reading the Torah through the liminal lens, the entire book becomes one wrinkle in time after the next. Isaac digs wells. The Levitical priests build a whole theological matrix on how to negotiate and travel between pure and impure states. Extant versions of the *Akeidah* (the almost-sacrifice of Isaac) describe Isaac actually dying and being brought back to life. Elisha and Elijah do bring people back to life, offering

9. George Savran and Andrew Mein, *Encountering the Divine: Theophany in Biblical Narrative* (London: T. & T. Clark International, 2005).

a template for the later miracles of Jesus of Nazareth. We could call Elijah the prophet of the liminal. Tradition says he never died, and still walks the earth today, as a kind of one-man black hole into the liminal. He shows up at lifecycle moments like a bris or a baby naming, at the close of the Sabbath, on Passover (the Night of Watching) – all times of turning, all moments when we are in the midst of becoming. The Torah is a shamanic document, a map for future initiates in a state of what Christina and Stanislav Grof called "spiritual emergency"[10] to follow.

Rabbi Jonathan Sacks writes that human beings are perpetually in the space between the place they are escaping from and the place they are escaping to. Think of Jacob on the run – leaving his homeland and the brother he thinks wants to kill him, going God knows where. Sacks calls this being between the known danger and the unknown danger.[11]

In more ways than one, the very definition of a person is a transitional being. If this is so, how are we to shape our laws? The whole system of Jewish law functions categorically. There are commandments to do if you live in the land of Israel and there are commandments to do if you live outside it. There are commandments to do if you are a Jew and those to do if you are a non-Jew, those to do as a man and those to do as a woman. The rabbis spilled so much ink around figuring out and legislating appropriately because they knew the binary system was an imposed system that did not fully reflect reality. Tellingly, way ahead of their time, acknowledging that the duality of male and female left a lot of territory uncovered, the rabbis identified as many as eight genders in the Talmud. The rabbis were obsessed with the liminal – out of fear, curiosity, and a need to create a language and a law that could create and support governable societies.

On one level, their question was what were the ethics of liminality? This was not just legalistic musing. If there is an ethic for when it is a time of peace, and another for when it is a time of war, what about those times when it is some kind of mixture – which we could argue is most of the time. If there is one set of obligations incumbent upon an individual when it is daytime and another when it is dark, what does one do when day and night are blended?

The Talmud says, "This world is like the night."[12] Moshe Chaim Luzzatto, in his seminal Mussar work, *Messilat Yesharim*, wrote that darkness has two effects on the sight: "We either see nothing at all, or we mistake one object

10. Christina and Stanislav Grof, *The Stormy Search for the Self: A Guide to Personal Growth Through Transformational Crisis* (New York: J.P. TarcherPerigee, 1992).

11. Jonathan Sacks, *Covenant and Conversation: A Weekly Reading of the Jewish Bible*, Vol. 1 (Jerusalem: Maggid Books & The Orthodox Union, 2009).

12. Bava Metzia 83b.

for another. A pillar may be taken for a human being, or vice versa."[13] The night is talked about as the place of greatest vulnerability, because we cannot see. Dusk and dawn may be even more dangerous, however, because we are more likely to mistake one thing for another. We shall return to Luzzatto's specific example in a moment.

God is the one who "forms the light and creates darkness" (Isaiah 45:7). In the evening prayer, we name God as "removing the light from before the darkness and the darkness from before the light." We imagine God is then present – right there – at the moment the dark is being rolled away from the light, and vice versa, at the moments when we cannot tell one from the other. The liminal space belongs to God. It is the place where the Divine is found, and, as such, it has both great power and contains great danger. Judaism holds that God is most accessible at such times. This is why we are simultaneously commanded to pray at exactly these times, and also why we are warned to be careful. Dawn and dusk are the re-enactments of creation, re-imagined every day. The Midrash tells us that in the dead of winter before solstice, the first human being feared that the earth was again returning to its primordial darkness (in the Hebrew it is called formlessness and void), but at dawn he learned that it was the way of the world.[14] We repeat this cycle. Avivah Zornberg wrote (paraphrasing Paul Valéry) that God made everything out of nothing, but the nothingness shows through.[15] The nothingness waits in our peripheral vision, off to the side, ready to reclaim the earth and wipe out all our splendid order.

Wrestling with the perils of blended space, the Mishnah debates about when one is first allowed to pray the morning prayers: "From what time may one recite the *Shema* in the morning? From the time that one can distinguish between blue and white. R[abbi] Eliezer says: Between blue and green." The rabbis of the Gemara continue the discussion:

> What is the meaning of "between blue and white?" Shall I say: between a lump of white wool and a lump of blue wool? This one may also distinguish in the night! It means rather: between the blue in it and the white in it. It has been taught: R[abbi] Meir says: [the morning *Shema* is read] from the time that one can distinguish

---

13. Moses Hayyim Luzzatto, *Mesillat Yesharim: The Path of the Upright*, introduction and commentary by Ira F. Stone, trans. and original introduction by Mordecai M. Kaplan (Lincoln, NE: The Jewish Publication Society, University of Nebraska Press, 2010).

14. Avodah Zara 8b.

15. Avivah Gottlieb Zornberg, *The Murmuring Deep: Reflections on the Biblical Unconscious* (New York: Schochen Books, 2009).

between a wolf and a dog; R[abbi] Akiba says: between an ass and a wild ass. Others say: from the time that one can distinguish his friend at a distance of four cubits.[16]

The very discussion above is fueled by a concern about how one is to make order of one's life and not misstep when one is in an indeterminate space. While the rabbis try to pinpoint the place within the dawn, within the mixture, when day is actually born, they talk about the language of discernment – maybe it is when one can see the distinction between two different colors of thread? Maybe it is when one can discern the difference between an animal that might be dangerous from one that is harmless? The first part of the Gemara recognizes the risk involved – what if we get it wrong and approach a wildness that is not for us to approach? Remarkably, in the end, they settle on this: when one can recognize the face of a friend from a short distance, it is appropriate to pray. Remember Luzzatto's warning, a pillar may be taken for a human being, or vice versa. This is the gravest possible warning because it is just this sin that humanity has been so devastated by – seeing a living person as nothing but a thing. The sin of incorrect seeing.

The rabbis could have chosen any way to illustrate the moment day emerges, but they chose to do it in these relational terms. In some Native American traditions, if a stranger is approaching and you cannot recognize them, if you come in peace, one is told to call out, "I am a you!" The response called back is, "You are an I!" An affirmation that this is indeed the case.

Maybe the most liminal space is the place between two people. It is also a place of mixture, like dawn or dusk. What do we call that space that is not self and not other, that charged emptiness of relationship? Martin Buber has described it as the "I-Thou space,"[17] the space of true encounter where God is to be found. Many have pointed out that in the book of Exodus, God tells the people as part of the instructions for building the cover of the Ark:

> Make two cherubim of gold – make them of hammered work – at the two ends of the cover. Make one cherub at one end and the other cherub at the other end; of one piece with the cover shall you make the cherubim at its two ends. The cherubim shall have their wings spread out above, shielding the cover with their wings. They shall confront each other, the faces of the cherubim turned toward the cover. Place the cover on top of the Ark, after depositing inside the Ark the Pact that I will give you. There I will meet with you,

16. Berachot 9b.
17. Martin Buber, *I and Thou*, trans. with a prologue and notes by Walter Kaufmann (New York: Touchstone, 1971).

and I will impart to you — from above the cover, from between the two cherubim that are on top of the Ark of the pact — all that I will command you concerning the Israelite people.[18]

"There I will meet with you." There you will experience me, precisely from that in-between space, the space of the gaze. In Emmanuel Levinas' philosophy, the trace of God is only to be found on the face of the other. However, it is not a foregone conclusion when two people face one another that the existence of I-Thou space will infuse the air. Hypothetically, it can. That charged emptiness can invite mystery and holiness, or it can, in the self's anxiety, cause the self to further inflate and fill that space, making it into what Buber would call the "I-It space."[19]

When I say self and other I am not solely defining self and other according to the physical boundaries of our respective bodies, though that can be a rough starting point. When we feel threatened, when we are unconscious, our self, in a sense, tries to occupy the other, or at least the space between us. It often does this with no ill will or evil intent; it is simply the default position of a self that is used to feeling besieged, even on a largely unconscious level. The besieged self either colonizes or shrinks back and retracts.

The challenge is to let the other be sovereign, to let the other be ultimately mysterious and unknowable. The other is a stand-in for every other we encounter, and ultimately, for God. We have to know where we end and the other begins, or we will not be able to be of deep service.[20]

The Mussar masters work with the precept of humility through this lens. They note the human tendency to flinch in the presence of the other. They note that our impulse towards self-protection (*yetzer ha'ra*) becomes self-absorption. While legitimate in certain contexts in terms of protecting the self, the *yetzer ha'ra* becomes the default setting in any encounter. The task in working with humility becomes remembering to ask ourselves, "Am I really in danger here?" It means noticing our tendency to colonize the space between us; it means noticing our fear and the subsequent recoiling or aggression that comes out of it. It means learning to ask the question, "How can I make the other my teacher?"[21]

The Zen teacher and poet Norman Fischer recounts a friend of his who noticed that in moments of intimacy with another he would always flinch — imperceptible to all except himself. He began to offer a one-word prayer

---

18. Exodus 25:18-22.
19. Buber, *I and Thou*.
20. For more on this, see the writings of Rabbi Ira Stone, including *A Responsible Life: The Spiritual Path of Mussar* (Eugene, OR: Wipf & Stock Pub., 2013).
21. These teachings are gleaned from the work of Rabbi Ira Stone and my other teachers at the Center for Contemporary Mussar (see http://mussarleadership.org).

at such moments: "Help." Even though he didn't have a defined belief or
existent prayer practice, somehow through noticing and opening, he was
able to keep the emptiness empty. To me, this is an example of a liminality
practice.

Sometimes the liminal state pulls us in and we have no choice but to
wade into the sea and pray that it parts, to meet the angel by the banks of
the river and throw our body against him. But the meeting between two
people is a perfect example of the necessity of having a liminality practice
– to learn and to be vigilant about entering the space where transformation
can potentially happen with open palms and an intention, as appropriate,
to be changed.

A poem of Celan's:

> Once,
> I heard him,
> he was washing the world,
> unseen, nightlong,
> real.
>
> One and infinite,
> annihilated,
> they I'ed.
>
> Light was. Salvation[22]

The source of the annihilation is not God's retreat, but people who "I."
When we are engaged in a particularly extreme form of self-absorption, the
awareness of "Thou," of the other, is absent – this annihilates God. If we
do not become adept at identifying the Holy liminal space between two
beings, we block the Holy.

The human responsibility is awesome. It is up to us whether or not God
is annihilated. And we have collectively failed at this obligation through
our actions and inactions – not just in Nazi Germany, but before and since.
Put differently, we have failed the liminal. Jane Hirshfield has written that
the great sin is one of turning away: "I begin to believe the only sin is
distance, refusal. All others stemming from this."[23]

We learn to see these liminal spaces in sacred text, and this trains us to
identify them off the page, in our lives and relationships. The first rule, if
you will, for learning to do this, is to try to study and live with a sense of
wonder.

22. Paul Celan, *Breathturn,* trans. Pierre Joris (Los Angeles: Sun & Moon Press, 1995).
23. Jane Hirshfield, "Salt Heart," in *Lives of the Heart* (New York: Harper Collins,
    1997).

Ouaknin writes: "The Talmud . . . begins with astonishment. Astonishment and questioning throw man out of the engagement of everyday familiarity with the world, with preset traditional and archaic familiarity, with a world that has been debated from time immemorial, leading him to the creative penury of unknowing."[24]

The function of Judaism's placing a premium on asking questions, or interrogating the text ceaselessly, is not just sophistry, or rattling the cage for its own sake. Again, Ouaknin: "Through astonishment and questioning, man is able to free himself once and for all from the domination of certain thinking habits, convictions, theories accepted without verification, opinions, prejudices, ready-made decisions, which decree what the world, things, people, knowledge, etc., are." [25]

In a Sefer Torah, we are trained to see the black letters of the actual text. However, if we can soften and readjust our eyes, as we do when looking at an Escher, say, we notice the white space around the letters and its patterns. Famously, we say the Torah is black fire written upon white fire. What is the white fire in the Torah? Traditionally, it is considered the space where Midrash and commentary comes from. The liminal. If it is just the black letters, we are idolators, but, if the black letters lead us into the white, we breathe life into the text as it breathes life into us. Ouaknin calls it a ventilation.

Commentary is never just commentary. It is a way of opening the text up. It is a reminder that the Torah is our primary portal into the liminal realms. In the *beit ha'midrash* (house of study) one finds a chaotic scene not unlike how the Torah describes the crossing of the sea. There is no quiet and peaceful scene, but instead a kind of wild hubbub, the air filled with voices and gesticulations. Here, *machlochet* (disagreement or debate for the sake of heaven, not ego) is celebrated as the prime tool to break through the dialectic into the white fire, to constantly challenge us to imagine other ways of interpreting and understanding. Interpretation and commentary are ways of opening the text up. Once this has happened, the text as we have known it has been dislodged and now points towards something unknown. Another reminder that there is loss in the liminal. It is not a bloodless affair, a simple act of moving between the old and the new, and getting to keep each. There is always incalculable loss involved.

The liminal space is a space of awe – and, as Chris Abani teaches, awe can come to us through many channels, including terror and confusion. The liminal is not for sissies. Abani writes about what could be called the courage to enter the liminal as a writer:

24. Ouaknin, *The Burnt Book*.
25. Ibid.

This is what the art I make requires of me: that in order to have an honest conversation with a reader, I must reveal myself in all my vulnerability. Reveal myself, not in the sense of my autobiography, but in the sense of the deeper self, the one we keep too often hidden even from ourselves. This revelation is not designed to engender sympathy, or compassion, or even pity. These sentiments, while generous on the part of the reader, obscure the deeper intent, the deeper possibility. The point is to dissolve oneself into the journey of the protagonist, to face the most terrifying thing in narrative, the thing that has been at its heart since the earliest campfire and story. To dare ourselves to imagine, to conjure and then face all of our darkness and all of our light simultaneously. To stand in that liminal moment when we have no solid ground beneath us, no clear firmament above, when the ambiguity of our nature reveals what we are capable of, on both sides. The intensity of that confrontation is the only gift the writer has to offer, the only redemption that is possible. . . . As terrifying as things we see are, perhaps more terrifying are the things that, once seen, cannot be unseen. This is a difficulty I think we all recognize in the most instinctual way, and perhaps this is why we all look away as often as we can from the things that have the power to unmake us. We do this in every way, every day.[26]

We are a community of the in-between, sharing this liminal passage of life. Because we are in a place neither here nor there, our default emotional state is often one of anxiety, and so our spiritual and religious practices become ever more paramount in helping us exhibit friendliness towards those places we do not understand. At the very least these ancient teachings can help us gird our loins. To see as clearly as we can. To see with heart. To do our best to turn towards.

---

26. Chris Abani, "Ethics and Narrative: The Human and Other," *Witness*, 22, no. 1 (2009), 167.

6

Hope in the Dark Passage

Michelle Trebilcock

As I listen, Loba – ragged and no longer young at age thirty – displays her pain through an absence of tears. She is too used to the burden of her story to emote anymore; she has been defeated by the constancy of her distress, and, in this moment, she has lost all hope that life will ever be any different. Then, sensing there is so much more that will never be spoken, I take a single, slow, and deep breath. For my part this breath has several intentions – it is a disciplined act of attention, a formless prayer, a complex feeling of sorrow, and yet, at the same time, nothing more than a simple, biological imperative. Loba responds to my heavy-laden breath with one of her own and somehow in the midst of our sacred conversation, a space opens up for something different, and we sit quiet for a time. Here in the wordless, thought-less silence, it becomes ok just to be here, without reference to any end or outcome. We feel. We sense. We let it be. And then, with her spirit substantially altered, Loba takes another single, slow and deep breath and her words return.[1]

* * *

I am a chaplain. I serve in a denominational agency that "works toward an Australia free of poverty." The conversation above is commonplace. It is my duty to listen to such accounts of life gone wrong and to provide guidance to those who are in the midst of it.

In theological school I was taught several frameworks through which I might understand the ministry of chaplaincy, and even more theories by which to understand crisis, trauma, grief, illness, stress, relationship

---

1. The details of Loba's identity and circumstances have been altered to protect her privacy.

breakdown, and so on. However, I came to this role after my own major life crisis, which led me into academic study of the themes of this book. Liminality theory has greatly stretched the way I understand my vocation as a priest and as a person, and it has transformed the way in which I approach the ministry of pastoral and spiritual care.

Liminality is essentially and always a middle. It is the moment of in-between-ness where what has been is gone, but what will be has not yet arrived. In Christian spirituality it is the moment of Holy Saturday, when Christ has died, but is not yet risen. There is nothing to be done on Holy Saturday except to learn how to die with Christ, in the hope that one day – but not today – life will be restored by resurrection.

Something of the essence of Holy Saturday hope was restored to Loba in the single, slow and deep breath of our conversation. In this chapter, through the lens of liminality theory, I hope to demonstrate what, why and how that was the case. I will share some of Loba's life story and some of my ministry story, in the hope that I might show how the practice of liminal spirituality is the best resource we have to offer to those for whom life is difficult and out of control.

Liminality in the Unfolding Process of Human Experience

Late in his career, Victor Turner embarked on another ambitious project, mapping how the observable process of liminality in social action might also describe the inner unfolding of psychological experience. With reference to the philosophies of William Dilthey and John Dewey, he proposed that the dialectical process of structured social form, liminal anti-structured social form, and restructured social form aligns with Dilthey's description of the dynamic nature of psychological experience, which is not static but constantly unfolding through a regular process of "breach – crisis – reflexivity – reintegration." [2] In the inner and the outer worlds, this process of constant evolution is an utterly natural and normal part of being human, enabling us to be in real relationship with all that is other to ourselves (both human and non-human), while also in a continual process of re-formation in relationship.

In the translation of this process in non-ritualized social drama, the ceremonial conditions are replicated in diverse forms, but the conditions of the liminal structure must still be met. The liminality of the ritual space is

---

2. Victor Turner, "Dewey, Dilthey, and the Drama: An Essay in the Anthropology of Experience," in *The Anthropology of Experience*, ed. Victor Turner and Edward M. Bruner, with an epilogue by Clifford Geertz Turner (Urbana, IL: University of Illinois Press, 1986), 35.

encountered through some kind of disruption to public life – a breach – an interruption of what had previously been experienced as normative. Next, there is a threshold – a limen, an invitation to move through the immediacy of the crisis to something else, the moment in which the person considers his or her committed response to the new situation. After the threshold comes redressive action – an authorized agent organizes what needs to be done and begins the process of reintegration. The agent might be certain people, if the experience is social, but it might also be an internal voice or principle, if the experience is within the inner life of an individual. This is the creative stage of liminality in de-ritualized form. It is experimental and surprising, often utilizing elements of ritual in the "performance" of the redress. Finally, the process leads itself to reintegration – the re-establishment of order integrated with the fresh insights or necessary re-formations gleaned from the disruption.

In his engagement with Dilthey's work, Turner began to see how experience and social drama operate together for the creation of shared meaning systems. Wisdom is born out of a constant dialectical unfolding, in-between what is normative and what arrives as unexpected and foreign. Meaning is constructed in the social process, just as it is constructed internally in a parallel process. By "experience" Turner refers to the individual, internal processes that occur prior to "expressions" of social roles and identity – the cultural manifestations of these processes. The source and scale of the breach largely determines the conditions of the liminal experience: whether it occurs on an individual level, or at the level of group or society; whether the participant has actively chosen to enter into the liminal sphere; and whether or not there is a pre-determined edge to the other side of the liminal experience.

The Conditions for Transformation

If Turner is correct, there is a consistency of process from ritualized liminality to de-ritualized liminality, when the conditions of form are met – that is, it is only with the suspension of what has been taken for granted that human beings are able to evolve in relation to the world around them. Meaning never unfolds out of nothing; there is always a prior experience, a context, a history, a set of relationships already in place. Hence, if new meaning is to emerge, then it must necessarily re-form what is already there. To step over the threshold of the breach is to step into disturbed, disrupted, and disordered experience but, if the arena of liminality can become conscious, then this experience returns to something ordered, to a transformed sociality.

On the other hand, if the forms of liminality are not met – if the thresholds are not firm, or the liminal space is not felt safe and secure, then the potential of this movement into crisis is either diminished or lost altogether. Turner labeled this experience "liminoid" because it might mimic some of the characteristics of liminality (for example, ambiguity of roles, deconstructed identities, suspension of social rules and norms) but without the transformative capacity of liminality, without the possibility of transition. When there is no demarcation of a pre-liminal and post-liminal experience, there is no journey from one world-of-life to the next, and therefore no progression, no growth, no maturation for the individual in terms of his or her relationships. For example, if an individual ages but does not "grow up" through the cycles of the social structure, the personal and the social eventually slide out of sync.

Liminoid phenomena are transitory, fragmentary, plural, and intermittent. They often "play" at ritual without enacting any of the social processes of ritual. Hence, in post-ritual societies, they are often leisure performances like sport or theatre. They are also, however, the terrible crisis moments of deconstruction without hope. For Loba, the entirety of her life has become subsumed in crisis and disorientation. What should have been transitory has become permanent and overwhelming, and she feels trapped in a permanent state of disaster. Losing what has been good, what has made life worth living, without any hope that it might be replaced by something else in the future, ceases to be a liminal experience and the power of transformation is lost. For those caught in crisis that is no longer just a stage onto something better – the millions of displaced people in refugee camps worldwide; the hundreds of thousands of Australians who are born into intergenerational poverty and expect nothing but lifelong unemployment; those whose childhood wounds predispose them to self-loathing and terrible decision making – for such as these, constructing a new hope which might frame their crisis and enable a different relationship to it is an exceedingly difficult task.

In his theory of liminality, Turner also emphasized the role of a master of ceremonies (MC), who hosts the boundaries of the liminal space and ensures that its participants safely and successfully pass through the ritual transformation. Turner warned that, in a context of unwieldy, societal or epochal liminality, the participants in transition are vulnerable to the play of the trickster personality. In place of a trusted (and trustworthy) MC, a charlatan or tyrant has the opportunity to step into the breach and offer false certainties and resolutions. Such are the environments in which criminals overcrowd desperate asylum seekers onto boats, politicians sell overblown certainty without compassion, and soap opera stars make a fortune from "self-help" books.

When liminality is applied in this broader way, as an underlying process to all human experience, both socially and individually, we begin to see the complexity of human life and its ongoing need for transformation. Participants might enter into a liminal sphere individually, as a group, or even as a whole society. They may or may not have exercised choice in entering the liminal sphere and they may be in that state momentarily, for a number of days, or for an entire lifetime. However, if each of these different types of liminal state shares an underlying structure, then, I suggest, it may be that we can translate between them. In fact, in my own particular experience of liminality out of control, it was through the discovery of deliberately invoked liminal spiritual practices – meditation, dance, mindfulness – that I began to develop the resources to frame the liminal arena and make it through to "the other side." Time and again, I have seen that the skills required for transformation in the midst of chaos exist within the experience itself.

Loba arrived in Australia as a refugee almost a decade ago. With the assistance of a man who took a keen interest in her plight, she was able to negotiate the labyrinth of immigration law and enroll in study to update her business qualifications. She was lucky because as an educated woman her English was very good. She married the seemingly kind man but, within a year, was both pregnant and fearful for her life again; his physical and emotional violence abruptly shattered her new home. Loba's resilience and skill enabled her to find work so she could support herself and her newborn daughter, but, six years after leaving the marriage, she is still in constant legal battle with her now ex-husband, and has frequently been forced to move house in order to be free of his abuse. Loba is raising a child here in Australia, but her family are in East Africa; she is divorced but still beholden to a violent husband; and she pays tax as a permanent resident of Australia, but remains a citizen of her birth nation. The occasion for our conversation arose when her team was informed that the program she is employed to manage might lose its government funding, so Loba is now also faced with the fear of unemployment. Day to day she must abide in the liminal space between two countries, two homes, two cultures, two states of marriage and family relationships, and the unending threat of job insecurity. She is exhausted and she does not know when she will be able to rest.

For Loba, periods of tension that could have been resolved have fallen into distressing forms of long-term or permanent uncertainty, such that very little of her life presently feels dependable. She is more fortunate than most refugees and asylum seekers – she was able to start participating in Australian society quite quickly through study and then meaningful employment. Her daughter is in school and she has a roof over their heads. This should have led to an end to the difficult transition from one country to another but, in the vulnerability of the refugee experience, other forms of chaos have emerged to perpetuate her feeling of a life beyond her control. It is the multiple layers of liminality that have ruined Loba's hope; the compound effect of unresolved instability in multiple areas of her life have robbed her of any sense of a "middle" through which she might transition into some new day. The absence of hope in turn destroys any faith that liminality might be an opportunity for growth.

Liminal Spirituality

It is my experience – in life and in my ministry as chaplain – that the tools which I need to negotiate these kinds of unwieldy liminoid states, have arisen in more securely held states of liminality. This experience is backed up by the ancient wisdom traditions, which teach that suffering can be a pathway to love, spiritual strength, and transformation. Personal, intentional, liminal spirituality has been my medicine in the deep deconstructions of my life, and it is now the key to my chaplaincy.

To me, spirituality is simply that aspect of being human that expresses our desire for deep connectedness. It has as many forms as there are human beings, for it is a project of integration between us and the complex web of life beyond ourselves. Spirituality is thus expressed in any number of spiritual practices, which may or may not be accompanied by a religious narrative.[3] Spiritual practices take place in real time and place, in real people's lives, individually and communally, and are the concrete forms of spirituality that give expression to the ineffable.

Not all spirituality or spiritual practices are liminal, though Turner did argue that the liminal state of being often refers to that which cannot be explained, the magical or mysterious, sacred and transcendent. In the breadth of human spirituality, there are many examples of rigid belief systems and ascetic disciplines that function to close down uncertainty

---

3. It may be useful to note that this definition of spirituality intentionally stands independent from any theological narrative, which is consistent with the work of Sandra Schneiders. See, for example, Schneiders, "The Study of Christian Spirituality: Contours and Dynamics of a Discipline," *Christian Spirituality Bulletin* 6 (Spring 1998), 1, 3-12.

and direct ecstatic experience, rather than create space for it. At its most basic, liminal spiritual experience is that type of spiritual experience and its associated practices that function without a predetermined rhetoric of sense-making. It is direct engagement with what is underneath the stories and propositions that usually make sense of one's life, by the temporary suspension of those forms in order to create movement into a liminal middle.[4]

Some liminal spiritual experiences arise without any intention on behalf of the individual – they are spontaneous, even mystical, events that defy all previous explanations of the ways of the world. Charismatic gifts of the Spirit fall into this category: the receiving of tongues or a word of prophesy, the gift of a vision or a spiritually significant dream. They are experienced as arriving from outside oneself or one's control. Moments of personal epiphany might also fall into this category: the sudden uprush of memory or awareness from the unconscious, prompted perhaps by a recognized smell, sight or sound; being held in a way reminiscent of the infant self with an accompanied response of longing, loss or lack (or, indeed, the opposite). Similarly, an encounter with beauty might "take one's breath away" and a brush with violence might "pull one up short." In each of these examples there is an unexpected moment where ordinary experience is suspended. There is a break in normality which brings with it an opportunity to reconsider what you had previously assumed to be true or real.

Other liminal spiritual experiences arise as a hoped-for consequence of an intentional spiritual practice. For example, the practice of meditation is a disciplined setting aside of time and attention, with its most profound effects often not experienced immediately but rather over the long term as our awareness of an inner stillness emerges. Intentional engagement with art also falls into this category; we go to the theatre "to be moved" or listen to poetry for "a different perspective." The desire is to feel a suspension of everyday life and have our minds and hearts elevated to higher things, however variously those are conceived.

It may be that beauty has an important part to play in liminal spirituality, for it is often observed to have a capacity to move us beyond the ordinary planes of empirical, physical existence. Beauty is put to use in many forms

---

4. Readers may note here the thinly veiled reference to apophatic theological method, as opposed to kataphatic theological method. In particular, the Christian mystical tradition understands the apophatic movement, into what cannot be thought, to be in dialectical relationship with the Scriptures and tradition. It is therefore to be distinguished from more recent existential hermeneutics, which rebound from the limit of thinking from positive into "negative," rather than remain in relationship to it.

of sacred space, marking out the "specialness" of what might happen there. Even in an inner space, beauty can have a particular way of demarcating a liminal encounter with the sacred that manifests in a sharp intake of breath, a gasp, a loss of words or total silence.

In many traditions, liminal spiritual experience has been referred to as contemplative spirituality. It is associated with silence, stillness, and meditation. The borders of the liminal practice might be held by a particular sitting position, the use of a mantra, a visual focal point or attention to the breath. Like individuals, groups may practice contemplation by sharing their experience simultaneously, or adding the quality of contemplation to other social forms of spiritual expression. For example, a Christian Eucharist that invites focus on the symbolic representations rather than on the literal words of consecration, invites the participant to move into a liminal spirituality rather than a prefigured form.

Mindfulness

The current mindfulness movement is a movement of liminal spiritual practices that is enjoying a growing amount of influence. Jon Kabat-Zinn, often referred to as the father of the modern mindfulness movement, defines mindfulness as "moment-to-moment, non-judgmental awareness." When this quality of mind is coupled with a meditation practice, such as is taught in Kabat-Zinn's Mindfulness-Based Stress Reduction course, it has been shown to effect significant health and well-being outcomes.[5] Neurological research into the effects of meditation suggests that in the meditative state, prefrontal cortex brain activity is suspended, which allows the flight-fight response in the amygdala of the brain to rest, thereby improving our impulse control and emotion regulation. In other words, we allow some breathing space in-between our body's sensory receptors, and the mind's choice of response. We learn how to feel our emotions and think our thoughts with more creativity and awareness.

The quality of mindful attention can be brought to any number of activities – walking, talking, listening, dancing, eating, making love, doing chores, and so on – but, as with prayer, not all mindfulness is liminal. For a mindfulness practice to function as a liminal arena it must have a designated border, a beginning and an end, a time during which to practice the skills of disciplining the mind; this is what the formal practice of mindfulness meditation does. Like anything that is exercised with regular repetition,

---

5. Jon Kabat-Zinn, *Full Catastrophe Living: Using the Wisdom of Your Body and Mind to Face Stress, Pain, and Illness*, 2nd ed. (New York: Bantam/Random House, 2013).

however, the brain begins to lay down new neural pathways and the body remembers the lessons of the liminal sphere. The more we practice, the more easily the body returns to the relaxed state acquired in meditation.

Personally, a regular practice of meditation has enabled me to know the terrain of my inner world, which in turn equips me to sense the demarcation between my inner world and another's. This clarity of "me, you and the space between us" increases my capacity for love – to give to the other without need for return, to serve without reference to myself. In addition to my sitting meditation, I am deeply grateful to have discovered conscious dance, and participate regularly in Open Floor movement meditation, which has given me an extensive language of the body, with its physical, emotional, mental, and spiritual dimensions. This wordless language of the body, listens, and speaks that which cannot be said but might be sensed, intuited, felt in liminal awareness.

Furthermore, I can map the journey through my own personal experience of liminality – a life crisis which started with desolation – with the development of these internal strengths. First came the ability to allow the questions without answers, then an increasing capacity to face pain without turning away. Next came an invitation to add curiosity and creativity, and, finally, a patience with living with what is, as it is, and letting the future unfold as it will. The more I learnt these skills for myself, the better I was able to remain in relationship with my communities, which are also to a large extent in liminality – my neighbourhood, my church denomination, our political systems, the global economic crisis, the existential uncertainties of the climate crisis.

I notice that, whilst Loba's head is downcast and her shoulders droop forward, her hands are fiercely clenched. The fingers are pressed in hard against each other with the thumbs pulling the fist in tight. In the instant when my eyes register her hands I sense their tension in my chest, in the muscles around my heart. Her hands are white, but my heart is red, raging with blood. I shift my attention to feel this sensing of my own body and invoke one of the familiar pathways of breath that I know I can trust from years of experience. "In through the nose, around the thinking center of the brain, down the channel of the throat and into the chest, around the feeling center of the heart. Let the breath carry awareness." Breathe in. Find an ease as it turns over. Breathe out. Rest. Breathe in awareness. Breathe out tension. Rest. I do this once, slow and deep, and return my attention to Loba. She has heard the invitation and joined me in the place of rest. Her hands have opened their clasp, just a little. We begin to breathe together.

Bringing Hope to the Hopeless

The single, slow and deep breath that transformed my conversation with Loba illustrates how the conscious practice of liminal spirituality can become a resource for those stuck in the middle. It is no small thing to be able to offer someone a breath full of invitation. As a chaplain, it is something that I have trained for and continue to practice regularly in order to maintain my skills. Breathing into chaos is about finding a frame of reference small enough to make a start, and, when we find that liminal space, time and again, hope builds. Our bodies and brains remember what it feels like. We get better at it.

There are three liminal spiritual practices that were influential in the sacred encounter with Loba: the creation of sacred space, deep listening, and meditation. They are characteristic of my chaplaincy ministry at the Brotherhood of St Laurence in Melbourne, and, whilst it is not an exhaustive list, unpacking these three spiritual practices might serves to illustrate the potential resource that liminal spirituality can provide when negotiating liminoid experience.

Sacred Space

The context in which our conversation was taking place was also not incidental. My organization has worked hard in recent years to affirm spirituality that supports the flourishing of everyone in our community, staff included. The Brotherhood of St Laurence is a social services organization that works toward an Australia free of poverty through research, advocacy and programs that target the root cause of inequality and exclusion. One innovative initiative in recent years has been to collaborate with local government and service providers to create a "hub" where vulnerable people can have a better experience of receiving services, and organizations can more effectively work together to empower local communities. The Community Services Hub in Epping has recently opened a "well-being room" for staff and volunteers who provide their services. This is where my conversation with Loba took place, and it is the first place where liminal spirituality was hosted in liminal space.

The opening of a well-being room at the Epping Hub gave concrete recognition to the value of spirituality in the context of social service provision. It has been carefully set up to create a space for momentary withdrawal and refreshment during a working day. The room was blessed in a multi-faith ceremony where it was officially named *Tarnuk*, a local indigenous word for welcome and wholeness. At the entrance to the room – the liminal threshold – a felt nameplate marks the space as a quiet one with an encouragement to pause on the threshold and "check in" by placing a circle of felt onto the nameplate to signal to others that you are in there. Green and white circles mean others are free to enter with you and red circles are a request for privacy.

The room is equipped with a variety of sensory supports for mindfulness. There are fluffy rugs, essential oils, an MP3 player and headphones, comfortable chairs, meditation cushions, and a large abstract painting of a peaceful forest. There is also an array of more religious spiritual symbols that might reconnect a person with their tradition: a Bible, an Islamic prayer mat, an Aboriginal message stick.

Encouraging an active spirituality among the staff that provide social services at the Hub demonstrates the Brotherhood's vision for holistic flourishing, and encourages participants and clients to aspire to a "good life," not just a life where they can scrape by. We can only achieve this if staff offer their service from the best of themselves – with love and attention to the individual. This has become increasingly difficult to do in an age where the demands on social service organizations have become severe. The *Tarnuk* Room is our statement of faith: lay your work down for a moment, then take it up again with renewed strength, compassion and grace.

Deep Listening

As chaplain, much of my pastoral work is liminal – I enter in and out of offices with no agenda, making myself available to whoever comes forward. This, for me, is essentially a spiritual practice of deep listening, and is the second resource of liminal spirituality that framed the sacred encounter with Loba. There are a variety of ways that I have learnt to conduct a pastoral visit as an act of deep listening. At the first level, the visit has a defined geography and space. I come in, the liminal space opens; I leave, the liminal space closes. During my time in the building I know that I am operating by different rules – I am awake to the notion of simply being at service and sense into the unspoken where, who and how of this particular visit. The routine acts as my MC, which in turn frees me up to offer the gift of holding liminal space for others.

Each encounter is a potential moment for listening. Sometimes, a staff member will make a more assertive approach and we arrange a suitable time for him or her to take a break from work and enter into an intentionally invoked liminal space of deep listening. At other times, by the careful choice of words and attention, I begin to notice who is in need of some open space to "fall into" for a time, who needs some breathing space, and who needs to "let things out." By holding a stillness, I have come to trust that individuals will sense that invitation and either step into it with their own choice of words and attention, or step away from it with the time-honored practice of small talk.

For me, deep listening is a liminal spiritual practice that can take me into the role of participant in the liminal process, or into the role of master of ceremonies hosting the liminal encounter. In this practice, we learn to listen without interruption and to listen to what is not spoken with words. Deep listening pays attention to body language, recurring words and phrases, the tone of voice. It goes beyond the literal to discern what is underneath. More than that, the purpose is not to fix, or to judge, but simply to witness. It is a space where there is nothing to be done except give expression to the liminal moment. The listener holds the open space for the speaker, like a master of ceremonies holds the ritual circle. They open the space through their attention, and they close it through their attention.

Meditation

The third liminal spiritual practice that was integral to the transformative moment in conversation with Loba is a regular practice of meditation. The disciplined skills of empathic awareness are only developed over time, with practice. Through meditation, my brain has learnt that it does not need to "freeze, fly or fight" in the presence of intense emotion. I have learnt that allowing conundrums and complexity to sit without resolution often leads to creative solutions. I have learnt to sense the concrete boundary between myself and another, and how to sustain the relationship between the two with more love than fear. This personal discipline made me a trustworthy MC of a liminal space that Loba could choose to enter.

I sometimes host a ten-minute "meditation at midday" at our Brotherhood offices. Ten minutes might not seem like much of a spiritual practice, but it is designed as a kind of "reset" and is, in essence, a liminal moment in-between a structured morning of work and structured afternoon of work. By experimenting with different forms of meditation, I have found that the most efficient way to anchor in the present is with a guided meditation on the breath, using the breath as a way of suspending logical thinking and allowing the brain and body to relax a little. Into this more relaxed space I then invite a little curiosity; when you have slowed down well enough to feel yourself breath, what else is here? Together we sense that this practice not only helps us to relax, it reminds us why we do what we do, and we return to work with more gentleness, compassion, and commitment to serve. With love.

With her spirit substantially altered, Loba takes another, more full and intentional breath, and her words return. She starts to contemplate the immediate rest of the day, rather than the unending drama of her life. Perhaps she can be grateful for the supportive friends she has at work. Perhaps she can remember that tonight she is staying in a house where she won't feel the need to heave the heavy chest of drawers across to block the bedroom door. Perhaps she can trust that her daughter will be happy when she picks her up from school in exactly 48 minutes' time. Our sacred conversation draws to a close as Loba shuffles her attention back into work mode, our bodies wriggle out stillness, and we smile at each other in satisfaction. Hope has been recovered – just a little – enough to sustain another day of living through chaos.

7
The Two Liminalities of War
Kate Hendricks Thomas

War is a universal experience of social liminality. If the scale of hostilities is sufficiently large, war can expand to even global liminality. Societies and nations are cast into a time between the times, a state of being filled with uncertainty and dread. For warriors within these societies, war represents a rite of passage, a transition that changes the identity of those who enter war and the community of those who share it. The warrior becomes a liminal person, a person living between pre-war structure and post-war resolution. Those who share it together develop the unique relationship of communitas – a community of the in-between. This affiliation is so intense that it may last a lifetime and transcend geography and time.

In ancient, indigenous, pre-industrial societies, the tribe specifically provided for the reincorporation of the warrior. This was accomplished through rituals conducted by tribal elders who were themselves already initiated. The healing and purifying process included communal story-telling, drama, dance, song, and feasting. Only such communal rituals reincorporated the warrior into peacetime existence. They were welcomed by the same tribe who sent them to war on their behalf.

* * *

Looking back now, I smile at the young woman who thought she knew it all. She had to feel that way, though. In Iraq she did not simply have to avoid incoming fire and stay safe on convoys all through Al Anbar, she also had to carry a knife into the showers and get lectures about how she should never walk around the forward operating base alone for fear of sexual assault. She had to have thick skin, a belief in her own invulnerability, and a powerful ability to compartmentalize. Those were survival skills – sanity-savers.

To understand my story, it is important to understand the demanding culture of the U.S. Marine Corps as a service branch. For me, the training started at home. I grew up in a family with a military dad. Anyone on active duty will tell you that the military is more a lifestyle than a job. Your work tends to come home with you and impacts basically everything you do. It is not just what you do, it is who you are.

Military culture was part of our home life from birth. My father asked us to seek excellence at all times, even if we thought we were already there. As kids, we got assigned summer book reports that my father graded. I always earned a grade of D or F on my first try, which was hard for a bookworm like me to accept. While it felt like a big, fat blow to my academic ego, my father meant it as a learning experience. He had no problem letting us cry as we chafed at the challenge presented.

We were an organized and hard-working little tribe – or else. My siblings and I still joke about the black trash bag that came out on weekend mornings if we had failed to pick up toys. We only had to see one favorite truck or doll thrown away before we learned to keep our gear in order.

Our family might have been a little more intense than normal because my father was a career infantry officer. He was dedicated to the Marine Corps in the true-believer way that a career officer must be. As a result, my decision to join the Marines was not a tough one.

After joining the Marines in my twenties, I realized how much the culture of my household prepared me for the physical and mental hardships of officer training. Sometimes I wondered whether I could handle the physical things I would be asked to do. I doubted whether twenty-mile hikes or sky-high obstacle courses were within the scope of things I could accomplish. Sometimes on my first try, they were not, but I trained hard and threw myself at walls until they became easy to hop. I bruised my arms learning to chicken-wing over parallel bars. I surrounded myself with people a little stronger and faster to benefit from the push they offered me. I was proud of every single bruise. I drank the Kool-Aid, gladly. My entire identity was being a Marine.

* * *

My little brother joined the Marines a year after I did. I commissioned him on a sunny day with lots of smiles and more than a little pride. We went through training pipelines and compared many notes, both proud to be Marines.

I was already deployed to Iraq when he e-mailed me to share his grand romantic plans to propose to his girlfriend before he headed over. She was a civilian schoolteacher that I had yet to meet. I was in my cynical deployment mode and groaned a bit when I received his note. At the time, I lived and worked with many Marines receiving what we call "Dear John" letters. I suspected some sort of template for these sad missives existed because they often read exactly the same: "The grind of deployment is too much. Our relationship is over. I already have a new significant other. The end."

I did not think his proposal would wind up any differently because he was headed to Iraq right behind me. Like a good big sister, though, I wanted to be supportive. I told him I did not have a problem with the proposal but advised him to buy her a ring made out of cubic zirconia. No sense in buying a diamond he might never get back. As younger brothers often do, he ignored my advice and bought her a beautiful ring.

I rolled my eyes but made a mental note not to give him too hard a time when he landed in Al Anbar. I knew his timeline and followed his unit's progress towards us. Around the time they were coming in, I convoyed south to be there at the hangar in the middle of the night. As they landed, my heart started to sink a bit. Even armed and incredibly well-trained, my brother will always look like a little kid to me. He was walking towards me with a huge pack on his back, a Kevlar on his head, and a rifle in his hands. All I could see were his big, blue eyes peeking out like a turtle under all that gear, and I thought, "Who let a ten year-old on the plane with a rifle?"

As I stood watching his C-130 aircraft unload on the tarmac, I forgot to feel invincible for a moment – I knew where he was heading and I knew what was happening there. I had some big sister notions of telling him what he needed to know to stay safe during his deployment and for the first time it occurred to me that that might not be enough.

Soon after, I was sent home to the United States, and I did not know it at the time, but he was as well. Except that an improvised explosive device (IED) made sure that his trip home was wounded and on a stretcher.

Once I found out, my job was to get to him. This time it meant making my way to a hospital ward in Maryland. When a service member is medically evacuated and they make it to the Stateside hospital, there are no guarantees and a lot of unknowns. When my brother arrived at Bethesda, we did not know what he might be facing. Our family came together to be there for him, but, even with our support system gathered, Bethesda was a dark place some days. Into this world walked my brother's civilian schoolteacher. Frankly, I did not yet know whether she could be part of our close-knit family. I had stereotyped her on sight – mostly because she was a pretty girl who often wore makeup and always had on matching accessories. I was waiting for her to fall apart.

She never did.

When her leave ran out at work, she went back to teaching all day long in nearby Virginia but made the drive every night to sleep in a chair at my brother's bedside. I was terrible in that hospital room, always dropping things – just graceless. She kept him smiling and focussing on their future together. She kept him connected to their community of friends when he left the hospital and had to spend his days in a reclining chair. She kept him looking forward to new plans to build a family, even when they had to install bars over his bed at home and he needed help with the most basic tasks.

That makeup had fooled me; she was more than serious. She showed up, and she was a foundation for my little brother when he really needed one.

As he began healing and moving forward with a new life as a medically-retired warrior, I vacillated on whether or not to leave the military. I did not feel ready to head off to graduate school and leave my tribe – we were still at war, after all. I think I was afraid of the transition. Control freaks are never terribly comfortable with that kind of ambiguity.

Although our present-day military is superb in the preparation of warriors for their service, it does not excel in providing them with resources of mental and emotional resilience that can serve them in the liminal domain. Unlike ancient societies and warriors, our present-day military and society do not provide adequately for the reincorporation of former soldiers into a civilian community, a society that typically does not understand them or what they have experienced. When warriors do not transition back into tribe and family, they often enter a second liminality, a post-war liminality. This world is unlike the one that was left the first time; it is at once the same and very different because the warrior has changed. In the worst-case scenario, the warrior who has not transitioned back is left in a state of permanent liminality, neither here nor there.

When reintegration occurs with an ideal level of social support, the veteran's reintegration story is like my brother's. In our family, he is still everyone's favorite. He is now a dad and a slightly intense high school English teacher. His wife is hilarious and keeps us all on our toes.

Too often, the reintegration story is like mine and like that of too many of our service members leaving active duty today. This is the second liminality of war.

I struggled with pulling the right people around me after my deployment and that time at the hospital. I was angry, guilty, then angry some more. I drew inward and sought to surround myself with people who had similar experiences to my own. I was looking for other Marines who were seeking balance in the same way I was.

That is how I met Kyle.

The story started the way many do, with sparkly attraction that morphed into friendship, then into love. We met by accident – I made a spontaneous decision to go meet an old friend. I walked into a restaurant in rumpled jeans with my hair casually tossed into a ponytail. That friend was seated at a table with a stranger by his side. I had not expected to have my head turned romantically, but he smiled at me, and he had a smile that seemed to light up the room.

I still grin when thinking about that first dinner, and the way our eyes meeting felt like the decision to become inseparable was made for us both in that instant. Kyle made me laugh at every turn. He was charming and outgoing – the life of every party. He had some of the same dark stories I did, and we connected on that level.

We were both Marine officers, which meant he understood my tribe and my dedication to what I did for a living. We worked hard and played even harder, which was all perfectly normal in the Marine Corps. Free time was a rare commodity, making us feel like every night out should be as epic as possible. We were sensation seekers who were always up for a challenge or adventure. To us, epic nights out often meant heavy drinking and keeping late hours at bars.

Kyle and I got serious quickly. Soon after we started dating, Kyle was packing bags to head overseas again, and we had to make quick decisions about what we were to one another. Moving in together, getting married, and spending as much time together as the Marine Corps allowed wove the tapestry of our early relationship. We were at once both wild and wildly happy.

It is hard to explain what my tie to Kyle felt like. He was the first person I shared almost everything with, and he was never judgmental. We both held unresolved experiences close to our chests and our shared resentments bred feelings of closeness that allowed me to ignore certain things.

First came the red flags that I ignored because I had all the same problems. Kyle drank in binge fashion, early and often. He was reckless and took risks at any opportunity, always up for some untried, new experience. Most of the time I was right there with him.

Then there were the flags that I somehow chose to ignore and excuse because I was blindly smitten. Kyle would mix prescription pain medication with alcohol, or go out until late and then head to work without sleeping at all.

Things got worse once we left the active duty Marine Corps. We lived in a new city, had new jobs, and were a bit disconnected from our families who resided hundreds of miles away.

It still seems embarrassing to admit out loud that I did not see the downhill slide. I was at once too busy and too proud. At the time, I did not see Kyle's behavior as symptomatic of anything larger than boredom or a bad attitude, and I railed against each episode with righteous anger. It became a cycle of fights, promises, and forgiveness, always on repeat.

I got very good at keeping up appearances. When one of his angry outbursts left a foot-sized hole in our wall, I moved furniture and arranged pictures to cover the damage. When family and friends came to visit, I had clever explanations for why the doors in our house were off the hinges. Loud yelling became shoves into walls or furniture. Our fashionable apartment and put-together life started coming apart, and my self-denial got harder to keep up. One sunny afternoon, he dragged me across the living room floor by my hair and threw me out of the front door. I remember being glad that our industrial-style concrete floors were smooth and polished – at least I slid easily.

I cannot even recall why he was angry. The neighbors who called the police never asked me any questions, and I never offered them anything but averted eyes. I could not tell anyone about it, even as forgiving and forgetting each incident was getting harder and harder to do. I was all alone at this point by choice. I was too invested in seeming smart at all times, and I knew smart women were not supposed to have problems like these in their relationships.

The influence of culture on my behavior during that period of time and on human behavior in general cannot be understated. It never entered my mind that Kyle had a problem with depression or stress injury, and that all of his self-medication had a source. It never entered my mind to go ask someone for help with an abusive relationship that kept escalating.

Never.

As things got worse in our home, I was truly not equipped to be a real source of help to Kyle. I was as invested in presenting an image of strong silence as he was, trained and driven to disregard symptoms that were staring me right in the face. I did not have the language to explain my own problem drinking or unresolved sadness and anger. I did not have the distance and objectivity to see Kyle's problems as real problems.

I was sitting alone in our apartment one day reading an article for a graduate school paper that made me gasp. It was a detailed anthropological analysis of military and law enforcement communities that explained why becoming a civilian again is so incredibly hard for service members. We are literally trained and culturally-programmed to avoid processing problems: "Warrior subculture tends to promote the belief that acknowledging emotional pain is synonymous with weakness and, specifically, that asking for help for emotional distress or problems is unacceptable."[1] The author

---

1. Mark Mamin, "Warrior Culture, Spirituality, and Prayer," in *Journal of Religion and Health* 52 (2013), 740-58.

made plain the consequences of my cultural buy-in and explained how warrior culture can distort critical thinking and good judgment in cases where warriors suppress emotional pain, fail to apply sound cognitive thinking, fail to acknowledge real health or wellness issues, and intentionally choose not to seek help that might remedy a mental health problem. If strength is a virtue, becoming a patient is antithetical to being virtuous.

I was excellent at suppressing emotional pain, and my decision-making left more than a little to be desired at this juncture.

The result of such a firmly entrenched value system is feeling a whole lot of shame associated with emotional struggle, patient identity, and mental health conditions. They are simply not options. This does not just mean that service members deny needing help; it means that we avoid recognizing any symptoms as such in ourselves or in those to whom we are close. If forced to address displayed symptoms, we will take denial to new heights and even actively dodge treatment when prescribed.

The U.S. Department of Defense and the U.S. Department of Veterans Affairs work tirelessly to provide treatment options for service members with depression and stress injuries. Within the military community, the issue is not lack of screening for depressive disorders, nor in the medical care available to service members suffering from depression. Rather, the problem is getting veterans to use treatment services.

I was a leader who had directed Marines working for me to Family Services for Combat Stress many times. Use them myself? Not an option.

A major reason why service members avoid treatment is that recommendations to seek it often come from civilian mental health providers. Because warrior cultures have their own temperaments, members are typically exclusive and mistrustful of outsiders with different life experiences. The military is an insular world, and well-intentioned providers are simply not a part of it. Research has shown that after deployments, service members separating from active duty feel incredibly disconnected from civilians.[2]

At no time in my military career was this feeling stronger than right after coming home from Iraq. Spending time in my brother's hospital room was always followed by time in the "real" world, where people asked inane questions or seemed to have no idea what was happening with the young wounded warriors I had just left.

I had no one to speak with about the guilt I felt for being safe and physically untouched while my little brother was not. My experiences in Iraq on convoys and with incoming indirect fire had been characterized by excellent timing and good fortune; I came home totally unscathed by

2. Charles Hoge, *Once a Warrior, Always a Warrior* (Guilford, CT: Lyons Press, 2010).

either contact or injury. In fact, the most I ever saw on the road was a controlled IED detonation. My service felt subpar, and I wished I could take my brother's place, and that I had been there for him in better fashion. I remember being ticked off that I had not known he was hurt right away so that I could have tried to finagle my way to him. I was peacefully packing gear not far away in another Al Anbar forward operating base. The thought that he might have waked up scared or alone when I could have been there killed me.

All of my thoughts left me simmering with rage and with a desire to surround myself with others who "got it." Everyone in the civilian world seemed so casual and happy, oblivious to the pain and sorrow facing my community, my family. I no longer knew how to speak to civilians, and my resentment of their complacency seethed under the surface. I was simply angry with no words for why. I stopped wanting to speak to anyone who did not speak my chosen language of alienation and latent anger.

I can look back and bemoan my lack of awareness about reintegration, but having tons of skills might not have mattered either. Lots of people had the same issue. I was struck reading the story of a professional who was formally trained in combat stress and skillful reintegration. She knew more than anyone how to avoid feelings of disconnect, yet she herself was not immune. A mother and Navy mental health provider, Dr Heidi Squier Kraft returned from serving with the Marines of Al Anbar around the same time as my brother and I to resume her Stateside practice. Of the experience she wrote:

> And so, I returned to life as a clinical psychologist in a peacetime hospital. Despite my clinical knowledge that each individual's suffering is real and important, I often found myself staring in disbelief at my patients. I could not fathom the crises that my patients made out of their life events, nor could I empathize with the petty relationship, work, or financial stressors that brought them to tears in my office. Only months before, I had held the hand of a twenty-two-year-old hero who gave his life to save two of his men. I had witnessed courage in the face of injury and pain, loyalty in the face of grief. Everyday psychological problems not only paled in comparison, they struck me as frankly absurd. Despite the personal toll seven months of war had taken, I found myself wishing I worked on a Marine base. At least then I would know what to say to my patients.[3]

3. Heidi Squier Kraft, *Rule Number Two: Lessons Learned in a Combat Hospital* (New York: Back Bay Books, 2007).

The feeling that American civilian culture was just as foreign as any far-flung land stuck with me, and it prompted me to stay in the Marines when my contract was up, to select a new duty station, and to move more completely into the mindset that characterized my time with Kyle. We moved into the liminal space of reintegration together, with our shared imbalances further exacerbating our problems.

Both card-carrying, warrior culture members who adhered rigidly to all its norms and values, Kyle and I became a dysfunctional duo in the last year we were together. We both ignored symptoms and put Band-Aids on wounds that were both figurative and literal.

Our days were very, very dark toward the end. They were a haze of alcohol and bad choices, walking on eggshells, crying, and making shameful compromises.

This isn't me.

This can't be who I am.

Is this the future I choose?

Still, I had no idea yet that I needed help, and I would not have known how to accept it if someone had offered.

It was not until one of Kyle's particularly scary benders left me alone in our apartment searching for places to hide our ammunition that I realized something had to change. He was mixing alcohol with Valium at the time, and I could barely understand his speech. He had become paranoid, obsessively checking my whereabouts, phone records, and e-mail inbox.

I had no idea where he had gone that night, but I knew he always came back drunk. I searched for places to secret away rounds so that, even if he went for one of our weapons when he came home, he would not have anything to load them with. I knew he needed help, and a tiny doubt began to creep into my mind about whether I was ever going to be able to get him to seek it before something bad happened to me. It was the first time I considered leaving, knowing I might be leaving him drowning.

Without ever making any of these admissions, I filed divorce papers and packed the car. I called Kyle's sister and left her a message that asked her to look out for him without giving away any in-depth information. I was still being loyal, in my own mind.

I left everything material I owned with him at our former home and drove off, a completely broken version of myself.

* * *

Perhaps today I work on military reintegration because my own experiences leaving the Marine Corps were not ideal – it just was not as easy to leave and re-invent as I had expected. The Marine Corps offered me education, challenge, the chance to push my limits and to lead other people. I loved the Marine Corps, but I never quite learned how to exist outside it.

It was hard to be a civilian who had never quite resolved her feelings about war, but it was also hard to be a civilian woman who had once been a leader of Marines. For most people the very word veteran calls to mind the image of a man, especially a combat veteran. But there are over 1.6 million women veterans in the United States. Of these, thirty percent are post-9/11 era, meaning younger veterans. Many of us served in Iraq and Afghanistan. We may be a sizable percentage of the women vet population, but post-9/11 women vets stand a bit apart in a normal crowd.

In general, fewer Americans serve today. The American veteran population (both male and female) has been declining for decades. What this means for my community of peers today is that only about twelve percent of young men and three percent of young women have served during the last fifteen years we have been at war.

It is easy to focus on how things are not optimized for military personnel leaving active duty, but I always turn back to notions of preventing some of that transition stress. "If I had only known to do this," became a familiar refrain for me. Today, I believe that it does not have to be as hard to reintegrate into a civilian community for tomorrow's service members. Many of us return from military service meaningfully changed – physically, mentally, emotionally, and spiritually. These changes encompass the whole person and hold the potential to transcend whole communities. Shifting our focus from post-service problems to pre-reintegration, mental fitness training for the active duty component is what we need to do. Here, rigorous evaluation of existing outreach efforts provide the foundation upon which savvy programmers must build. Our best chance for making a difference in both the post-service and training environments (before a service member faces transition stress) involves designing programs from a baseline of proven success.

To operate in training commands requires great cultural competency, making mental fitness programming relevant to warfighters working to maintain readiness and improve performance. The narrative must become about mission success, not mental health treatment. To train is to participate actively, and this is a wellness concept with which service members are already familiar. Framing self-regulatory training as a way to "bulletproof the brain" renders palatable a training opportunity specifically designed to create more effective warriors who possess mental endurance. Framing mental fitness training as promotion of combat fitness, resilience, and mental endurance renders it accessible to the military population. We are interested in building strengths, after all.

When we talk about resiliency-cultivation for those warriors who have been immersed in combat operations for over fifteen years, we have to speak their language. PowerPoint simply will not cut it. By establishing mental fitness as another component of optimal combat readiness, we establish its training as a crucial component of mission preparedness. As a benefit, we remove the stigma of such practices for post-deployment troops who may be struggling with stress illnesses of varying degrees. The message can become directive; just as soldiers learn mission-essential skills and train their bodies for arduous combat, we must adopt practices designed to train and promote health in the mind, body and spirit in a holistic sense. This training does not succeed in sustainable fashion in a vacuum. Knowing the importance of social support to well-being and generally wanting to contribute to improved quality of life for service members requires a focus on the larger community in which a warrior operates. Social and family fitness is part of mental fitness, and we must consider family readiness programming that is more extensive and progressive than our current offerings.

When we consider how we could apply these basic recommendations to military veterans seeking relief from reintegration stress or to active duty military preparing for it, we must consider how to make stress management a testable metric. Biofeedback tools exist that can do this. Checking for the adrenal hormone DHEA and blood cortisol ratios or conducting periodic blood cortisol checks can be as important as other physical standards are in the military. Biomarkers tell us quickly whether someone is taking time to practice balanced wellness. This is an exciting area of future work: helping active-duty service members learn to de-escalate their nervous system response as a performance metric can make resilience itself a performance metric. It turns self-awareness and resilience into standards, and motivates learning, training, practice, and performance in our community's culture. Training warriors to embrace a mental training regimen can make them better at their jobs and more resilient in their lives, both during and after their service for their country.[4]

The way back for warriors in our own time parallels ancient rites of passage. We need to re-establish our sense of community and belonging,

---

4. Kate Hendricks Thomas and David Albright, *Bulletproofing the Psyche: Preventing Mental Health Problems in our Service Members and Veterans* (Santa Barbara, CA: ABC-CLIO/Praeger, 2018).

the role of ritual elders to transition the warrior home, spiritual resources for purification and healing of the soul, opportunities for story-telling, and we need to improve the general population's understanding and awareness of the warrior's journey. In this way, the inevitable liminality of war may avoid becoming permanent, and what should be the solace of homecoming may not become a second liminality – sometimes deadlier than the first.

8

Out of the Whirlwind

Jill Cameron Michel

There we stood in the cavernous expanse that was our Quonset hut. Decades earlier the church had received the hut from a nearby Army base. Since that time the building had become home to basketball leagues and Sunday school classes. More recently it hosted a Friday evening neighborhood ministry. But most of the time it stood empty and dark. In the minds of many it was an eyesore that detracted from the stately beauty of the neighboring Carthage limestone church building. I had many times jokingly commented that, though the Army found this building useless after World War II, we did not; the church held on to things. So here we were in 2011 and we still had the Quonset hut.

Just days earlier an EF5 tornado (the highest category) had torn a gaping wound through our town. It left a six-mile-long, one-mile-wide scar; thousands of houses, half of the public school buildings, our primary hospital, nearly forty churches, and over 500 businesses were either destroyed or damaged. Hundreds were killed or injured. The tornado peeled back the roof of our church and broke out the windows.

But the old Quonset hut stood fast, seemingly unscathed. Perhaps the arched shape allowed the winds to blow over it. Or maybe some cosmic sense of humor needed to pester me in the midst of disaster. For whatever reason, the building stood. And we stood in it.

A new friend, a member of a partner denomination with long experience in disaster recovery, looked around and said, "This building would be great. We could just rough in a few showers in the back. People could bring their cots or mattresses. I slept in semi-truck trailers in 100-degree heat after Katrina. This could be luxurious compared to that."

That surprise came after we had walked round the entire church building looking for spaces that could serve as housing for volunteers. We had all but exhausted the possibilities when I unlocked the door to the Quonset hut. I expected others to see the same dismal place I saw. Instead, a new possibility was imagined and a dream began to take shape.

Nine months later, church buildings and grounds repaired and back in good shape, volunteers were staying in our Quonset hut, a space that had been transformed. Rather than simply creating an open space for air mattresses with some showers roughed in, we built an intentional space for volunteers to relax after a hard day's work. We constructed large restrooms, complete with shower enclosures and private changing areas. The team crafted two bunk rooms with bunks stacked three high. And all that was accompanied by a great room with kitchen, dining and living room facilities. Before we knew it, the Quonset hut, which I once imagined as having blown away, became known as the Hilton of mission stations.

Something had changed. We had changed.

But where did this all begin? The tornado ushered us across the threshold into an involuntary liminal space. But what happened in the years before that prepared us to respond to this disaster?

Before the Wind Blew

More than ten years earlier I had been called to serve in Joplin, Missouri as pastor of The First Christian Church (Disciples of Christ). On paper there was not much to write home about. It was a traditional, mainline Protestant congregation doing traditional, mainline Protestant ministry. The numbers were not especially encouraging. My first impression of the town was not fantastic. In spite of all that, however, I fell in love. I fell in love with the people I met. After my initial visit, I knew this was the place that I was going to move.

Upon arriving I discovered more challenges than I expected. There were some "old guard" versus "new guard" battles. There were some people among the congregation who seemed compelled habitually to work against the pastor. They liked to hang out in the shadows and stir things up.

Maybe I was too young to know better. Maybe I was too hopeful, too naïve. Whatever it was, it worked. Day after day, year after year, I responded to secrecy with honest, open conversation and to resistance with understanding. I worked hard to be true to myself and my calling while at the same time knowing that, should some tragedy occur, I needed to show up and be pastor to each and every member of the congregation.

While there were certainly situations I could have handled differently, by and large that leadership approach worked. We moved together from handshakes to hugs, from a closed community to an open and welcoming one, from a people who doubted our congregation's longevity to a people who were embracing the future with hope, from a people who said no to change to a people who asked how we could change.

This did not happen overnight. I had been serving the congregation for over a decade before the tornado blew through town. Change happened incrementally as we built memories, relationships and trust. We became a different people through loss and addition. We became a different congregation as we faced difficult questions about our future. We were changed as we claimed that God was not finished with us and that the community would not be better off without us.

Many of the positive changes occurred when we quit worrying about being numerically smaller and traveling a road toward congregational death. We finally embraced the belief that there was a future for our congregation. Once we accepted that belief, we were more able to dream that future and get excited about the possibilities that lay ahead. We became a place where people were happy to be. Those who were already part of the congregation became more committed and those who were new saw something they wanted to belong to.

We did not grow by leaps and bounds. In fact, some of the losses we sustained, especially in the form of the departure of people with a different vision, meant a numerically smaller congregation. But those who stayed were committed to making a difference in their community and world. We were committed to offering a safe place for people to explore their faith, to ask questions, to be welcomed no matter who they were or where they came from. We were committed to a future even without knowing the details of that future.

What that meant was that, when the winds of the tornado died down that unforgettable May night, and we walked outside to behold the destruction that had occurred, when we tried to drive to find a friend or loved one only to discover roads blocked with debris, landmarks and street signs blown blocks away, when all this happened, we were ready. We were ready not only to face the painful realities that were thrust upon us, but ready to be transformed into a better version of ourselves than we ever could have imagined.

Involuntary but Ready

Our liminal event was a natural disaster. It was not something we chose. Nevertheless, without realizing it, it was something for which we had prepared.

We had not prepared for a tornado. We did not have a stockpile of chain saws and bottled water. We had not set up a calling tree. We did not even have signs posted in the building to direct people to safe areas when the sirens howled.

But we were ready nonetheless.

We had built trust and deepened relationships. Therefore, after the tornado had gone, one of the first responses of many in the congregation was to go out and discover ways they could help others from the church. One young couple, initially called upon to help some good friends, turned their attention to others and carried a ninety-year-old, fellow church member from the rubble of her home. Several people went into the most deeply impacted areas where they wandered the unmarked streets looking for familiar signs that could point them to the homes of church friends, as they sought to make sure everyone was safe and to see whether they could help comb through what remained in hopes of salvaging some evidence of earlier life.

I had been serving that congregation for a good number of years and had built up knowledge of the people. From knowing the names and numbers of family members who lived out of town to having been in people's homes enough that I could recognize a home by the foundation's footprint when everything else was gone, I had the ability to connect with people in a time in which it was hard to find each other. I remember watching a colleague who had moved to town only months before the tornado who was at a loss to do the same. At that point I was grateful for the history that I had.

We had already done the work of wondering whether we had a future and had chosen to believe we did. We had learned to let go of some of our need to control. We had learned to put our energy into more important questions. We had learned to build enough trust that even when we disagreed with each other, we trusted that the other had our collective best interest in mind. This put us in a good position to be flexible. We benefited from this flexibility in everything, from deciding where we would worship and how we would handle logistics for the six months we were out of our building, to being able to make a quick decision about the opportunity to share our space for the city's recovery, to empowering people who had a track record of making good decisions for the congregation with the authority to make decisions on our behalf. We trusted each other to make good decisions and to engage in the necessary conversations without being restrained by yards of red tape.

When we embraced the belief that our congregation had a bright future, we also shifted from piecing things together to doing things well. This was reflected in our intentional processes to call people into leadership positions because they had the skills and commitment for a ministry (rather than just filling slots with warm bodies). This was reflected in the work we did on our facility, which transitioned from being duct taped together to being a point of pride. This commitment to excellence was evidenced in the way "The

Station" (which became the new name for the Quonset hut, our volunteer lodging) was put together as well as the hospitality that was shown to each group of volunteers who passed through our church.

One of the things we discovered was the necessity of hope. It was really the hope for our future that caused us to be well positioned and able to respond to both our own needs and the needs of the community when the tornado hit. None of our specific preparation was done with a tornado in mind. Rather, our preparation was that of a congregation hoping for a long and healthy future of making a difference in the community and the world. Consequently, when the tornado ravaged our city, we were ready. We might have been ready for anything.

The Creation of Communitas

Our liminal experience opened up a beautiful space for healing and transformation. Before the tornado I never had a strong sense that our people were proud of their city. Though they held a collective identity based on place, I wouldn't have called it pride. Whatever challenges the tornado brought, it also revealed many of the great strengths of our people. And by the end they knew it.

While in many ways the early efforts were focused on a survival response to a disaster, the long-lasting impact materialized in an unexpected and unanticipated way. What we experienced was a community that came together in a remarkable way and became better than it was to begin with. What I witnessed was a transformation during liminality that created a whole new post-liminal state. This positive transformation was not only for our congregation but for our whole city.

After all, tornadoes are not choosy. Its destructive force blew down new expensive homes and older homes that were barely standing. Renters and homeowners alike lost their shelter and possessions. Neighborhood stores and schools, businesses and churches were destroyed. One of the immediate post-tornado realizations was the widespread poverty of our city. Rather than ignore it, our community leaders and government entities worked to respond in ways that paid attention to that disparity. People were not simply returned to their pre-liminal state; they were helped to move beyond poverty. This included recognition that many systems were available to homeowners but not renters. As a result, many in our city worked to make resources available for those who rented as well.

As one might expect, in the initial hours and days after the tornado, neighbors helped neighbors and strangers became friends. People looked for survivors. They dug through debris, provided meals, and offered safe places to stay. They did all this across lines of economics, race, religion, and other demographic details that often create barriers.

What amazed me most was how this work continued. The city's Long-Term Recovery Committee (LTRC) was populated with leaders from helping agencies, government institutions, and faith communities. This group worked together with an ease that surprised and delighted me. It's not that there were no difficult decisions, no times when people disagreed, no moments when one institution just went on and did their own thing. Those things happened. But in spite of all that, the city came together and worked to recover as one. At the very least they kept each other informed so that "the left hand knew what the right hand was doing."

Time would show this was not a short-term function of recovery. It was rather a permanent outcome. One of the most striking examples of the transformation of our city occurred over a year after the tornado, in response to an unrelated event.

On a Monday morning in August 2012 we awoke to the news that our local Islamic Society building had been burned to the ground. Though not immediately confirmed, people suspected an act of hate. This was not the first time the Islamic community had experienced arson; on a previous occasion, surveillance cameras confirmed an intentional act.

Many of us wondered how we could respond. Several congregations had already begun interfaith work after the previous year's tornado. In fact, a number of us had been at the Islamic Society just two nights before the fire. We were there during Ramadan, sharing prayer and an *Iftar* dinner as Muslims broke the day's fast. Because of these relationships of trust, interfaith partners offered places for the Islamic congregation to gather for worship and the next week's meal. But we wanted to do more, and we did. We invited representatives from congregations across the city to gather and discuss how we could best respond.

My congregation had the pleasure of hosting that conversation, and I remember being pleasantly surprised by the turnout. People I expected to attend were there, but so were people I did not expect. Some of these were folks who held a theology that did not generally move them toward interfaith (or even ecumenical) cooperation. I barely knew some of them until the tornado reminded us that we were one.

That group sat in the fellowship hall of our church building and wondered aloud how to respond. It became clear that, in addition to offering personal support and encouragement, we needed to do something public. We decided that we would take out a full-page advertisement in the local newspaper to demonstrate our support for our Muslim friends.

The statement was simple: "Deeply saddened by recent events, the faith communities of the Joplin area stand by our neighbors from the Islamic Society in their time of tragedy. We believe that 'Love thy Neighbor' has no restrictions."[1]

The statement itself was impactful, but what impressed me most was the list of names who signed it. Signatures included individual clergy and lay persons, secular individuals, and whole congregations. Most strikingly, I was aware of how the names of Christians whose faith traditions restricted sharing communion with those of other traditions were listed right alongside everyone else who supported the Muslim community.

In a town that has a preponderance of conservative Christians, it was notable that the immediate and overwhelming response to the burning of the Islamic Society building was outrage at such an act of hate and support for our Muslim friends. Person after person, even those I did not expect, expressed their sadness, distress and anger. Though we cannot know for certain, I suspect that had this fire occurred two years earlier our collective response would not have been nearly so robust.

As a community drawn together through involuntary crisis, we were transformed in that liminal state into a people who discovered hidden truths. We now understood our connection to our neighbor was much deeper than we originally knew. We experienced the truth that "those who share the liminal passage develop a community of the in-between, a connection that transcends any former distinctions between status and station created by social structures."[2] In responding to our Muslim friends, I was reminded that the impact of the tornado on our community was not short-lived, but in fact had changed us in ways that would prove to be long lasting and far reaching.

This Is Hard Work

I confess that I routinely keep a pair of rose-colored glasses nearby. I often prefer them to the ordinary lenses through which one may see the world. Those glasses do impact the way I experience and tell my stories. Nevertheless, upon reflection, nearly seven years after the tornado, I know more than ever that there is no minimizing the difficulty of that time. There was nothing about that transition that was easy or without its angst.

Yes, we were prepared, even when we had not intentionally prepared for this particular type of crisis. Our preparation had led us toward being

---

1. *Joplin Globe*, 12 August 2012.
2. Timothy Carson, *Liminal Reality and Transformational Power: Transition, Renewal & Hope*, rev. ed. (Cambridge: Lutterworth Press, 2016), 4.

a community. Even when we were displaced from our congregational home, personal homes and workplaces, it was possible to move forward with decision-making and rebuilding. It was easier because of our future orientation and the hope we had claimed in becoming who we were intended to be, both physically and spiritually. This resilience provided us with balance in the face of inevitable angst. In fact, in many ways, this gave us the ability to choose something other than angst.

While angst was certainly a part of our new reality, I was often amazed to see that it was seldom the primary focus. Yes, stress levels were high. After all, thousands of people in our city were trying to navigate unfamiliar disaster recovery systems. Thousands more were learning how to be helpful in the midst of recovery. Volunteers from elsewhere were streaming in, some willing to help in exactly the ways we needed, others insisting that they knew what we needed or asking much of us even though they could help very little. Meanwhile we were going from home to work, from a disaster recovery office to a worksite, from the lumber yard to the dump, and not even recognizing the landscape of some places that we had known so well.

Yes, grief became our constant companion. From grieving the deaths of 161 people to the loss of homes, keepsakes, routines and familiarity, grief was real, even for those who were not directly in the tornado's path. I remember times when I would turn a corner and be shocked all over again by the barrenness of what lay ahead. I remember going to a charity ballgame in a nearby city intended to raise money for our town and in the middle of the game wondering why I thought it was a good idea to come. After all, the reality of our tornado was a daily thing. I did not need to talk or hear about it more.

In the aftermath of the tornado, liminal time moved at its own pace, mostly slower than we might have preferred. Grief would well up unexpectedly. Sometimes people just needed to take a break and not drive through town and see it again. Questions piled up:

When would things get back to normal?

Would there be enough money to rebuild?

Did rebuilding or buying an existing house make more sense?

Would schools be ready to open in the fall?

How would resources be allocated?

Would our city ever seem like our city again?

How long would all this take?

Even with this stress and grief, questions and angst swirling around, somehow we kept moving forward. My friend, Kenny Foster, wrote a song about this experience of the tornado:

Mother Nature ain't around to answer questions, but what she tore down, we're building right back up. When you've got everything to gain, well then what's a little rain gonna do to folks that don't know when to stop.[3]

It did indeed seem that ours was a community that just did not know when to stop. When we felt like we could not move forward, we borrowed energy and hope from the many, many people who had come to lend a helping hand.

Post-Liminal Growth

Seven years later what has changed and changed for the good? At this point my observations about both the congregation and city that I knew are from a distance. Three years after the tornado my husband was offered a job that required us to move. I still pay attention, however. Here are the observations I can make about the community.

First, while many cities that experience disasters also experience a significant reduction in population, that was not true in our case. In 2015 the City of Joplin estimated that the population was up more than 1,000 people since the 2010 census:[4] "Although more than 30% of Joplin residents had been displaced, few left the community. As a result of aggressive efforts at student re-enrollment, public school attendance had declined by less than 10% on opening day [of the 2011-2012 school year]."[5]

Second, the Interfaith Coalition that began following the tornado and amped up after the mosque fire continues to thrive. The Coalition is doing the important work of sharing stories, nurturing understanding, and building relationships between people of various backgrounds and religions. It also recently pooled its resources and worked together to respond to those impacted by hurricanes in 2017.

Third, having recently returned for a visit, I believe that life in Joplin looks mostly strong. Yes, I notice that some areas still seem a bit abandoned, neighborhoods where the density of houses never returned to pre-tornado levels. However, I am also aware that when the new high school was built, they did not just rebuild what they had before; they created a school that matched their new dream for a new day. For the most part businesses returned, even if relocated, and many new ones have come to town.

---

3. Kenny Foster, "Hometown," 2011. Found at https://kennyfoster.bandcamp.com/track/hometown-single.
4. Lynn Iliff Onstot, Public Information Office, Joplin, MO at http://www.joplinmo.org/DocumentCenter/View/1985.
5. Robert K. Kanter, M.D., and David Abramson, Ph.D., M.P.H., "School Interventions After the Joplin Tornado," in *Prehospital and Disaster Medicine* 29, no. 2 (April 2014), 214-17.

There is evidence that this is a place where people want to live.

Within the congregation, changes seem lasting as well. As I said earlier, we had already done the hard work that positioned us to be more present in our community. We believed in our future. We were nurturing leaders and helping people respond to their call. We built trust among us. We were, I believe, on the cusp of finding our place in the community.

The tornado brought all that to fruition. First, we responded by saying yes to hosting a mission station. The congregation created a beautiful space for people to stay and also embraced a ministry of hospitality. The people who stayed in the mission station were not treated as nameless faces or unidentified groups who simply cycled through. Rather, every week people in our congregation were baking cookies for volunteers, hosting meals, telling their stories of the tornado, and listening to the volunteers talk about what motivated them to come and what they were experiencing. Relationships were being built and joy was shared each time a group returned.

Shortly after opening the mission station we also decided to hire a Minister of Mission and Outreach. The inception of this position was occasioned by the tornado, but not meant to work only with tornado recovery. We made it clear from the outset that this role was partially about tornado recovery and partially about helping us to find our calling in the community and the world. Over the next three years, our new minister worked diligently with those who came through the station, represented us on the LTRC, and helped us to identify and meet needs in our community for which we were gifted. More than that, she helped people understand that serving the world was part of the calling of their faith. She helped individuals and the congregation to discover the passions that motivated them to engage in the community.

One of the most sustaining results of the Minister of Mission has been the relationship that the congregation developed with a local elementary school. This relationship began early in the recovery when the new school building had not yet been built and much of what was asked was connected to the tornado. After all, the population of the school was largely made up of children who had lost their homes. Even today, however, the relationship continues. Today there are volunteers from the congregation serving in the school on a weekly basis as lunch and reading buddies. The congregation has hosted special events such as a children's art show. School families have passed through emergency situations to which the congregation has responded.

When I return to the city or when I read the church newsletter, I find myself amazed again and again by how this community has been strengthened. People are resilient. I have long believed that, but nowhere have I experienced it more than in the endurance and fortitude of this community in the days and months and years since the tornado hit.

Forever Changed

In September 2011 our church choir gathered for ice cream after their first practice following a summer break. My five-year-old son was present. He sat at the table with the choir members, looked around at them, and asked, "So, which of your homes got hit by the tornado?" While I was first taken aback, worrying that it was still too fresh for some of them to want to discuss with a five year-old, it was simply part of the standard conversation he expected to have. Meanwhile, our daycare provider observed that she now found herself watching young children play tornado when they used to play school or house. She had not experienced this in twenty years as a child care professional, but now it was part of the children's life experience.

One of the results of this experience was that what had previously been an abstract possibility was now something real that had happened and could happen again. For some that caused heightened anxiety. But for many, my children included, it simply increased their vocabulary and their experiences. While, as a parent, I may have mourned the loss of their innocence, they now live with a realism that allows them to recognize that tornadoes happen, houses and buildings blow away, communities come together, and we all do our best to take the next step forward.

Maybe that is okay. While I would never wish a tornado or any other disaster for myself or anyone else, the reality is that each experience we have becomes part of who we are. Our transitions, whether they are expected ones like graduating or getting married, or those that come out of the blue, become part of our story and change how we respond and how we think about life.

Yes, in this community you will see more tornado shelters than you used to and you will notice people responding differently to spring storms and sirens. Yes, in this community, there is some continuing grief and some people do not feel changed for the better. Nevertheless, what I have seen more often are the examples of people and a community that grew stronger in the face of very real fear, angst and loss.

As we speak of the liminal experiences that are anticipated, those for which we plan, I sometimes wonder what would have happened if we could have planned for this. I suspect that there would be some ways in which such planning could have been helpful. There would have been some systems in place that could have been stronger and nimbler in their response. All things considered, however, I am not convinced it would have been better. Different, yes, but not necessarily better. The gift of this involuntary liminal event revealed our great resilience. What we did not realize before the tornado was just how strong and connected our community actually was. When the winds blew, both were revealed and, as a result, we have been forever changed.

9

Adoption and Cross-Cultural Parenting

Colleen Warner Colaner

Adoption is a centuries-old practice still enacted with tens of thousands of children each year.[1] Each one of these child placements changes the course of not only the adoptee's current and future family, but also the numerous family members in the birth and adoptive families of origin, thus touching the lives of millions of individuals worldwide.[2] At its core adoption is simply transferring parental rights from biological to legal parents. However, there is nothing simple about adoption. Adoptees find themselves between two families for the duration of their lives – in a place of permanent liminality.

The liminal nature of adoption has long been unacknowledged by practitioners and families. Adoptees were historically told very little about their adoption – if at all.[3] Open conversations about adoption were certainly rare. Thus, biological families existed primarily as questions in the minds of adoptees, not known or discussed in the adoptive family. This had a number of negative outcomes, even in the most loving and well-adjusted adoptive families. The reality was that adoptees yearned to know answers to fundamental questions of identity: "Where do I come from?" "Why is my nose shaped this way?" "Where do I get my musical talent?"

The answer to this longing for identity was open adoption: birth families were no longer to be strangers but rather known by adoptees and their legal families, at times with ongoing interaction. Open adoption is associated with a number of positive outcomes for adoptees, birth

1. Paul Placek, "National Adoption Data," in *Adoption Factbook IV*, ed. T. C. Atwood, et al. (Alexandria, VA: National Council for Adoption, 2007).
2. Kathleen Galvin, "The Family of the Future: What Do We Face?" in *The Handbook of Family Communication*, ed. A.L. Vangelisti (Mahwah, NJ: Lawrence Erlbaum, 2013).
3. Ibid.

parents, and adoptive parents.[4] Again, however, there is nothing simple about open adoption. These complex relationships require considerable collaboration, negotiation, and emotional distance regulation. Importantly, these relationships are created and maintained through talk, thus placing communication at the center of these complex relational webs. Adoptive parents, in particular, are the gatekeepers of the open adoption relationship while their children are in their formative years, regulating how, when, and who from the birth family communicates with the adoptive family.[5]

Because adoption, in general, and open adoption, in particular, involves the linking of two families, adoptees naturally find themselves in the in-between. The liminal space occupied by adoptees necessitates that adoptees consider their identity, their place, their belonging.

Permanent Liminality in Adoption Experience

> That was an interesting day. To stand on the doorstep realizing that the people behind the door were responsible for my birth but I'd never met them. . . . What do you say to your mother when your mother's standing beside you? You know, long time no see?[6]

Adoptees exist between families for their entire lives. They are products of legal and biological families, but not fully either. This liminal space is their reality, and from it comes complex identity work. The extent to which adoptees engage with the liminality of their adoption status emerges as a product of individual, contextual, and familial characteristics.

Individual Characteristics of Adoption Liminality

Universally, adoption calls upon adoptees to enter the liminal space between adoptive and birth families. However, the degree to which adoptees engage with this liminality is dependent on individual factors.[7] Individual tolerance

---

4. Harold Grotevant et al., "Contact Between Adoptive and Birth Families: Perspectives from the Minnesota/Texas Adoption Research Project," *Child Development Perspectives* 7 (2013).

5. Colleen Warner Colaner and Kristina Scharp, "Maintaining Open Adoption Relationships: Practitioner Insights on Adoptive Parents' Regulation of Adoption Kinship Networks," *Communication Studies* 67 (2016).

6. Colleen Warner Colaner, Danielle Halliwell, and Phillip Guignon, "'What Do You Say to Your Mother When Your Mother's Standing Beside You?' Birth and Adoptive Family Contributions to Adoptive Identity via Relational Identity and Relational-Relational Identity Gaps," *Communication Monographs* 81 (2014).

7. Colleen Warner Colaner and Jordan Soliz, "A Communication-Based Approach to Adoptive Identity: Theoretical and Empirical Support," *Communication Research* (2015).

for uncertainty and adoption curiosity are traits that trigger some adoptees' reflections on their adoptions.[8] Those with low tolerance for uncertainty and high adoption curiosity will be more apt to seek out and interact with birth families to explore the meaning of their adoption for their definition of self, and thus more likely to feel the pull between the family groups.

In interview research with adult adoptees, this pull between birth and adoptive parents is apparent – and at times painful. Adoptees often report an innate desire to know their birth parents' characteristics as a way to better understand their own characteristics, proclivities, and appearance.[9] Those without access to birth records or in situations where birth parent contact and open adoption is not an option often have to grapple with these questions with very few resources and answers. These individuals' experiences of permanent liminality grow out of a lack of connection to a family they desire to know but will never get to know.

One woman, for example, described to me her experience of living in permanent liminality.[10] She recalled spending hours of her childhood poring over the thin folder of records that accompanied her adoption placement, looking for clues that would help her better understand herself. The few facts in her paperwork, however, did not bring clear answers to questions of origin and identity. In adulthood, she attempted to add to the small list of facts about her birth family. Eventually, she located her birth mother, who was institutionalized as a result of a brain condition that severely impaired her ability to care for herself and interact with others. She also eventually identified her birth father. However, she found him a few years too late, after his untimely death in a car accident. After decades of wondering and searching, she found herself with her birth parents' identities, but without a path to gain more information or insight. This devastating realization was existential in nature. She summed it up, saying, "I just kind of think that I am going to wander the earth forever just kind of wondering." Her permanent liminality and connection to a family she did not know was palpable.

Her experience is not an isolated case. Adoptees without access to birth records similarly feel trapped in a nether world of identity stalemate.[11] Across the U.S. states differ with regard to accessibility of birth records. According to the American Adoption Congress, only nine states currently

8. Harold Grotevant et al., "Adoptive Identity: How Contexts Within and Beyond the Family Shape Developmental Pathways," *Family Relations* 49 (2000).
9. Colaner, Halliwell, and Guignon, "What Do You Say to Your Mother?".
10. Colleen Warner Colaner and Haley Kranstuber, "'Forever Kind of Wondering:' Communicatively Managing Uncertainty in Adoptive Families," *Journal of Family Communication* 10 (2010).
11. Colaner, Halliwell, and Guignon, "What Do You Say to Your Mother?".

allow adoptees unrestricted access to their birth records.[12] Twenty-two states have sealed records. The remaining states allow access for adoptees born in certain years and/or access only to certain information. Restricted or denied access to birth records feels particularly hurtful to adoptees seeking information about their identity. The fact that information exists that they cannot access exacerbates their uncertainty. One adult adoptee reflected on her permanent lack of information about her birth family, saying, "They didn't know my mom's name or anything about her. . . . I would just wonder a little bit about what she looked like or what happened. I never really asked because I didn't think they really knew either."[13] The ongoing denial of access to information about origin and identity was distressing to individuals who were hungry to know basic facts of their birth and biological family. In response to this permanent lack of information, individuals created fantasy versions of their biological families. One woman envisioned that her birth mother was either Judy Garland, Gloria Estefan, or Karen Carpenter.[14] Another imagined every woman she saw in public with blonde hair as possibly her mother, drawing on the one characteristic she knew to make sense of her identity and belonging.[15]

Adoptees have presented varying responses to this liminal space between belonging and not belonging. Some individuals without information about their biological background became preoccupied with their adoption status, attributing the bulk of the highs and lows in their life and family relationships to their adoption status.[16] These individuals tended to be highly dissatisfied with their adoption, not as connected with their adoptive parents, and exhibited lower levels of self-esteem.[17] Individuals also noted the myriad ways they did not fit into their adoptive family, thus emphasizing the lack of belonging. As one woman explained, "Jeepers, I really don't fit in with these people," referencing her adoptive parents.[18] Another similarly emphasized the differences between her and her sister, saying, "We were both just completely different people. And . . . we're both raised by the same parents, and we both came out so completely different."[19] Emphasizing the lack of belonging served to heighten the liminal nature of their adoption

---

12. American Adoption Congress, "State Adoption Legislation," https://americanadop tioncongress.org/state.php.
13. Colaner and Kranstuber, "Forever Kind of Wondering."
14. Ibid.
15. Ibid.
16. Colleen Warner Colaner, "Measuring Adoptive Identity: Validation of the Adoptive Identity Work Scale," *Adoption Quarterly* 17 (2014).
17. Colaner and Soliz, "A Communication-Based Approach."
18. Colaner, Halliwell, and Guignon, "What Do You Say to Your Mother?".
19. Ibid.

status, as these individuals were not able to anchor belonging in a birth family due to closed adoption records. Thus, these individuals permanently existed in spaces between family relationships.

Alternately, many adoptees emphasized belongingness within their adoptive family in response to the liminal imperative of the adoption status. These individuals credit their adoptive parents with creating their unique identity, thus de-emphasizing their biology and focusing instead on their socialization in the adoptive home. One said for example, "My entire identity, who I know I am . . . is . . . formed by my adoptive parents."[20] Similarly, another adoptee assumed the role of family historian in her adoptive family as a way to emphasize connection. Despite a lack of genetic connectedness to her family, this adoptee became central to the adoptive family by functioning as the family expert and gatekeeper of the family ancestry. This was particularly important as her connections became less tangible in generations further up the family tree. As she explained:

> I see it as the way that I make myself a part of the family. You know, I know all of my aunts and uncles, you know, feel like I am a part of the family, like no doubt about it. But . . . you know, once those branches get a little farther and farther out, I . . . I want to feel like I'm a part of that by helping to bring it together, I guess.[21]

Thus, connection in an adoptive family lessened the experience of liminality by emphasizing belongingness.

While adoptees with a strong sense of belonging to their adoptive families tend to be more satisfied with their adoption and their family relationships, the liminal placement between two family units remains. Connection with an adoptive family may lessen the expression of the liminal existence, but the pull between the families is an inevitable component of adoption experience. Gravitating to one family unit rather than another is a natural human response to suppress the liminality, but doing so has relational implications. Analysis of data from adult adoptees revealed that the more adoptees identified with their birth mother, the less they identified with the adoptive parents.[22] Even though adoptees are intimately connected to both families and report moderate to strong levels of attachment to each family, these family identifications may be at odds with one another, repelling one from the other like opposite magnetic forces.

---

20. Ibid.
21. Ibid.
22. Colleen Warner Colaner, Haley Kranstuber Horstman, and Christine Rittenour, "Negotiating Adoptive and Birth Shared Family Identity: A Social Identity Complexity Approach," *Western Journal of Communication* (2017).

For many adoptees, opposing family identification was expressed as a suppression of efforts to seek out the birth family. Adoptees reported not wanting to search for their birth parents because it would be upsetting to the adoptive family.[23] One woman tearfully explained how she waited until her adoptive mother was deceased to meet her birth mother. Once her mother had died from breast cancer, she reached out to her biological mother, only to find that her biological mother had also recently died of breast cancer.[24] This adoptee was motherless twofold, further reinforcing her feelings of permanent liminality.

Familial Considerations of Adoption Liminality

Liminality is embedded in the adoption experience. This experience is not just for adoptees, however. The liminality is collective. Not only is the child suspended between two families, but the families themselves exist on the margins of how society defines family. Adoptive families offer legal justification for their family relationship, showing court decrees and revised birth certificates listing adoptive parents as mother and father.[25] Yet adoptive parents and siblings face intrusive questions that call the family's legitimacy into question:[26] "Who is her real mother?" "Are they real sisters?" "Could you not have children of your own?" Adoptive families at times are perceived as and feel more "family-like" than family, stuck in a liminal space of connected yet not fully viewed as a legitimate family unit in society.

Similarly, birth families face ambiguous loss upon placement of a child into adoption. The child who grew in her body and has his blood in its veins – this child is both theirs and not theirs. Birth families face day-to-day life without the biological child. The birth family bears the emotional, mental, and spiritual scars and relinquishment, and the mother the physical scars of birth.[27] How many children do you have? How does one answer that question? It depends – how do you count children who are yours but not yours?

---

23. Colaner and Kranstuber, "Forever Kind of Wondering."
24. Colaner, Halliwell, and Guignon, "What Do You Say to Your Mother?".
25. Kathleen Galvin, "Diversity's Impact on Defining the Family," in *The Family Communication Sourcebook*, ed. L.H. Turner and R. West (Thousand Oaks, CA: Sage, 2006).
26. Elizabeth Suter and Robert Ballard, "'How Much Did You Pay for Her?:' Decision-Making Criteria Underlying Adoptive Parents' Responses to Inappropriate Remarks," *Journal of Family Communication* 9 (2009).
27. David Brodzinsky and Susan Smith, "Post-Placement Adjustment and the Needs of Birthmothers Who Place an Infant for Adoption," *Adoption Quarterly* 17 (2014).

Of course, the liminal family experience is not relegated to just the parents – biological and legal – of the adoptee. The extended family of the child is also implicated in the in-between. Grandparents, siblings, aunts, uncles, cousins, and so on through the family trees also exist on the margins of the family relationship.[28]

Contextual Factors of Adoption Liminality

In addition to the liminal experience embedded in the fabric of adoption, certain adoption scenarios add additional layers of liminality, including transracial adoption, foster care, and legal transfers.

The Transracial Adoption Paradox

Adoption often comes with diverse and at times competing identities. In the case of transracial adoption, liminality expands beyond group belongingness within families to racial identity. Transracial adoption most often occurs with white parents adopting minority children.[29] In this scenario, the minority child is placed into a unique racial existence. The minority child functions largely within majority-white spaces, including neighborhoods, social groups, schools, and places of worship. As a function of existing in their parents' majority-white communities, most children of transracial adoption report having few individuals in their day-to-day interactions who share their racial in-group, particularly within their closest circles. Thus, transracial adoptees tend to have the values, privileges, and opportunities of children in white families as a product of their predominately-white racial socialization.[30]

However, the child cannot fully be a member of the race identity group of their white parents.[31] The child's skin tone prohibits the child from fully existing in these majority-white structures in ways similar to their white peers. Transracially adopted children face racial biases and prejudices in public spaces, and at times in the family and community spaces long occupied by their white parents. At the same time, the adoptee does not fully exist in the racial minority identity group of his or her biology.

28. Colaner and Scharp, "Maintaining Open Adoption Relationships."
29. Kathleen Galvin, "International and Transracial Adoption: A Communication Research Agenda," *Journal of Family Communication* 3 (2003).
30. Sara Docan-Morgan, "'They Don't Know What It's Like to Be in My Shoes:' Topic Avoidance About Race in Transracially Adoptive Families," *Journal of Social and Personal Relationships* 28 (2011).
31. Leslie Nelson and Colleen Warner Colaner, "Becoming a Transracial Family: Communicatively Negotiating Divergent Identities in Families Formed through Transracial Adoption," *Journal of Family Communication* 18 (2018).

Children of transracial adoption are often unfamiliar with elements of culture attached to their race due to lack of exposure and racial socialization in their racial majority home, feeling out of place when interacting with individuals from their racial in-group. Scholars have termed this liminal space between biological race and socially-derived racial identification as "the transracial adoption paradox."[32] Adoptive parents attempt to mitigate the child's experience of this paradox by providing racial socialization in the form of cultural heritage camps, social events with others in the child's racial in-group, or linking the child with racial mentors. Still, the paradox remains, and for some adoptees is experienced as a feeling of cultural homelessness, described as not fully fitting into any racial group.[33] Thus, transracial adoptees exist in the liminal space between racial identities, further complicating their position between biological and legal families.

Foster Families as "Family-like" Caregivers
Another scenario of heightened adoption liminality is that of foster children. The complex legal system regulating the foster-care system places children in a series of temporary care scenarios.[34] Children have varying degrees of connection to biological parents. The goal of the foster-care system is reunification with biological parents. For some, reunification results after a lengthy process of proving the biological parent to be competent and fit to provide care for the child. For others, the goal of reunification is never realized as they progress through developmental stages while in care and without a permanent family. Court-appointed special advocates (CASA) workers are placed on children's case files to provide a semblance of stability for a child traversing through care. For children rotating through multiple foster homes, the CASA worker is the only thread of consistency throughout the process.

Foster children experience an interruption in the caregiving bond that is fundamental to human attachment. Thus, foster children face a host of developmental risks socially, mentally, and emotionally.[35] In addition to

---

32. Lee Richard, "The Transracial Adoption Paradox: History, Research, and Counseling Implications of Cultural Socialization," *The Counseling Psychologist* 31 (2003).

33. Veronica Vivero and Sharon Jenkins, "Existential Hazards of the Multicultural Individual: Defining and Understanding 'Cultural Homelessness,'" *Cultural Diversity and Ethnic Minority Psychology 5,* no. 1 (1999), 6-26.

34. Leslie Nelson, "The Evolving Nature and Process of Foster Family Communication: An Application and Adaptation of the Family Adoption Communication Model," *Journal of Family Theory & Review* 9 (2017).

35. Sylvia Oswald, Katharina Heil, and Lutz Goldbeck, "History of Maltreatment and Mental Health Problems in Foster Children: A Review of the Literature," *Journal of Pediatric Psychology* 35 (2010).

this robust literature on foster-care outcomes, the lens of liminality also illuminates the "in-between" experience housed in the foster-care system. Whereas adoptees exist between two families, foster children exist within a complex system of temporary care scenarios. Biological families remain part of foster children to varying degrees, but foster children float through childhood years without a consistent and reliable family unit to which to adhere. Foster families provide a "family-like" care situation, functioning and fulfilling roles in ways consistent with family structures.[36] Yet, foster families lack several features of permanency and authority which sustain other family relationships. For example, the courts provide limited parental rights to foster parents, with case workers heavily involved in – and, at times, unilaterally making – decisions about the foster child's care. Thus, the foster-care system exhibits perhaps the most heightened sense of liminality of family forms.

Murky Moments in the Transfer of Parental Rights

In addition to contexts heightening adoption liminality, certain time periods also exacerbate the liminality of adoption arrangements. Every adoption experiences some degree of legal limbo between relinquishment and finalization, an in-between space where legal rights to the child are murky. Birth parent relinquishment – whether voluntary or done by the courts – is final. Once a birth parent terminates rights (or has rights terminated by the court), legal ties are severed and can only be reconnected through formal adoption proceedings.[37] States vary on when birth parents can relinquish rights for voluntary infant adoption. Most states require that birth mothers wait seventy-two hours after birth to surrender parental rights.[38] These first three days of a newborn's life are ambiguous with regard to responsibility of care. Newborns able to stay in the hospital for this duration of legal limbo are cared for by nurses rotating through shifts over the course of their stay. At times, adoptive parents care for the infant without parental rights, assuming the birth mother will relinquish rights according to prior arrangements. About a third of the time, however, the birth mother exerts her right to parent the child and declines to relinquish her parental rights.[39] Because of this fact, adoptive parents assume the parenting role without parenting rights or the guarantee of placement. At other times, the child

36. Leslie Nelson and Haley Kranstuber Horstman, "Communicated Meaning-Making in Foster Families: Relationships between Foster Parents' Entrance Narratives and Foster Child Well-Being," *Communication Quarterly* 65 (2017).

37. Kathleen Galvin and Colleen Warner Colaner, "Created through Law and Language: Communicative Complexities of Adoptive Families," in *Widening the Family Circle*, eds K. Floyd and M.T. Morman (Thousand Oaks, CA: Sage, 2013).

38. Colaner and Scharp, "Maintaining Open Adoption Relationships."

39. Adam Pertman, *Adoption Nation* (New York: Basic Books, 2000).

is placed in temporary care with "Cradle Care," a very short-term foster-like arrangement where an approved family takes in a child drifting in the liminal space between legal families.

Hospitals find themselves navigating this liminal terrain during the initial days of the life of a child to be adopted. Legally, birth parents are the only parents recognized by the hospital staff up until the relinquishment of parental rights. In cases in which adoptive and birth parents have coordinated plans for placement of the child, adoptive parents may be present at the hospital, but with limited access and without a location to reside in the hospital. Accommodating hospitals at times offer an empty room to adoptive parents to visit the child, but such arrangements occur at the discretion of the hospital staff. At other times, hospitals have extensive policies. Prospective adoptive parents have reported being denied access to the child when the birth parent is not present (even when the birth parent requests that adoptive parents be with the child when they are not present). Adoptive parents have also reported being supervised by hospital staff at all moments of interaction with the child or placed in unconventional locations, such as supply closets, while staff handle legal and medical concerns with the birth parents. These first days of an adoptees' life can be tumultuous and legally precarious, with adoptive families, birth parents, and medical practitioners stumbling through interactions with and about the child in the liminal legal spaces.

Once the birth parents' legal rights are terminated, adoptive parents go through a process to receive parental rights from the courts. Again, states differ in their requirements as to how long this will take, but most states range from thirty days to six months between placement of the child and finalization of the adoption. In this pre-adoption stage, the adoptee functions as a child of the family in the adoptive parents' home. However, the placement is temporary and contingent upon the court's approval, which relies upon post-placement visits and a recommendation from a licensed social worker. The majority of placements in this phase proceed to finalization, but the placement of the child is somewhat precarious. Life transitions, such as the loss of a job, the death of a member of the adoptive family, or legal issues in the adoptive family could compromise the adoption finalization. Thus, adoptive families find themselves just on the other side of permanent placement, wading through the liminal space of temporary caregivers with the hope of fulfilling the parental role for the remainder of their lives.

Liminality is central to the adoption experience: adoptees navigate their identity in the space between two families; adoptive and birth parents wade through liminal "family-like" space; and contexts such as transracial adoption, fostering, and temporal legal moments muddy the waters of belonging and identity. By and large, adoption liminality is experienced as one of tension and difficulty.

Western Parenting Values and Adoption Liminality

Western notions of parenting embedded in U.S. societal norms have strong roots in a sense of ownership of children, with children positioned as products of parents. Western culture is dominated by individualism, with emphasis on the self as a unique individual positioned independently from a group.[40] A highly individualistic orientation emphasizes achievement as a personal (as opposed to a group) recognition.[41] Applying this individualistic, achievement-driven orientation to Western family relationships – specifically with regard to adoption practices – illuminates cultural forces contributing to adoption liminality.

This Western view of prioritizing ownership of children has emerged out of historical shifts in human experience which have changed the purpose, experience, and motivation for family relationships, with implications for child-rearing perspectives. Historically, marriage functioned largely as a kinship contract, organizing political and economic structures.[42] Marriages united tribes, constituted transfer of property, consolidated wealth, and brokered peace treaties for thousands of years. Because formal social institutions, including government regulation and law enforcement, were unformed or weak, family units supported survival. The primary function of marriage in this era was to pool spousal resources to meet basic needs such as food, shelter, and protection from violence.[43] The eighteenth-century revolution in views about love, and social development during the industrial revolution ushered into North America and Western Europe a companionate form of marriage. The ability to marry for love and affection emerged as a new concept, made possible by societal efforts to support survival through social rather than family systems. Most recently, another understanding of marriage has emerged: marriage as a form of self-expression. Following the civil rights and feminist movements of the

40. Bernadette Watson, "Intercultural and Cross-Cultural Communication," in *Inter/Cultural Communication*, ed. A. Kurylo (Thousand Oaks, CA: Sage, 2013).

41. Min-Sun Kim, *Non-Western Perspectives on Human Communication* (Thousand Oaks, CA: Sage, 2002).

42. Stephanie Coontz, "Revolution in Intimate Life and Relationships," *Journal of Family Theory & Review* 7 (2015).

43. Eli J. Finkel et al., "The Suffocation Model: Why Marriage in America Is Becoming an All-or-Nothing Institution," *Current Directions in Psychological Science* 24 (2015).

1960-70s, Americans began to prioritize authenticity, self-discovery, and personal expression. Marriages shifted again, now serving to fulfill personal needs such as self-esteem and personal growth.[44] As humans worked their way upmoved beyond addressing basic survival needs to understanding marriage as a form of self-actualization, s Abraham Maslow's "hierarchy of needs," spouses began to demand more from the institution of marriage.

Parallel to marriage, the expectations and functions of children within the family have shifted. Children were historically situated to be heirs or workers on family farms.[45] Adoption perpetuated this exact goal very distinctly during the Orphan Train Movement, in which homeless children were transported from urban areas on the American East coast to rural areas in the Midwest.[46] Families welcomed children into their homes as an "extra set of hands" around the farms. When families joined urban areas and child labor laws were enforced, children no longer were required to sustain the family's survival. Thus, parental motivation shifted to that of belonging, group identification, and family enhancement. Children were an expression of family life, central to the developmental stage of married couples in their child-rearing years. The shift to marriage as self-expression brought with it the motivation of child-rearing as a fulfillment of esteem and self-actualization needs, i.e. the ultimate goal of Maslow's hierarchy. Parenting has become increasingly self-expressive in the West in recent decades, and Western family structures prioritize the family unit as a realization of parenting self-expression.

As children serve to fulfill parents' desire for personal expansion and fulfillment, a cultural tendency has emerged to view children as products of parents, created by parents, and owned by parents. Evidence for this lies in observation of comments by and about parents vis-à-vis their children. For example, the word "own" has a prominent place in public discourse about children: "Do you have children of your own?" or "I may adopt but I also want children of my own." These comments not only perpetuate the notion that biological children are more legitimate than adopted children, but also suggest that children are extensions of biological parents. The implication is that parents have ownership of another human, suggesting an entitlement to their children: we created this child, thus we have parental rights to this child, and this child belongs to us. Another example of parenting as a self-expression is embodied in the celebration of children who are viewed as miniature versions of parents. Colloquially described as a "mini-me,"

44. Ibid.
45. Coontz, "Revolution in Intimate Life."
46. Jeanne Cook, "A History of Placing-Out: The Orphan Trains," *Child Welfare* 74 (1995).

these comments praise the replication of a parental persona in a child's appearance and mannerisms. The child is valuable by virtue of reflecting the identity of the parent.

Embedded in these parental self-expressions are Western, individualistic values of control and individual achievement, which Tsabary calls "the parental ego."[47] She argues that ego positions the parent as greater than and the authority over the child. Rather than honoring the child's autonomy as a human being, the child serves to extend the parent's will further into the world. The child's purpose, then, is to follow the parent so the parent can be fuller and more complete.

These Western-based notions of parenting as self-expression position children as belonging to one set of parents. This orientation does not allow children to exist between families, as ownership has to be negotiated in relation to specific individuals. U.S. legal practices grant legal parental rights to two parents at most, positioning the family unit as an exclusive entity regulating a child's livelihood. If an adoptee cannot peacefully co-exist between families, their experience of liminality is naturally then charged with negativity, tension, and discomfort. Western values embodied in such an individualistic family orientation may exacerbate the experience of liminality in the adoption experience by forcing an adoptee to adhere to one family unit over multiple identifications. Thus, the experience of liminality, of being stuck in-between the families, is heightened because the adoptees must make an impossible choice to prioritize one family membership over the other. The inability to co-exist in multiple family memberships in a communal orientation, then, subjugates adoptees to an uncomfortable liminal space of not quite belonging to either family unit.

Embracing Adoption Liminality Through Eastern Cultural Values

Eastern notions of family and communal communication practices offer shifts for embracing liminality as a productive component of the adoption experience. Adoptive family relationships in particular require members to embrace impermanence and transience between family groups, prompting us to rethink ownership of the parent-child bond. Eastern parenting values are communal in nature, involving multiple generations caring for the child and distributing parental tasks among a larger group of people. Eastern approaches to parenting also position children as autonomous beings who join family members' lives for a period of time.[48] Shifting away

---

47. Shefali Tsabary, *The Awakened Family* (New York: Penguin 2016).
48. Ibid.

from individualism and control in childrearing de-centers perceptions of ownership. The child came from the parents and through the parents; however, the child was not created by the parents, does not belong to the parents, and is not possessed by the parents.[49]

Shifting away from positioning parents as the child's creator prompts a release of ownership, allowing the child's authentic self to emerge in connection to multiple sources. Children are formed through biological processes. However, children are not created by humans, any more than humans create new skin cells or white blood cells to combat an invasive virus. The biological process of conception and birth can be controlled to some degree by human intervention, but these biological processes are not manifested as a result of human control and will. Rather, these are processes of life being done to parents and happening around parents. Adoptive parents embody a metaphor for reimagining parents' role in a child's life in this way. Without a stake in the biological process ushering in the child's life, adoptive parents are invited to take a role in the child's life without a biological claim to ownership over the child. Of course, the metaphor breaks down when we enter into the legal logistics that organize society and provide protections for children and families. Yet adoption provides a glimpse into the possibilities of loosely placing a child between two families, neither having ownership to the child, but each committed to the child's well-being, livelihood, and personal development. Adoption liminality in this way presents an opportunity for rethinking Western parenting ideals, allowing children to exist in families, attached to parents but not controlled by them.

Adoptive families are often stigmatized as less than, an option pursued only after biological processes – first natural and then medically assisted – prove unsuccessful.[50] However, open adoption places children at the center of two families, thus stretching family definitions and typical family processes housed in Western ideals. Open adoption allows us to understand families differently, embracing the possibility of what family can be in a more communal space. Rather than children positioned as products of parental control and subjected to parental ownership, adoptees have the opportunity to exist within a web of multiple caregivers. To the degree that adoptive and birth parents collaborate to meet the child's developmental needs, open adoption provides an opportunity to embrace the communal possibilities central to Eastern parenting philosophy and liberating for children regardless of adoption status.

---

49. William Martin, *The Parent's Tao Te Ching* (Philadelphia: Da Capo Press, 1999).
50. Nicholas Park and Patricia Hill, "Is Adoption an Option? The Role of Importance of Motherhood and Fertility Help-Seeking in Considering Adoption," *Journal of Family Issues* 35 (2013).

Collaborative communication practices play an important role in helping adoptees feel supported and unconstrained between two family groups, thus reducing the negative tone of adoption liminality. Collaborative communication allows adoptees to exist freely between the two families. Open adoption functions best when adoptive and birth parents work together to meet the developmental needs of the child.[51] These collaborative relationships offer connections between families that can embrace and support adoption liminality through open and responsive communication behaviors with birth and adoptive parents interacting with one another without ego, ownership, or entitlement to the adoptees. One adoptee described this dual membership by saying, "I suppose insofar as my adoptive parents have shaped me, that I in turn shaped them in ways that would echo my birth parents."[52] She viewed her identity as a product of both her adoptive and birth families simultaneously. Another adoptee described how her adoptive and birth father interacted with one another, celebrating her accomplishments and expressing pride in the person she became. She viewed this collaboration as providing "multiple layers of support" that allowed her to view her dual membership in both families as a positive and not limiting experience.[53]

Adoption communication openness (ACO) is a specific communication practice that encourages adoptees to exist more comfortably within adoption liminality.[54] ACO is open, direct, empathic, and sensitive communication used to support children's emotions about adoption. Adoptive parents practicing ACO invite conversations about adoption, providing a nonjudgmental environment for the child to seek information and process feelings about the adoption. ACO encourages development of an adoptive identity and relates to adoptees' feelings of self-esteem. Importantly, ACO can help reduce feelings of adoption liminality. Research revealed that feeling close to one's birth mother contributed to decreased feelings of closeness with adoptive parents.[55] At the same time, adoptees felt closer to their birth parents when they had adoptive parents who were high in ACO, suggesting that adoptive parents' communication behaviors play a role in adoptees' ability to connect with birth parents. Alternately, adoptive parents' lack of willingness to talk about birth parents contributed to adoptees feeling trapped between families.[56] Adoptive parents report

---

51. Grotevant et al, "Contact Between Adoptive and Birth Families."
52. Colaner, Halliwell, and Guignon, "What Do You Say to Your Mother?".
53. Ibid.
54. Colaner and Soliz, "A Communication-Based Approach."
55. Colaner, Horstman, and Rittenour, "Negotiating Adoptive and Birth Shared Family Identity."
56. Ibid.

saying that their child is able to ask questions about adoption at any time,[57] but ACO is not a passive quality of the family dynamic. Adoptees reported not asking their adoptive parents questions because they sensed the adoptive parents' discomfort with the topic or because the adoptive parent never brought adoption up as a topic of conversation. ACO requires that adoptive parents actively cultivate an environment in which adoption is an acceptable topic, model adoption talk in interactions with and around the child, and respond to the child's comments, needs, and questions with empathy, active listening, and compassion.

Actively cultivating belonging for adoptees requires adoptive and birth families to work together through open communication, without ego or ownership. Adoption is not a competition; it is a connection that grows and grows, and grows even bigger when adoptive and birth families work together. Drawing from Eastern parenting values can assist adoptive and birth families in connecting to adoptees in ways that allow adoptees to rest within a web of biological and legal relationships. Shifting permanent liminality to serve as a strength of the adoption experience allows adoptees to emerge from the collective experience of adoptive and birth parent influences, benefitting from layers of support instead of feeling stuck between opposing family groups. In this way, adoption liminality offers fresh insight for all parent-child relationships, reminding us that ownership attitudes constrain children to parental self-expressions and do not engender the development of the child's unique nature. Loosening the grip of Western parents on child development embraces the mystery of becoming for children in a variety of family forms.

57. Colaner and Scharp, "Maintaining Open Adoption Relationships."

10

Climate Change and Desert Spirituality

Timothy Robinson

The Earth is in trouble. This is not news. The planet is undergoing a fundamental transformation brought about by human activity. Population growth, consumption, and industrial-technological impacts are altering the biological and geophysical systems that sustain life. We stand on the brink of ecotastrophe.[1] The term "climate change" now names both the outcome of centuries of human insertion of fossil fuel-based greenhouse gasses into the atmosphere *and* a symbolic designation of the pervasiveness of human impacts on the biosphere. The influential nature writer Bill McKibben, whose 1989 bestseller announced *The End of Nature* has more recently argued that human influence is so pervasive that we need a new name for this altered world. "Eaarth," he calls it: "a tough new place."[2] The French anthropologist Bruno Latour says that we live in "the new climate regime," by which he means "the physical framework Moderns have taken for granted . . . has become unstable." Latour refers to the "backlash" that nature is causing in response to what humans have done.[3] The biologist Eugene Stoermer and chemist Paul Crutzen have put forth a term that is

---

1. As far as I am aware, I coined this term when I wrote the article "Nurturing Hope in the Face of Ecotastrophe: Advent, Eschatology, and the Future of Creation," *Liturgical Ministry* 19 (Winter 2010), 9-20. This is not to say that I invented the term, only that I was unaware of any other usage of it when I wrote in 2010. The term emerged for me as I read Elizabeth Kolbert, *Field Notes from a Catastrophe: Man, Nature, and Climate Change* (New York: Bloomsbury, 2006), and Frederick Buell, *Apocalypse as a Way of Life: Environmental Crisis in the American Century* (New York: Routledge, 2004).
2. Bill McKibben, *Eaarth: Making a Life on a Tough New Planet* (New York: Henry Holt and Co., 2010).
3. Bruno Latour, *Facing Gaia: Eight Lectures on the New Climatic Regime*, trans. Catherine Porter (Cambridge: Polity Press, 2017), 3.

now widely used in environmental circles to describe the geologic epoch in which we now live: the Anthropocene, or the age of human dominance and pervasive impact on the climate and the environment. Whatever moniker one settles upon to name the present moment, we can describe it as a liminal time. It is a "threshold" time in which we have moved out of one state of being, assumed to be stable, but we do not know what lies ahead. We know only that our environment will not be as it has been, or even as it is now.

Climate Change as Liminal Space for the Earth and its Religions

Bjorn Thomassen, in his article on the meaning and uses of liminality, suggests that the concept can be applied helpfully to understanding whole societies experiencing a crisis of "collapse of order." This contrasts with the understanding of liminality in rites of passage literature, in which the liminal is clearly defined, the rites proceed in generally linear fashion and resolve in reintegration into an established order, and the liminal period recedes. When applied to a "wholesale collapse of order affecting an entire society," liminality indicates an inherently unknown future and a vacuum in leadership because no one has been through such a liminal period previously.[4] Further, it suggests that the liminal extends indefinitely. Thomassen's application of liminality to large-scale societal crises helps us locate ourselves within the current ecological crisis. Within human history we have never confronted something on the scale of global climate change and all its attendant symptoms until now. The crisis is overwhelming, disorienting, paralyzing. The future remains something of a mystery, for although there is widespread – almost unanimous – agreement among climate scientists about the certainty and scope of the problem, scientific modeling continues to update or change predictions about precise impacts in particular places or time frames as, for instance, if/when the melting of the Antarctic ice sheets accelerates, or new technologies develop to help communities with mitigation and adaptation measures. There is, of course, widespread disagreement among politicians and policy makers, economists, scientists, and pundits about the scope of the crisis and what might be appropriate or effective responses.

All of this suggests that climate change is what might be called a "wicked problem." Wicked problems, a concept put forth by Horst Rittel and Melvin Webber back in 1973, have the following characteristics:

4. Bjorn Thomassen, "The Uses and Meanings of Liminality," *International Journal of Political Anthropology* 2, no. 1 (2009), 21-22.

1. they are hard to define clearly;
2. they have no clear-cut stopping point;
3. there are no absolutely right and wrong solutions, only approaches understood as "better" or "worse;"
4. they have multiple causes, and addressing one cause may conflict with addressing others;
5. any proposed solution will have unexpected consequences of its own;
6. they are socially complex, rather than merely technically complex;
7. they are constantly evolving;
8. they are all symptoms of other problems; and
9. they have multiple valid explanations, each of which determines the approach to the problem.[5]

The point in naming climate change a "wicked problem" in this context is that the concept adds a further layer of complexity to applying the concept of liminality to it. Definitive statements about causes and effects must be held loosely, while predictions about where we are going resist definitive prescriptions. The bottom line is that we live in a liminal time where the future is opaque and our leaders – or "ceremony masters," as Thomassen calls them – provide little direction as human communities look for ways forward. In fact, Riley and Bauman, viewing climate change defined as a "wicked problem," emphasize that, "It is not something to be 'solved,' but something to be lived with and through in better and worse ways."[6] This suggests that we are, perhaps, entering a state of permanent liminality. In the end, this wicked problem is the result of human activities and human impact on our environment.

Religions and theologies exist in this liminal space, too. Willis Jenkins writes, the "environmental crisis forms a new global dimension of religious experience."[7] Larry Rasmussen concurs, noting that Christian spirituality and ethics – his term is "religious discipleship" – "has never before lived with a globally threatened ecosphere."[8] Thus, religious practice and theological

---

5. Horst Rittel and Melvin Webber, "Dilemmas in a General Theory of Planning," *Policy Sciences* 4 (June 1973), 155-69. I have adapted the list from the way it is characterized in two places: Matthew T. Riley and Whitney Bauman, "Wicked Problems in a Warming World: Religion and Environmental Ethics," *Worldviews* 21 (2017), 1-5, and the Australian Public Service Commission, "Tackling Wicked Problems: A Public Policy Perspective," 31 May 2012, accessed 26 February 2018, http://www.apsc.gov.au/publications-and-media/archive/publications-archive/tackling-wicked-problems.
6. Riley and Bauman, "Wicked Problems in a Warming World," 2.
7. Willis Jenkins, "After Lynn White: Religious Ethics and Environmental Problems," *Journal of Religious Ethics* 37, no. 2 (2009), 295, fn. 15.
8. Larry Rasmussen, *Earth-Honoring Faith: Religious Ethics in a New Key* (New York: Oxford University Press, 2014), 234.

reflection takes place in a "new climate," and the starting point for theological reflection must be the fact of a fundamentally altered planet.[9] Because religious practice and thought has never existed in such a place, it is unclear exactly how to appropriate past traditions or what shape spirituality will take in the future: we are "betwixt and between."[10] Bauman uses the "ecotone" as a metaphor for the situation of religions in the contexts of climate change: the ecotone is a "transition space between two different ecosystems, in which a blending of the two ecosystems occurs." For Bauman, this names the current condition of "in-betweenness, flux and change" faced by the Earth itself as well as by its religious traditions.[11] This liminal space is not indicated only by what we refer to as "the ecological crisis," but also by other conditions and forces with which it is entangled: the signs of our ecotonal phase include climate change, economic and cultural globalization, refugee crises driven by environmental factors, war, and social disruption, resurgent ethno-nationalism, especially in the West, and so on.[12] The scale, scope, and complexity of this ecologically and societally liminal space requires religious people not simply to "update" their religious practices to include "stewardship" or "care for creation" through certain practices like recycling, buying local produce, or reducing waste, although it is true that religions must incorporate practices that contribute to the world's healing. At a deeper level, it requires a fundamental shift in world views, and, consequently, a complete revision of the foundations, assumptions, and tenets of faith; "it requires religious categories, values, meanings, cosmologies, etc., be re-thought in light of these issues and our new ecological contexts."[13] Our ecologically liminal circumstance is the catalyst and the context for religious liminality as religious persons and institutions dwell in this space and time in which the future – of humanity itself, not only of a particular theological or religious community or tradition – is unspecified.

Where might religious people look for resources to inform such a radical re-orientation of faith? Religions, and Christianity particularly, have been blamed for contributing to the problem. In 1967, Lynn White, Jr, famously pointed the finger at Western Christianity as "bearing a huge burden of guilt" for the ecological crisis. "Christianity," said White, "is the

---

9. The title of one of Sallie McFague's books is *A New Climate for Theology: God, the World, and Global Warming* (Minneapolis: Fortress Press, 2008).
10. Victor Turner, *The Ritual Process* (1969), 95.
11. Whitney Bauman, "Meaning-Making Practices and Environmental History: Toward an Ecotonal Theology," in *Routledge Companion to Religion and Science*, eds James Haag, Gregory Peterson, and Michael Spezio (Malden, MA: Routledge, 2014), 368-69.
12. Ibid., 369.
13. Ibid.

most anthropocentric religion the world has seen."[14] Christian theologians have been responding to White and defending Christianity ever since his brief article appeared, but his charge against Christianity as contributing significantly to exploitative attitudes and destructive practices toward the Earth is conventional wisdom to many. One significant factor in the history of Christian thought and practice, contributing to the perception that Christianity is hostile to ecological well-being, is the wedding of Greek, especially Platonist, thought with Christian theology in the early centuries. One of the effects of this wedding has been to devalue the body and the material world as corrupt, while elevating the spiritual realm as superior. Platonism and Neo-Platonism have not been the only contributing influences, but it is true that many aspects of Christian life and thought have assumed dualisms of matter and spirit, body and soul. Dietrich Bonhoeffer's notion of "abstraction" helpfully identifies these dualisms as a theological fallacy. For Bonhoeffer, "abstraction" is the result of the breaking apart of the union between God and the world in Jesus Christ, with God imagined as separated from or apart from the world. The human body – not to mention the bodies of other creatures and the body of Earth itself – becomes immaterial to spiritual concerns or eternal salvation. Lisa Dahill draws on Bonhoeffer's notion to name the way that our present ecological crisis is playing out. Humanity as a whole, and Christians in particular, have elided God's presence from the natural world. Thus desacralized, the material world becomes little more than an economic resource to be exploited for profit and pleasure, rather than the locus of divine encounter or, in Thomas Berry's words, a "communion of subjects" to be honored and protected.[15]

In light of the role that religions, generally, and Christianity, particularly, have played in supporting and justifying negative attitudes and destructive practices toward the Earth, scholars of religion and ecology have been urging the world's religious traditions to re-orient themselves to support more sustainable practices. Mary Evelyn Tucker implores religions to enter "their ecological phase," asking, "Can religious traditions help us to find our niche as a species that does not overextend our effects and overshoot the limitations of fragile ecosystems?"[16] A vast scholarly literature in the

14. Lynn White, Jr, "The Historical Roots of our Ecologic Crisis," *Science* 155, no. 3767 (10 March 1967), 1205. For evaluations of White's work and influence, see *Religion and the Ecological Crisis: The "Lynn White Thesis" at Fifty*, eds Todd LeVasseur and Anna Peterson (New York: Routledge, 2017).

15. Thomas Berry, *The Sacred Universe: Earth Spirituality, and Religion in the Twenty-First Century* (New York: Columbia Press, 2009), 86, and Lisa Dahill, "Addressing God with Names of Earth," *Currents in Theology and Mission* 43, no. 4 (July 2016), 27.

16. Mary Evelyn Tucker, *Worldly Wonder: Religions Enter Their Ecological Phase* (Chicago: Open Court, 2003), 9-10.

fields of ecotheology and religion and ecology has grown up in the last fifty years to attempt to help religious traditions do just that. Also, there have been many efforts in faith communities of all religious traditions to include Earth care and ecological justice among their range of concerns. However, many of these efforts fall short of undertaking the radical reimagining of religion and faith called for by the conditions of anthropogenic climate change. While our circumstance calls for a radical reimagining, the integrity of a religious tradition depends, too, on some degree of continuity with its past. If liminality names a state that exists on a continuum, then what role does the past play in transitioning to and shaping the future, when past traditions seem to be at the root of the problem and the future has no definitive or known shape? Are there resources that may be appropriated to aid the transition, wherever it may be leading, or to help us "live with and through in better ways?"

In the annals of Christian spirituality there is an abundant literature describing intimate contact between saints and "nature" that may help us think about this issue. The early ascetics of the Egyptian, Syrian, and Palestinian deserts became models, through the chronicles of their lives and sayings, for later generations of holy men and women. The lives of later Irish saints in the sixth through eleventh centuries echo the early desert fathers and mothers, the two traditions being closely linked historically and thematically. Their chronicles are filled with stories of close, intimate contact with the wilderness and its creatures and the way they responded to societal upheaval by migrating into the desert or voyaging at sea in search of uninhabited island refuges. The writings we have about each of these traditions reveal spiritualities shaped by the landscapes they inhabited and their encounters with "wild nature." As these ascetics entered into and moved beyond the ecotonal spaces of wilderness/culture, desert/city, land/ sea, they navigated liminal spaces that were both physical and spiritual; their interior struggles to confront their own demons and find "purity of heart" were mirrored by the exterior landscapes they inhabited.

Desert Christian Ascetics

The late third and early fourth centuries comprised a liminal time for both the Roman Empire and the Christian movement. Each went through interrelated periods of massive change during this time. Constantine spent the first decades of the fourth century advancing and consolidating his power, establishing himself as supreme ruler over the whole Mediterranean world. After experiencing intermittent persecution throughout the first two centuries after the apostolic era, the worst of which occurred under the emperor Diocletian at the end of the third century and in the early years of the fourth century, the Christian Church in the Roman Empire found relief under the reign of Constantine. Thus, the Christian Church moved from the position of marginalized outsider to state religion, enjoying increasing wealth, status, and power.

Some of the earliest desert ascetics, such as Saint Anthony and Paul of Thebes, went into the desert to escape the persecutions of the late third century. As the Mediterranean world settled into the Constantinian arrangement and Christianity became the religion of empire in the fourth century, other Christians followed their example for different reasons. Not all were pleased with the turn of events. The Church wrestled with the implications of its newfound prosperity and influence as a series of controversies emerged over doctrine, leadership, identity, and the meaning of discipleship. During this transitional time, as the texture and the shape of Christian religion underwent seismic reconfigurations, many decided that Christianity's newly established status as the official religion of the empire was incongruous with the spiritual and moral identity of those who followed a homeless, crucified peasant from Galilee, and that it dishonored the faith of those martyrs who had been joined to Christ's suffering and death during the waves of persecution that had washed over the Church in earlier times. To some interpreters, this is what drove many Christians to seek refuge from the creeping materialism, careerism, and political intrigue of the imperial Church in the deserts of Egypt, Syria, and Palestine, the wilderness spaces of North Africa and the Middle East. They sought solitude, attempting to escape from all worldly distractions in order to devote themselves, single-mindedly, to achieving union with God through prayer and ascetic discipline. While others before them had sought something similar by removing themselves to the edges of cities and towns, those who populated the desert in the fourth century are generally identified as the pioneers of Christian monasticism.

Much has been written through the centuries about these men, and some women, known as the Desert Fathers and Mothers. Philip Sheldrake observes, "Living on some kind of physical boundary symbolizes a state of liminality – of living between two worlds, the material and the spiritual."[17] The desert monks, living at the edge of civilization and beyond, confronted that which distracted them from the pure contemplation of God, understood in the first instance to be their material and bodily needs and desires. The explicit purpose for those who sought refuge in the wilderness was to escape the distraction and perceived corruption of more inhabited spaces in order

---

17. Philip Sheldrake, *Spaces for the Sacred: Place, Memory, and Identity* (Baltimore: Johns Hopkins University Press, 2001), 91.

to devote oneself to spiritual matters. Thus, the desert fathers and mothers may seem like an odd place to look for resources to confront a tradition that has abstracted the spiritual and the material, because in many ways they exemplify the dualisms at the root of human alienation from the rest of the world. Nevertheless, they could not escape the material world and its demands, no matter how they might attempt to discipline the needs and desires of their physical bodies. The spiritual dimension notwithstanding, wilderness demands close attention to the body's physical needs for survival, close attention to one's physical surroundings, and the establishment of a new kind of relationship to the land, as well. The desert has long signified both a physical place and a spiritual challenge in Christian experience, and in the case of the desert ascetics, the landscape they inhabited was not incidental to their spiritual questions. Rather, as Douglas Burton-Christie writes, the physical place they inhabited was "integral to those questions, giving them shape and substance." He adds that the "geography of the heart" is "*at once* [my italics] physical and spiritual."[18] The desert was not ancillary to their spiritual quest, as if another place could be substituted and produce the same results. For the desert ascetics, the particular ecosystem, the geography they inhabited, represented something particular. The barren desert was the place that one went to confront what kept them from God: it was the place where one went to have those things stripped away, whether that be material possessions, carnal desires, or ego. Belden Lane has observed: "deserts . . . confront us with a vast horizontal edge, a horizon of emptiness into which we find ourselves absorbed and lost. The desert is intrinsically hostile to the ego, threatening to swallow it up in its endless expanse of nothingness."[19] However, in its hostility to ego, the desert creates space for one to replace ego with single-minded devotion and the practice of virtue. To the monks, the desert was a place both foreboding and liberating. It was the haunt of demons and the paradise of God. It became the place where the monks would confront their innermost fears and frailties, the place where they would overcome the alienations they felt, between true and false self, society, and the world, and where they would find rest in God.

The purpose of the writings by or about the desert ascetics was not to reflect on the experience of "nature," per se, or the human place in or relationship to it. However, the literature of the desert contains many accounts of the

---

18. Douglas Burton-Christie, "The Place of the Heart: Geography and Spirituality in the *Life of Anthony*," in *Purity of Heart in Early Ascetic and Monastic Literature: Essays in Honor of Juana Raasch, O.S.B.,* eds Harriet Luckman and Linda Kulzer (Collegeville, MN: The Liturgical Press, 1999), 46-47.

19. Belden Lane, *The Solace of Fierce Landscapes: Exploring Desert and Mountain Spirituality* (New York: Oxford University Press, 1998), 39.

monks' direct encounters with wild animals, with the elements, as well as with their own souls in the liminal spaces of empire, desert, and the quest for holiness. Through narrating the physical challenges and encounters with places and creatures, the literature tells us of their spiritual struggles and suggests these ancient holy persons as potential sources of wisdom for us in navigating contemporary ecological challenges.

Saint Anthony was the archetype of the desert ascetic, in many ways. The fourth-century bishop of Alexandria, Athanasius, composed the *Life of Anthony* not as a straightforward biography, but as one of the earliest and most influential examples of hagiography: that is, a narrative of the life of a holy person designed to demonstrate the person's holiness, to teach important lessons about the spiritual life, and to inspire others to model their lives after the example of the saint.[20] In the *Life*, Anthony is portrayed as a young Egyptian man who was inspired by hearing a reading of the Gospel of Matthew 19:21 in church: "If you would be perfect, go, sell what you possess and give to the poor, and you will have treasure in heaven." Convinced that this was the path he must follow, Anthony sold his land and possessions, gave the proceeds to the poor, made provision for his sister with a company of consecrated virgins, and dedicated his life to the pursuit of spiritual and ascetic discipline, a quest which led him to seek solitude by moving incrementally further and further into the desert.

The narrative has Anthony first moving to the outskirts of his village to a place associated with ascetics, then to a place of greater solitude among some nearby tombs, and then to an abandoned fortress on the edge of the desert. In each of these places, Anthony faces temptations and struggles with demons, while practicing ascetic disciplines and giving himself more and more to the cultivation of his interior life. He spent twenty years enclosed in the fortress, in solitude, eating very little, and continuing his combat with demons. When he emerged from his enclosure, his friends were amazed at what they saw, for "his body had maintained its former condition, neither fat from lack of exercise, nor emaciated from fasting and combat with demons, but was just as they had known him prior to his withdrawal."[21] Anthony was luminous, the state of his soul showing forth as "one of purity." Further, he was endowed with the power of God to heal sickness, purge demons, and give wise counsel to those who sought it.

---

20. The *Life of Anthony* also played a role in Athanasius' ecclesiastical politics as he sought to exert his influence over both the desert monastics and those who dwelt in cities. See David Brakke, *Athanasius and Asceticism* (Baltimore: Johns Hopkins University Press, 1998).

21. Athanasius, *The Life of Anthony and the Letter to Marcellinus*, trans. Robert Gregg (New York: Paulist Press, 1980), 42.

Athanasius emphasizes the complete transformation God had wrought in Anthony as he lived in his desert solitude. However, since the "desert was made a city by monks," inspired by his example, Anthony longs for even greater solitude. He hears a voice tell him that if he wants true solitude he should "go to the inner mountain," a solitary place deep in the eastern desert. When he arrives at the place that will become his final home, Athanasius reports that "Anthony, as if stirred by God, fell in love with the place." It had a suitable place for a garden, "abundant water from a spring," and some date palms. Its beauty and simplicity moved him.

Anthony, not wanting to burden others with caring for his physical needs, procured some garden tools and seeds, planting vegetables and grain for bread. In the first human/animal encounter noted in the desert literature, "when the beasts of the wilderness came for water, they often would damage his crop and his planting." Anthony responds by "gently capturing" one of these unspecified beasts, and says to them all, "Why do you hurt me when I do you no injury? Leave, and in the name of the Lord do not come here any longer." After that, they did not disturb his plot.[22] In another version of the story, the animals returned after Anthony's rebuke, but only drank water and did not damage the garden again. Susan Power Bratton points out the simple nature of Anthony's lifestyle: it "was based on subsistence gardening and encouraged wildlife to continue to share the resources of the inner desert with him." She notes that, although the monks certainly altered their environment, Anthony and others limited their harvesting of resources so that they took only what they needed.[23] One of the themes in desert literature about holy persons as they come into contact with landscape and wild animals is the recreation of paradise. In the desert, Antony finds a way to paradise. His experience recreates a perfected humanity, restoring the lost harmony with creation known in the Garden of Eden.[24]

The *Life of Anthony* spawned many imitators. In the late fourth century Jerome wrote a hagiography, the life of a hermit named Paul of Thebes, who purportedly lived in the third and fourth centuries. One purpose of Jerome's work was to challenge the claim that Anthony was the first desert hermit. The work is full of encounters with wild beasts and mythical creatures. As the narrative goes, Anthony learned in a dream of a hermit who had been in the desert longer than he had and whose holiness surpassed his own. Curious, Anthony set out to find this person and was led to him by a thirsty wolf. As Anthony and Paul talked, a raven appeared with a loaf of bread for them to

---

22. Ibid., 68-69.
23. Susan Power Bratton, *Christianity, Wildlife, and Wilderness: The Original Desert Solitaire* (Scranton, PA: University of Scranton Press, 1993), 165.
24. Andrew Louth, *The Wilderness of God* (Nashville: Abingdon Press, 1991), 57.

share. After they had shared conversation, bread, and prayer, Paul informed Anthony that he was about to die, telling him, "You have been sent by the Lord to cover my poor body with earth, or rather, to return earth to earth." Full of grief, Anthony went away to retrieve a cloak in which to wrap Paul's corpse and, while he was away, Paul died. After wrapping the body in the cloak, Anthony was distraught to realize that he had no tools with which to dig a grave. At that point, a pair of lions "came running from the inner desert, their manes flowing over their necks." While frightened at first, Anthony gave his fears over to God and stood his ground. The lions went to the dead saint, wagging their tails and lying down at his feet in a display of devotion, "roaring loudly as if to show that in their own way they were lamenting the best they could." The lions dug a space for burial out of the ground, after which they approached Anthony, licking his hands and feet, hoping for a blessing. Anthony obliged, and, "Immediately he burst out in praise of Christ because he realized that dumb animals, too, were able to understand that there was a God."[25] While many interpret the story to indicate simply the holiness of the saints giving them authority over the wild animals, to Susan Power Bratton, this story illustrates "a *relationship* [my italics] between a human and animals, not raw power over nature."[26] Anthony is guided by a wolf, he and Paul are fed by a raven, and lions help him to revere the holy man he sought. They are capable of grief and capable of recognizing the power of God in both Paul and Anthony. From their desire for the saint's intercession and blessing, they, in turn, inspire Anthony to praise God.

In a tale from Palestine, a lion with a wounded paw approached Saint Jerome who instructed some fellow monks to tend to it: they removed some thorns, bathed the paw, and the lion's wound healed. The grateful lion remained among the brothers at the monastery and Jerome came up with a job for the lion: he was to shepherd the monastery's donkey when it went out to graze, protecting it from predators and potential thieves. One day, as the donkey grazed, the lion fell asleep and some passing merchants stole the donkey. The sorrowful and guilt-ridden lion returned to the monastery where the brothers assumed the lion had finally killed and eaten his charge, but Jerome instructed them to treat the lion with mercy, while requiring the beast to take on the donkey's previous responsibilities. One day, the lion encountered the merchants returning with the donkey. After scattering the caravan, the lion returned to the monastery with the donkey and three camels in tow. The newly vindicated lion enthusiastically moved among the brothers without bitterness at their false accusation and they, remorseful, embraced

25. Carolinne White, trans. and ed., "Life of Paul of Thebes by Jerome," in *Early Christian Lives* (London: Penguin Books, 1998), 75-84.
26. Bratton, *Christianity, Wilderness, and Wildlife*, 167.

him as a friend: "Behold, our trusty shepherd whom so short a while ago we were upbraiding for a greedy ruffian, and God has deigned to send him to us with such a resounding miracle, to clear his character!"[27] In this story, a wild beast and humans live in community, work to heal one another, take on responsibilities of community life, come into conflict, and experience reconciliation. The falsely accused lion holds no grudge against his accusers even as he does penance for a crime he did not commit, and the humans learn something of virtue, humility, and forgiveness from the wild animal. As Bratton notes, "the desert fathers saw their own values operating in nature and perceived wild nature as directly responsive to the Holy and to the Will of God."[28] Both human and animal communities participate in the economy of grace: communal responsibility, penance, forgiveness, and reconciliation.

Irish Saints

The Egyptian-Palestinian desert tradition was transmitted to Celtic lands, primarily Ireland and Wales, via Mediterranean Sea routes. As Esther de Waal explains, the monastic wisdom of the deserts landed among Celtic Christian communities who were, themselves, monastic and eremitical, "and it came from the desert to a deeply rural people who lived close to the earth, and whose religious beliefs were naturally shaped by their feeling for creation and the whole of the created world."[29] The sea figures prominently in the tales of Celtic saints, as they lived along coasts and valued sea voyaging; the theme of wilderness solitude shows up as monks seek isolation in forests and along lake shores, and as mariners seek uninhabited island paradises on which to practice their lives of contemplation.[30] Animal encounters figure prominently in the lives of Irish saints, too.

Seafaring and animal encounters converge in a remarkable tale about Saint Brendan, sometimes called "Brendan the Navigator" or "Brendan the Voyager." This mythical tale narrates his years-long seafaring venture in search of the island of paradise. As Easter approached during the first year of the voyage, Brendan's companions urged him to land somewhere so that they could celebrate the holiday rites. "God is able," Brendan replied, "to find a land for us in any place He pleases." When Easter came, a great whale raised its shoulders high above the surface of the waves, so that it formed dry land. And they landed on it and celebrated Easter. And they were there

27. Helen Waddell, trans., *Beasts and Saints* (Grand Rapids, MI: Eerdmans Publishing, 1996), 27-32.

28. Bratton, *Christianity, Wilderness, and Wildlife*, 169.

29. Esther de Waal, "Introduction," in *Beasts and Saints*, trans. Helen Waddell (Grand Rapids, MI: Eerdmans Publishing Co., 1996), xxii.

30. See Bratton, *Christianity, Wilderness, and Wildlife*, 182-84.

for one day and two nights. The great whale disappeared into the sea once the sailors had again embarked, but it returned at the approach of Easter each year for seven years so that the voyagers could celebrate the Mass.[31] One thing animals do in these tales is to assist the saints in their religious practices. As Brendan asserted, God made provision for them to carry out their celebration, but it was done with the cooperation of the whale.

Other-than-human creatures are also portrayed as capable of offering their own praise to their creator. As Saint Benno was wandering the fields in meditation and prayer, he passed a marsh where "a talkative frog was croaking in its slimy waters." The holy man, not wishing to be distracted from his reverie, wished the frog's voice to be muted. A short time later, Benno recalled a Biblical passage enjoining whales, cattle, and other beasts to bless the Lord, so he withdrew his complaint and commanded the frogs to "praise God in their accustomed fashion," fearing that their singing "might perchance be more agreeable to God than his own praying." Then "the air and the fields were vehement with their conversation."[32] Such tales indicate that nature and its creatures are of concern to God, that they have sacred worth and participate with humans in the economy of grace.

A story about Saint Bartholomew and some ducks indicates how animals can exercise rationality and turn to humans for help in distress. As a mother duck was leading her brood, one of her ducklings fell into a crevice which she could not reach. Distraught, the duck turned to the saint for help. "Let no one doubt she was then endowed with human reason," the writer says. Showing persistence, the mother duck tugged on the hem of Bartholomew's cloak, leading him to the cliff, and pointing to her trapped duckling, whereupon he climbed down to rescue the creature and return it to its mother, "who in high delight seemed by her joyous look to give him thanks."[33] In this tale, the bird displays trust in a human companion to come to her aid and ensure the well-being of her offspring, while demonstrating gratitude for his assistance.

Another tale takes up the theme of wild animals turning to humans for help, this one in the life of a saint called Maedoc of Ferns. Maedoc's sanctity was recognized at a very young age. One day, while tending the herd of sheep belonging to his foster mother, "there came towards him gently and fawningly eight wolves together, poor, weak and starving." Maedoc responded to their plight by offering them eight sheep from the herd for food, which they eagerly accepted. When his foster mother learned

---

31. Charles Plummer, *Bethada Náem Nérenn: Lives of Irish Saints,* Vol. 2 (Oxford: Clarendon Press, 1922), 68.
32. Waddell, *Beasts and Saints,* 65-66.
33. Ibid., 86.

of his actions, she came after him in a rage. Maedoc, more frightened of his guardian than of the wolves, prayed the following prayer: "O Almighty God, Lord Jesus Christ, help and assist me, for it was in honour of Thee that I gave food to the poor starvelings." Before his step mother could reach him, eight sheep, identical to the ones given to the wolves, appeared to replace them.[34] While the explicit moral of the tale in the *Life of Maedoc* is to evoke praise to God and to indicate the Maedoc's holiness, it also makes note of the hospitality he displayed toward wild creatures in distress. Such kindness toward wild animals indicates the saint's virtue, but it also suggests a reciprocal relationship between human and animal. The saint exercises hospitality toward animals, and nature returns the favor, replenishing the resources spent in his act of compassion (of course, the first eight sheep do not fare so well, but that might be fodder for reflection in another context).

A final example takes us back to the sea and demonstrates that not only do animals look to humans for assistance, but they also give aid to their human kin. Saint Cuthbert of Lindisfarne, while visiting a remote monastery perched on a cliff above the sea, maintained his customary practice of keeping an outdoor prayer vigil deep into the night. On this night he prayed in the sea itself: "wading into the depths till the waves swelled up to his neck and arms, [he] kept his vigil through the dark with chanting voiced like the sea." As dawn approached, Cuthbert exited the water and began to pray on the beach, whereupon two otters came out of the sea: "These, prostrate before him on the sand, began to busy themselves warming his feet with pantings, and trying to dry them with their fur." When they had finished and received Cuthbert's blessing, they returned to the water.[35] In this tale, the animals' response serves to indicate the saint's holiness.[36] However, there are many other tales in Cuthbert's life in which he and others receive the aid and provision of wild animals and of the sea itself. Such tales not only identify the holy man, they also suggest ways in which humans rely upon the Earth and its creatures to sustain human life and provide for human need.

* * *

The literature of the ancient desert monks and medieval Celtic saints is extensive and filled with many tales like these. In this liminal time, when climate change presents us with an opaque and uncertain future, can the literature that emerged from the liminal experience of Christian contemplatives in late antiquity offer us any wisdom for navigating our challenges in better ways? In her preface to Waddell's translation of the

---

34. Plummer, *Bethada Náem Nérenn*, 189-90.
35. Waddell, *Beasts and Saints*, 55-56.
36. Bratton, *Christianity, Wilderness, and Wildlife*, 188.

animal legends of the desert monastics and the saints of Ireland, Esther DeWaal suggests that these legends hold some special potential to contribute to the recovery of "the wholeness of the Christian tradition and of our own inner wholeness."[37] Can they also contribute to the wholeness of the planet and our neighbors, human and other?

One question that has been raised over and over again, beginning in the time of the first desert monks, is whether they were negligently withdrawing from society, washing their hands of responsibility for the challenges facing Church and culture while they pursued their own, private, "purity of heart." Sheldrake, while acknowledging the validity of the question, suggests instead that monasticism as exemplified in Christian antiquity "should be viewed as having a prophetic role vis-à-vis the human city rather than simply as providing an escape route into an alternative, purified universe."[38] Given the radical differences in context between the ancient desert and medieval Irish monks and contemporary Western Christians, let us ask, in what ways might this be true in the context of the anthropocene? I have three suggestions.

First, the desert monks immersed themselves in the wilderness; they thrust themselves into close intimate contact with the desert ecosystem. True, they did so in order to wrestle with their inner demons. On one hand, they went into the wilderness to escape worldly distractions to their spiritual quest for union with God; they have been criticized for an otherworldly, disembodied spirituality that sought to escape responsibility for societal problems and contributed to the abstraction mentioned earlier. From another perspective, though, their quest was completely embodied. Their awareness of their own bodies and their physical surroundings was amplified by close contact with the wilderness and its creatures. Such intimacy breeds knowledge of how things work: where water is, what plants are edible, nutritious, or medicinal, how to grow food in a particular environment, how to read weather patterns, how to ensure safety from the elements and from predators, and so on. Paying attention to their habitat was not optional, but necessary, and no doubt honed their knowledge of the ecosystem's functioning.

Such intimate knowledge of ecosystems is sorely lacking today. How many people in developed countries have even a cursory knowledge of their local flora and fauna, of where their food comes from, or of their local water supply? Public rhetoric about climate change suggests widespread ignorance about the basic science of it, suggesting that we don't know much more about planet-wide ecology than we do about the local. While educating ourselves about native plants or the migratory patterns of

37. de Waal, "Introduction," xxiii.
38. Sheldrake, *Spaces for the Sacred*, 94.

butterflies will not by itself overcome the ecological challenges we face, it is a place to begin. The desert ascetics and Irish monks challenge us to come into intimate contact and develop intimate knowledge of the places where we live, what lives in them, and what threatens them. Walter Burghardt has defined contemplation as "a long loving look at the real."[39] The real is the world all around us and those ancient contemplatives call upon us to look long and lovingly at it so that we may know it and treat it well.

Second, as we come into intimate contact with the world around us, we will begin to notice ties of kinship with it. One of the themes in monastic literature of wilderness is that humans and animals often treated one another as companions, neighbors, teachers, guides, and helpers. As they narrated their own values, endowing animal kind with human-like qualities, the monks were, perhaps unknowingly, expressing the truth that modern science tells us: that we are all bound together, human, animal, plant, Earth. Donna Haraway, a philosopher of science and technology, has written of the "entanglements" that species share, in terms of evolutionary biological and genetic connections, as well as in sharing space on the planet in our interactions with one another and in our common dependence on its resources. Humans, rather than transcending the material and animal world, share an evolutionary history with it and emerge from that history along with all other things. "I am a creature of the mud, not the sky," she writes.[40] Following Haraway and Latour, Bauman insists that we live in an evolving world: "always, already as natural-cultural beings. . . . Rather than maintaining some sort of human exceptionalism from the rest of the natural world, we might begin to re-narrate ourselves back into the planetary community as meaning-making creatures."[41] In the tales of encounter between monks and animals, the characters recognized their mutual dependence upon one another and relied on one another, not only for human well-being but for the well-being of the whole. They suggest that becoming fully human is something accomplished through participating in mutual relationships with humans and other-than-humans, through recognizing our interdependence, and through valuing the well-being of all.[42] Their wisdom is congruent with Thomas Berry's vision that we could see the world as a "communion of subjects rather than a collection of objects."[43]

39. Walter Burghardt, "Contemplation: A Long, Loving Look at the Real," *Church* (Winter 1989), 14-18.

40. Donna Haraway, *When Species Meet* (Minneapolis: University of Minnesota Press, 2008), 3.

41. Bauman, "Meaning-Making Practices and Environmental History," 371.

42. For a recent theological account of these ideas, see Celia Deane-Drummond, *The Wisdom of the Liminal: Evolution and Other Animals in Human Becoming* (Grand Rapids, MI: Eerdmans Publishing, 2014).

43. Berry, *The Sacred Universe*, 86.

Third, consider their ascetic discipline. As already noted, this could be regarded as problematic for us as we consider a new spirituality that values the Earth, and in some ways it is. However, in light of the rampant consumerism that has contributed so significantly to our current ecological crisis, perhaps asceticism is exactly what we need to practice. From a global perspective, the economies of nations – of First World nations especially – are grounded in assumptions of an endless supply of natural resources that must be turned into consumer goods to fuel a continually growing economy. Growth is an article of faith in capitalist economies and it relies on consumers to make it work. Consumption is often portrayed as a sacred duty to keep the economy growing. Thus, individuals are bombarded with messages about how consumer goods will fulfill and satisfy them, physically and spiritually. The message that we should not question our consumerist lifestyles or question the natural limits of growth, that we must only find and take the resources we need to maintain these lifestyles,, however, has resulted in the decimation of resources and their uneven distribution around the globe. The ascetic disciplines of the desert monks illustrate, perhaps, the most forceful prophetic critique of cultural norms. They practiced their disciplines – resisting many of the urges of their bodies and souls – by voluntarily forgoing certain pleasures: food, sex, wealth, sleep. They consumed modestly, living off what their land could provide for them. While some of their more austere practices – especially related to sex, sleep, and so on – reveal an unhealthy disdain for the human body and the material world, their simplicity for the sake of something greater is worth our consideration. They denied themselves things in order to devote themselves more fully to God. By living more simply and consuming less (of everything), we reorient our vision of the good life to be found in making room for our neighbors, human and other, and making space for God's presence and action within us.

Further, through their ascetic practices, the monks were anticipating the re-creation of paradise in their bodies and in their communities. In many of the tales of encounter between saints and the natural world, the theme is the restoration of Eden in the body and person of the saint. The holiness achieved through their ascetic practices is recognized in the re-establishment of Eden's harmony as malice between animals, Earth, and humans dissipates. Full restoration is only complete in the next life, of course, but the saints' lives anticipate here and now and show evidence of what God will do.

Such an eschatological hope may be inspiring to some, but our hope cannot be in a future afterlife or another world. People of faith can enact an asceticism that anticipates the healing of the Earth, but that healing must be seen as taking place in history. People of faith must take on an asceticism today that enacts a hope that we can pull back from the brink, as we commit ourselves to practices that reduce energy use, reduce the emission of greenhouse gases, reduce consumption of precious and scarce potable water, and that ensure a more just distribution of resources and of responsibility for those who will experience the worst effects of climate change. Our sense of agency in the work of redemption must shift, too, until Christian people regard this as their work and not God's alone, or even primarily. Just as in the tales of God providing for Saint Cuthbert or Saint Anthony through the help of animals, so we must view ourselves as the primary agents of healing in the face of climate change. As we face a "wicked problem," there may be effects that cannot be undone; we can, however, act in ways that help us navigate current conditions in the best ways possible, given the circumstances. Along the way we are enacting our hope for healing. Perhaps the lives of those ancient and medieval ascetics can supply us with some wisdom to help us find our way in this liminal time.

Falling Down the Rabbit Hole

Nicole Conner

Never knowing which way was up
Until I drank the bitter cup
And then the sky it disappeared
And I was falling without fear
Falling falling without a sound
Down down down down down down down
This is who I am, this is what I need
Falling down the rabbit hole
This is how I live, this is how I bleed
Falling down the rabbit hole
This is what I know, this is how I think . . .

Joel Sattler

* * *

Meandering Paths

Storytelling is the aorta that runs through my family and ancestors. It has nourished us for generations. The traditional German *Kaffeeklatsch* may start with just two or three people drinking coffee and eating *Sahnekuchen*, but within minutes the room is filled with invisible guests, jostling for their stories to be heard from another time and place. I was a fortunate child to grow up surrounded by such rich narrative.

The stories of war and displacement were never far from the lips of my Oma. She lost her husband, my grandfather, in the battle of Stalingrad. As a young mother, with my aunt who was a toddler and my father who was a three-month-old baby at the time, she had to flee her hometown of Lyck (Elk, Poland) as the Soviet Army approached in 1945. Her survival stories were harrowing: stories of despair, hunger, abuse, but also of hope. The man she married six years later would provide a safe haven for a young widow and her children.

My mother suffered from Post-Traumatic Stress Disorder all her life, most of those years without a diagnosis and unable to understand her own sense of consistent, heightened anxiety and insomnia. She was older than my father and remembers the war – running for bomb shelters, shaking violently as the fighter jets approached, the sound of Gestapo boots on the street, and her Jewish neighbor jumping off her balcony to her death so she would not be arrested. Her childhood was turbulent and traumatic.

The stories my parents and grandparents told shaped so much of my world. I grew up in a loving and nurturing home, but I was not shielded from these stories, and for that I am so grateful. It prepared me for what I was about to experience as a seven year-old when my parents packed up house and moved from Germany to South Africa.

Most immigrants can relate to the sense of disorientation and disconnection experienced when one settles into a country that is very different from their accustomed culture and social norms. I felt as if I was caught in a giant tidal wave of learning and new experiences, and I did not find my feet for several years. I had to learn English and Afrikaans – an apartheid-torn South Africa had a dual language approach. I also learnt Zulu. But all that took time. In the meantime, I became the focal point of playground fun and belittling. Children show little mercy when they can distract potential bullies to a prey that is more vulnerable than they are. The school library became my safe place during recess and the Giant Illustrated Catholic Children's Bible became a source of wonder.

I had no embedded idea about the blue-eyed, blonde-haired man I was looking at in that Bible. He reminded me of someone from Norse mythology or a Viking character that featured in one of the many stories my Oma told. It would be quite a few years later before I would encounter this man again. At that time, I learnt his name: Jesus.

It was the system called apartheid – an ultimate form of marginalization, bullying and oppression of people based on the hue of their skin – that reminded me that the world is not really a safe place. My lack of friends at school was quickly compensated for by the children of the cleaners and helpers at my mother's hair salon. It was with their help that I mastered Zulu long before Afrikaans. It was their presence that exposed me to the cruelty I now witnessed in person, not in stories. My Zulu friends could not go into the shops I visited, they had separate drinking fountains, it took them a long time to find a public toilet they were permitted to use, and they often had random grown-ups shout at and abuse them. They were not permitted to be in the streets of the area where I lived. I have a distinct memory of the neighbor across the road beating an African man unconscious because he took a shortcut across a nearby field. That neighbor then dusted off his suit and got into his car to go to church. I later found out he was an elder at the local Dutch Reformed church. To me he remains immortalized in my historical narrative as the archetypal arsehole.

These were some of my pre-liminal stories and life experiences. I would dream of a better world. In my imagination I was the super-hero who would put every bully in his place and liberate the oppressed. I was a child waiting to become a zealot, looking for a cause. More than that, I was a child desperately looking for belonging, safety, and predictability. I found it in institutional fundamentalist religion.

The Safety of Institution

I was "saved" in the Newcastle Full Gospel Church when my father randomly decided he would go to church, prompted by an invitation from his supervisor at work. A visit by aliens would have been less surprising. I walked down the aisle that day and "gave my heart" to the Viking-look-alike-god I encountered all those years earlier. I waited for the magic to happen as I was told I was now saved and transformed and a whole new being. In a sense I did experience magic – suddenly I belonged to a group of people who smiled constantly and fed me delicious South African desserts. The wandering little girl, now in her teens, had found a home.

Like a woman possessed, I frantically built the structures of certainty and absolutism around my life, following my coming to faith. I embodied the zealous figure of Saint Paul before his conversion, slaughtering any and all ideas that contained seeds of doubt and paradox. Fundamentalism, with its overtures in literalism and dogmatism, became the strong tower that produced my concept of God. I was a loyal soldier to the cause. Finally, I had found something that soothed my angst over what appeared to be a harsh, confusing and meaningless world.

In the meantime, on the geographical front, we had returned to Germany for a year and then migrated to Australia. It was in Rockhampton, Queensland, in 1984 that I would meet the man who would become my life partner. He was travelling up the coast with a friend and dropped in to visit my church, an offshoot of the large Pentecostal faith community called Waverley Christian Fellowship based in Melbourne. His father was one of the ministers there. So, one bright, sunny day in February 1985, I packed up my old Valiant station wagon called "Boris" and drove for three days to Melbourne, sleeping at the side of the road along the way. So begins the story of a three-decade-long journey as an integral part of a conservative religious institution and my addiction to certainty.

Certainty Addiction

Kierkegaard was an admirer of Socrates and the Socratic dialectical method. He observed how Socrates would consistently examine a student's certainty in an area of knowledge because certainty eventually leads to paradox. Paradox provided a pathway to higher truth. Kierkegaard believed that engaging in this dialectical process would offer more valid glimpses of the Divine in one's journey. This, for him, was the only developmental certainty – the trek through the "stages of life's way."[1] This provides me with a helpful reflection as I consider thirty years lived within a conservative Pentecostalism that had little room for questions or paradox, and which held a collective tradition that often resisted critique and is known for its frequent anti-intellectual stance.[2]

I often wonder why it took me nearly thirty years to wake up in the matrix. I think my internal fear of chaos and confusion collaborated so well with the structural ideologies in a place that refused to question. I do not want to give the impression that these were in any way bad years – they were not. I experienced a sense of happiness and fulfillment in the various roles I filled in the mega church of which my husband would become Senior Minister in 1995. They were heady days of success, expansion, and admiration. I developed as a speaker and was travelling the world delivering profundities from various platforms about everything certain and absolute. People cheered. I had found truth.

In our structure-building phase of life, we often find safety and solace in organizations that exude confidence and assurance. For religious institutions that hold to literalism of the Bible as a form of orthodoxy, the framework of certitude and conviction are irresistible for anyone seeking guarantees or formulas that will work in this wild ride called life. Unless we foster a strong culture of critique and self-reflection in these settings, we will mistakenly confuse our flourishing ego as faith and our elitism as community. With such a narrative, held in place by praise and success, it becomes increasingly

---

1. Sylvia McMillan, "Kierkegaard and a Pedagogy of Liminality," (Ph.D. diss., Brigham Young University, 2013), https://scholarsarchive.byu.edu/cgi/viewcontent.cgi?article=4623&context=etd.
2. Marius Nel, "Rather Spirit-filled Than Learned! Pentecostalism's Tradition of Anti-intellectualism and Pentecostal Theological Scholarship," *Verbum et Ecclesia* 37, no. 1 (2015), https://verbumetecclesia.org.za/index.php/VE/article/view/1533/html.

difficult to change and grow. Richard Rohr writes, "The human ego prefers anything, just about anything, to falling, or changing, or dying. The ego is that part of you that loves the status quo – even when it's not working. It attaches to past and present, and fears the future."[3] My ego had hired my love for certainty and structure as labourers – it was a perfect match. Success and accolades dull the senses. They have us cling to fantasies and keep us blind. Maybe that is why I didn't question hierarchical structures or patriarchal dominance for such a long time. My love affair with certainty ensured that I obediently nodded to ideas and doctrines that were presented as absolute truth, yet jarred deeply with my values. At least I submitted in the early years, when influential leaders would propagate the myth of male headship. However, both my husband and I began to fall down the rabbit hole as we opened ourselves to voices outside our tight-knit community,[4] and the wheels of change began to slowly move and creak. Questions started to arise, often uttered in hushed tones, questions that prodded at some of the communal ideology adopted through the adherence to dogma stemming from the Holiness and Latter Rain Movement. This was not easy. Holy Cows are very precious. However, paradox was calling.

The Emperor has No Clothes

I understand why people do not want to engage with questions and critique. It is a humbling, terrifying, and ego-destroying exercise. Many of us will never go there willingly. Yet once we engage with that niggling doubt that will not leave us alone, like an itchy mosquito bite, we crack open Pandora's box – and all hell breaks loose.

It came to me in the quiet, dark, early morning hours. We had just hosted another successful conference that was overflowing with people and goosebumps. Our lives and our schedules at this stage were stretched to maximum capacity. We were adrenaline junkies doing God's will – and God was clearly "blessing" us. Lying in bed exhausted, I wondered whether this is what Jesus had in mind when he referred to his "church." It was the question that never left me, and, like someone who had been under water for a very long time, I came to the surface gasping for air.

Questions were the red carpet on which Paradox made her appearance and entrance. Once you see her, you cannot look away. I became like a paranoid version of Truman Burbank of *The Truman Show*, suspiciously

---

3. Richard Rohr, *Falling Upwards* (San Francisco: Jossey-Bass, 2011), 29.
4. Pentecostalism is an insular movement. Barring a few exceptions, leaders and parishioners usually limit their reading and listening to Pentecostal sources. This sectarian trend continues to this day.

staring at some of the hyper-reality I was part of and helped create. The safe ivory tower of Evangelical Pentecostalism that has carved such a mega place for itself in modern Christianity started to crumble for me.

I began to notice the consumerism that was hiding under the idea of "blessing." If we are convinced that God's blessing is inadvertently tied to more stuff, buildings, growth, and numbers, then the pursuit of more becomes a holy crusade. If there is one word that describes the motivational factors behind the empire building of modern-day Christianity, it is more. More is the trophy held up in individual and community life as the proof of God's blessing. Is it any wonder that the key question at the many pastors' conferences I attended was, "How many people are in your church now?" How beautiful the golden calf shimmers in the light of "blessing."

Consumerism was but one of the many concerns that now hounded me in the "mega" space of religion. I began to notice the blindness I carried to my own privilege. I had become accustomed to living in an empire that influenced politics, policed morality, dominated social structures and was very quick to cry foul, or rather "persecution," if it felt threatened. It held little regard for voices on the social margins, and it had no time for anyone questioning the parade. "A cold commodity culture in which everything is reduced to its market value will blasphemously obscure our vision that all this earth is hallowed ground," writes Brian Walsh.[5] He is right. The dualistic attitude held in these ivory towers of us and them, holy and secular, consistently reduces those who differ to other or sinful. We are told to ignore it all because the parade must go on. Whenever the emperor waved, I normally waved back. But paradox and questions had come into my life, so all I could do was stand and gape in horror: the emperor had no clothes.

Disenchantment

I started to tap into what felt like a bottomless pit of red-hot, bubbling anger. When there is a head-on collision of values that have been denied, a deconstruction of idealism that had to do with identity and belonging, and a deep disappointment of personal and community expectations, anger is often the prevalent emotion and lead member of the "rescue team." I also faced the dilemma that in fundamentalism anger is frowned upon – everyone is just nice. The niceness culture in some parts of Pentecostal Evangelicalism is as caustic as rat poison mixed with icing sugar. It breeds shallow relationships that are held in place by the fear of judgment.

---

5. Brian Walsh, *Kicking at the Darkness: Bruce Cockburn and the Christian Imagination* (Grand Rapids, MI: Brazos Press, 2011).

My inner torment was amplified by the fact that critical and robust dialogue was often interpreted as negative, and everyone was terrified of being "negative." I had very few safe places or people with whom to process my questions, doubts, and thought processes. Pentecostals hold to a triumphant happiness theology. The rhetoric from pulpits is one of "victory," "triumphs," "breakthrough," "better," and "greater." It is a victory over negativity, poverty, sickness, anxiety, and depression. The result is that anyone who is unable to live in that suspended, Eden-like utopia is considered with caution. When I began to raise some of the doubts I was wrestling with, I recall being asked by one church leader whether I had adopted a "new kind of spirituality." It was a question that silenced me for a few more months. Institutions of any kind tend to guard the structure of certainty over people. It can become a dangerous place for anyone who has begun to fall down the rabbit hole of questions and started deconstructing embedded dogma.

At the end of 2010, I resigned from a prominent role as Associate Pastor. I was terrified. It was a massive step made far more complex as my husband would continue to serve as Senior Minister for the next six years. My decision to step away from the high-profile role was complicated. Perhaps I can simply say that I fell out of love with certainty. The black and white absolutism required of leaders in conservative fundamentalist institutions was something I could no longer hold on to with any form of integrity. My self-assured stance on life and the world had been shaken and found desperately wanting. Perhaps, with a bit of fierce intentionality and some open conversations, my continued dislocation from the community would have been salvageable. However, in the words of Frodo Baggins, "How do you pick up the threads of an old life? How do you go on, when in your heart you begin to understand there is no going back?" There is no going back once you wake up in the matrix – and, more importantly, once you begin to engage with people who have been shunned by some of these very institutions. For several years leading up to my resignation, for example, I had many conversations with LGBTIQA people of faith. I soon discovered that these friendships would be both a gracious, healing gift and the final severing sword to thirty years of ministry in this particular context.

Betrayal

The last blow to what was left of my extravagantly structured system of certainty came via a very familiar medium: stories. It started with just one conversation between me and a gay friend. Since then I have listened to many people who have had to navigate exile from their homes or faith communities based on their gender identity or sexual orientation. I am indebted to them. They opened their hearts to me and through their vulnerability they opened my eyes to a dominant, patriarchal system of ideas that cloaks itself as orthodoxy and truth. The stories were hard to hear. The cruelty and brutality so many faced in the name of God were unfathomable. I realized that I had supported, enabled, and helped build a ministry within a wider religious structure that was responsible for much trauma. My own blind privilege had not even considered those who were suffering. It is so easy to dehumanize another when you are removed from their pain, ignorant of their plight.

My eyes were also opened to the effect that ex-gay "ministry"[6] had on people. It works on the assumption that there is something intrinsically "broken" about anyone who identifies as anything else other than heteronormative. The idea that drives it is that this "brokenness" can be healed by God and ultimately that this person can then go on living as a "normal," straight human. It continues to operate in churches and para-church organizations to this day,[7] and many desperate, vulnerable people, convinced they are displeasing God seek help and a "cure." The toll of this quackery is hard to put into words – anguish, disillusionment, mental health issues, and suicides. There came a day when I was asked to talk about what I had observed in the last several years. I could no longer remain a silent, horrified witness. So, I agreed to be interviewed on Melbourne's JOY FM – and all hell was unleashed.

The hysteria that unfurled was spectacular. The interview even managed to raise an extreme right activist out of retirement in order to write one more e-mail to his faithful followers – an e-mail that mysteriously made its way to many of our church parishioners. He demanded that my husband should keep his wife "under control" – a violent rhetoric that seemed to find support from many others based on the e-mails and letters we both received. After several unpleasant confrontations and conversations, I became hesitant to darken the doors of the church. Until that day I had a lot of sympathy for people who found their lives consumed by anxiety, but this was the season when my sympathy became empathy. I had never known the crippling effect of anxiety until I became the focal point of the angry religious faithful. My earnest prayer became, "Lord, save me from Your followers."

Once you break any sacred tribal rules of conduct and belonging, you often find yourself at the blunt end of a tribe's most devastating weapon: shame. Elizabeth Gilbert writes:

---

6. http://insideexgay.org.
7. Farrah Tomazin, "I Am Profoundly Unsettled: Inside the Hidden World of Gay Conversion Therapy," https://www.smh.com.au/national/i-am-profoundly-unsettled-inside-the-hidden-world-of-gay-conversion-therapy-20180227-p4z1xn.html.

Shame is the most powerful and degrading tool that a tribe has at its disposal. Shame is the nuclear option. Shame is how they keep you in line. Shame is how they let you know that you have abandoned the collective. Violence may be fast and brutal, but shame is slow . . . but still brutal.[8]

The interview created the final rift. Friends I had known for years stopped speaking to me. The pain was overwhelming. I let go of the trapeze bar and found myself free falling into liminal space.

Escaping the Matrix

It is hard to recognize the kindness and mercy of Providence when your soul seems to convulse with heartache. These days I can see it much more clearly. It was mercy that led me to the shadows and the margins. C.S. Lewis writes, "My idea of God is not a divine idea. It has to be shattered from time to time. He shatters it Himself. He is the great Iconoclast. Could we not almost say that this shattering is one of the marks of His presence?"[9] My fervently constructed ideas of God and church lay shattered. I looked at the pieces and knew there was no rebuilding – I had to let it all go. Yet it is so hard to trust that letting go process.

As David Foster Wallace wrote, "Everything I've ever let go has claw marks on it." Liminality is the ultimate life lesson in trust. We do not choose to trust – we simply have to trust. I do not think anyone intentionally throws themselves down some random rabbit hole in order to experience this other dimension of their own free will – all that appears too risky and too painful. Rather, we are thrust down there through crisis or suffering – a moment when there is a glitch in our matrix, when the ocean comes calling and we cannot go back.

For thirty years I had kept the oceans of mystery and paradox at bay. The niggling doubts, the contradictions, the many questions that I used to wave to from a far and safe distance suddenly loomed like a tidal wave above me. The ocean was no longer friendly. It had invaded my life and turned my world upside down. This poem became my metaphor and mantra through this flood-filled time:

I built my house by the sea.
Not on the sands, mind you,
Not on the shifting sand.

---

8. https://www.facebook.com/GilbertLiz/posts/806653502750100:0.
9. C.S. Lewis, "A Grief Observed," quoted in Sheila Cassidy, *Sharing the Darkness*, Maryknoll, NY: Orbis Books, 1991.

And I built it of rock.
A strong house
By a strong sea.
And we got well acquainted, the sea and I.
Good neighbours.
Not that we spoke much.
We met in silences,
Respectful, keeping our distance
But looking at our thoughts across the fence of sand.
Always the fence of sand our barrier,
Always the sand between.

And then one day
(and I still don't know how it happened)
The sea came.
Without warning.
Without welcome even.
Not sudden and swift, but a shifting across the sand like wine,
Less like the flow of water than the flow of blood.
Slow, but flowing like an open wound.
And I thought of flight, and I thought of drowning, and I thought of death.
But while I thought, the sea crept higher till it reached my door.
And I knew that there was neither flight nor death nor drowning.
That when the sea comes calling you stop being good neighbours,
Well acquainted, friendly from a distance neighbours.
And you give your house for a coral castle
And you learn to breathe under water.

                    Carol Bialeck, RSCJ[10]

There is a moment in the film version of Tolkien's *Lord of the Rings* when
Gandalf, having slain the Balrog, lies lifeless on the rock face, drifting in
nothingness – and then he takes a deep breath and returns to Middle Earth,
forever changed. I remember the day when I returned to Middle Earth –
the day I took that breath underwater that Bialeck describes, and despite
the pain, knew I would go on.

It was the observation of a friend that brought me back from the house
of sadness. "Nic, I don't even pretend to understand what this must all feel
like, but as your friend I can tell you that the world and structure you were
part of is really, really small. Your world is about to get so much bigger." He
was right. Falling into liminality was about letting go of so much. I do not

---

10. Quoted in Cassidy, *Sharing the Darkness*.

want to downplay the grief associated with the loss I experienced. It felt as if I was saying goodbye to something or someone else nearly every day. But I was also saying hello – to a new world, to new friends, and to a whole new way of being. I had jumped on a ferry that was pulling away from my tribal and ideological island, and every day that island becomes smaller and the universe becomes vaster and more spectacular.

Betwixt and Between

A couple of years down the track, my husband and I find ourselves living in the lush hinterland of the Sunshine Coast in Queensland, Australia. A "green womb" was how a friend described our home. We are very much removed from the structured, differentiated, and hierarchical system that shaped the first half of our life together. We put two states, and two thousand kilometres, between where we live now and the social structure we left behind. It has been a time of healing, detoxifying, learning to breathe again, and acclimatizing to a whole new and glorious world. There is a sense of standing on a threshold, "betwixt and between," as Victor Turner once described liminality.[11] According to Turner, it is temporal space – the midpoint between a starting point and an ending point. It holds the idea of temporarily having fallen between the cracks of social structure. However, I would tend to agree with the wisdom of a friend who remarked that our whole life is a liminal space. It is a way of being in this world, a lens for looking at life.

This gift of liminality, presented to me wrapped in pain, exile, and humiliation, has assisted me in recognizing many of my ego's trappings and yearnings. In this place I have been confronted and stripped of much of the baggage that I carried over the years and of trying to live up to all sorts of expectations. I had been continually feeding a need to be the "good girl." Liminality, like the character V in the film *V for Vendetta*, simply showed me the bars of my ideological and structural prison, all dressed up in religious moralizing – and once you see, you cannot un-see.

I also experienced a reunion with old friends I had left behind when entering my idea of structural utopia all those years ago. One of them was the joy of not knowing, and the other was the delight of wonder. That most ignored and banished exile of fundamentalism, wonder, has returned to me. Tentative at first, and then, detecting a safe place, she brought her suitcases and moved in. Every day she delights me with her songs. Every day she teaches me to return her gaze and open my eyes.

---

11. Turner, "Betwixt and Between," https://brunel.rl.talis.com/items/FC0877AE-B1 34-D5B3-FD41-E1C2D991F889.html.

Liminality has also changed my taste for music. There is a new rhythm: an unforced rhythm of grace that is now free from being reduced to a necessary tick on our doctrinal boxes of orthodoxy – something that is tangible, warm, comforting, strong, and relentless. Like a sunrise in slow motion, it suddenly dawns on me: all is grace! In this place of the great unknowing I, like Jacob of old, suddenly recognize what my head once knew but now my heart confirms: "You have been here all along and I was not aware of it!"

So, Dear Liminal Traveler, I offer you my story in the hope it will bring you a sense of connection to the many others who, like you, may have fallen down the rabbit hole. For me liminality is the "thin space" of which the Celts have spoken, the rabbit hole where the door between this world and the next is cracked open for a moment, a most uncomfortable place that the world around us often fails to understand. May you be present in it, for it is indeed a most confusing sacrament and gift. Holy.

> Don't surrender your loneliness
> So quickly.
> Let it cut more deeply.
>
> Let it ferment and season you
> As few humans
> Or even divine ingredients can.
>
> Something missing in my heart tonight
> Has made my eyes so soft,
> My voice
> So tender,
>
> My need of God
> Absolutely
> Clear.
>
>   Hafiz

12

Intersections, Kairos, and Cyborgs

Adam Pryor

Though long assumed at odds, theology and science has become a robust field of study, growing up in the space between formal disciplines. But rather than explaining how a scholar brings two fields together methodologically, I interpret theology and science in terms of an animating trajectory in which theology and science research seeks to re-enchant our experience of the world. Scholars have established that scientific facts need not threaten the process of religious meaning making. Nor are we restricted to hard and fast models of independence – isolating religious belief from the realm of the "real" world science dutifully studied in its workings. At its best, theology and science research (regardless of the religious sensibility informing the theological reflection) is a particular type of public theology engaged in a process of worldview formation.

Theology and science research as a field has had a broader intention in its history, particularly insofar as it is public facing; as it is committed to interpreting sets of religious symbols as a means to ordering existence in congruence with ultimacy,[1] it summons us to a particular way of being in the world with others that constrains how we might live humanly together.[2] In this way, symbols speak to a primordial sphere of vulnerable relationality – a co-constituting, interhuman depth.[3] The relevance and potential meaning of this primordial sensibility communicated by symbols cannot be restricted to any singular, originating community: thus, the public quality of such a theological approach.

---

1. See also Robert Cummings Neville, *Ultimates: Philosophical Theology, Vol. 1* (Albany: SUNY Press, 2013), 15.
2. See Edward Farley, *Deep Symbols: Their Postmodern Effacement and Reclamation* (Valley Forge, PA: Trinity Press International, 1996), 3-4, 113-15, and 126, ns 4-6.
3. Ibid., 4-6 and 21-23.

Liminal phenomena can provide potent symbols for this public approach to theology and science research. Specifically, liminal phenomena represent kairotic moments in the midst of our everydayness. These moments convey an experience of the divine that challenges our assumptions about what it means to be a self in the midst of the wider world: to understand our ontological status of "being-with" such that we are fundamentally "betwixt and between."

Liminality and Being-With

In Victor Turner's descriptions of liminality, he draws a fascinating connection to Martin Buber's now famous concept of the I-Thou relationship. The connection to Buber provides an existential grounding to Turner's terms: it locates them in wider existential or phenomenological categories that would be familiar to theology and science researchers. Locating liminality in relationship to existing categories used in theology and science research provides a ready-made way to incorporate liminality as a concept.[4] For instance, in describing liminality Turner writes:

> The attributes of liminality or of liminal personae ("threshold people") are necessarily ambiguous, since this condition and these persons elude or slip through the network of classifications that normally locate states and positions in cultural space. Liminal entities are neither here nor there; they are betwixt and between the positions assigned and arrayed by law, custom, convention, and ceremonial.[5]

The liminal is this space between; it is a state in which the classifications of the everyday are bracketed to reveal an alternative order, a more basic relatedness, which undergirds the everyday power and position exemplified by given cultural norms. When this experience of liminality is consciously recognized, it has an event structure; it is what we might call a "happening" in various forms of philosophical theology. In the liminal event, a dynamic interplay emerges that disrupts or dislocates everyday sensibilities about individuality, socio-spatial borders of convention, and clearly identifiable cultural roles.

It is this dynamism that parallels Buber's account of the I-Thou relationship. For Buber, the experience of relationship – as a "happening" – occurs as a direct and immediate encounter between individuals wherein each recognizes the other as a complete and concrete person. Neither one subsumes

---

4. It could even be argued that Buber's existential work on the I-Thou relationship is what gives philosophical grounding to Turner's reflections on liminality and communitas as expressions of a relational ontology of co-existence. I have not found any research that makes this case specifically.

5. Victor W. Turner, *The Ritual Process: Structure and Anti-Structure* (New Brunswick: Aldine Transaction Publishers, 2011), 95.

the other to a wider universal category.[6] The I-Thou relationship represents the co-constitutive power of a wholly subject-to-subject relationship. Of course, Buber famously contrasts this I-Thou relation to the attitude of an I-It existence in which the other is objectified.[7] Crucially, though, in neither pairing can we separate the sense of "I" from its partnered term; when we use the term "I" it stands as a shorthand for one of these pairings.[8]

6. See also Robert E. Wood, *Martin Buber's Ontology: An Analysis of I and Thou*, Northwestern University Studies in Phenomenology & Existential Philosophy (Evanston: Northwestern University Press, 1969), 38.

7. For a helpful, basic introduction to Buber's work, see Sarah Scott, "Martin Buber," Internet Encyclopedia of Philosophy, accessed 3 February 2018, http://www.iep.utm.edu/buber/#SH2b. Of course, the seminal descriptions of these relationships, particularly as they are conditioned by the eternal, appear in Martin Buber, *I And Thou*, trans. Walter Kaufmann (New York: Touchstone, 1971)."number-of-pages":"192","source":"Amazon","event-place":"New York","abstract":"Martin Buber's *I and Thou* has long been acclaimed as a classic. Many prominent writers have acknowledged its influence on their work; students of intellectual history consider it a landmark; and the generation born since World War II considers Buber as one of its prophets. The need for a new English translation has been felt for many years. The old version was marred by many inaccuracies and misunderstandings, and its recurrent use of the archaic \"thou\" was seriously misleading. Now Professor Walter Kaufmann, a distinguished writer and philosopher in his own right who was close to Buber, has retranslated the work at the request of Buber's family. He has added a wealth of informative footnotes to clarify obscurities and bring the reader closer to the original, and he has written a long \"Prologue\" that opens up new perspectives on the book and on Buber's thought. This volume should provide a new basis for all future discussions of Buber.","ISBN":"978-0-684-71725-8","language":"English","author":[{"family":"Buber","given":"Martin"}],"translator":[{"family":"Kaufmann","given":"Walter"}],"issued":{"date-parts":[["1971",2,1]]}}}],"schema":"https://github.com/citation-style-language/schema/raw/master/csl-citation.json"}

8. This point is stressed repeatedly by Buber. See *I And Thou*, 3-4, 21-22, 62, 66-67, and 70."number-of-pages":"192","source":"Amazon","event-place":"New York","abstract":"Martin Buber's I and Thou has long been acclaimed as a classic. Many prominent writers have acknowledged its influence on their work; students of intellectual history consider it a landmark; and the generation born since World War II considers Buber as one of its prophets. The need for a new English translation has been felt for many years. The old version was marred by many inaccuracies and misunderstandings, and its recurrent use of the archaic \"thou\" was seriously misleading. Now Professor Walter Kaufmann, a distinguished writer and philosopher in his own right who was close to Buber, has retranslated the work at the request of Buber's family. He has added a wealth of informative footnotes to clarify obscurities and bring the reader closer to the original, and he has written a long \"Prologue\" that opens up new perspectives on the book and on Buber's thought. This volume should provide a new basis for all future discussions of Buber.","ISBN":"978-0-684-71725-8","language":"English","author":[{"family":"Buber","given":"Martin"}],"translator":[{"family":"Kaufmann","given":"Walter"}],"issued":{"date-parts":[["1971",2,1]]}},"locator":"3-4, 21-22, 62, 66-67, and 70","suppress-author":true,"prefix":"This point is stressed repeatedly by Buber. See"}],"schema":"https://github.com/citation-style-language/schema/raw/master/csl-citation.json"}

When the equality of the I-Thou relationship, where each is a person of dignity before the other, is extended beyond strictly binary relationships, one I and one Thou, the "essential We" begins to emerge.[9] The community of the "essential We" is one in which each person exists solely in I-Thou relationships to the host of other people who are part of the community. As soon as one member of the community violates the spirit of the I-Thou relation in its fundamental respect for the dignified subjectivity of the other, the "essential We" begins to break apart.[10]

The mutual dignity of the I-Thou relationship creates a feeling of betweenness and belonging to one another. Whether describing the I-Thou, the "essential We," or the liminal phenomenon, Turner's foundational work indicates that liminality provides an experience not of solitary being, but an original way of being-with.[11] Liminality is an entry point to describing a minimal ontological premise; it describes the originating and universal experience of existent being as fundamentally an in-between phenomenon. For public-facing theology and science research, this point is crucial in that it locates liminality in a wider tradition of philosophical theology.

For instance, interpreted this way liminality prefigures Jean-Luc Nancy's compelling parallel argument in *Being Singular Plural*, namely, that our being in the world is always a form of being-with that determines our existence from the start. Or, it offers a similar parallel to Martin Heidegger's recognition that there is no being-in-the-world without "being-with" one another.[12] Liminality could denote the fleeting experience of the *mitsein*, being singular/plural, the I-Thou, the chiasmic flesh, relational being, theopoiesis, agentive realism, or processual experience that, when understood, theologically emphasizes the pre-eminence of panentheism. These approaches stress the primacy of relationship to religious or theological thinking because it is through relationality as a fundamental, if impermanent, mode of our experiencing that the divine is made manifest in the midst of the world. Instances of liminality are the symbolic spaces where the premise of ontological relationality is manifest.

9. Buber stresses that this "we" is not simple collectivism – a conglomeration of individuals. See *Between Man and Man* (Mansfield Centre, CT: Martino Fine Books, 2014), chap. 5.
10. Others have noted the importance of this concept for anthropology and sociology. See, for instance, Maurice Friedman, "The Interhuman and What Is Common to All: Martin Buber and Sociology," *Journal for the Theory of Social Behaviour* 29, no. 4 (1 December 1999), 403-17, https://doi.org/10.1111/1468-5914.00110.
11. This is the *Zwischenmenschliche* that Turner twice identifies as the critical piece of Buber's thinking for his own work. See *The Ritual Process* (2011), 127 and 136.
12. Martin Heidegger, *Being and Time*, trans. John Macquarie and Edward Robinson, Reprint (New York: Harper Perennial Modern Classics, 2008), secs. 25-27.

Religion and Science as Discovering Moments of Liminality

Theology and science research are in the business of re-enchanting our experience of the natural world.[13] At its best, this would entail equipping individuals to discover experiences of liminality in the world around them and providing a framework for analyzing those experiences to become more aware of our grounding in relationality. Within the Christian tradition, these moments of discovery or re-enchantment have been called kairos moments.

For Paul Tillich there were three theological conceptualizations of time: *kairos*, *chronos*, and *eschatos*. Kairos refers to an in-breaking of eternity. It is a moment of opportunity, a qualitative time of an "event" or "happening," designating a special time in history that reorders our subsequent experience.[14] The kairos moment is specifically an event in which the ambiguities of life's station and status are overcome in an experience that manifests the unifying power of the Spirit of God.[15] It is an experience of ultimacy to which all other moments of time might be subjected.

Theologians usually contrast kairos with chronos. Chronos describes the quotidian experience of time. Specifically, we understand kairos as the "right" time and chronos as "formal" time, or kairos as qualitatively fulfilled and chronos as an expression of quantitative measurement.[16] There is a dialectical movement between these two. Kairos moments are meant to condition the ongoing action of chronos. Chronos time is the scale of history on which our decisions are played out, made manifest in the kairos moment. The kairos moment remains fleeting, though, and its permanent fulfillment in the ordinary history of chronos time is impossible.[17] The dialectic of these two remains inherently incomplete, provisional, and in need of persistent reinterpretation.

---

13. Implicitly, I am also suggesting that religion and science research should *not* be primarily pursued, or interpreted, as a form of confessional apologetics: offering a defense of specific religious doctrines in light of scientific discoveries.
14. See also Mary Ann Stenger and Ronald H. Stone, *Dialogues of Paul Tillich* (Macon, GA: Mercer University Press, 2002), 168ff. The approach I am outlining with regard to these three terms is heavily influenced by Tillich's approach, though it is not exactly the same as that found in the final section of Tillich's *Systematic Theology*.
15. Paul Tillich, *Systematic Theology, Vol. 3* (Chicago: University of Chicago Press, 1963), 369-72.
16. Paul Tillich, *The Protestant Era* (Chicago: University Of Chicago Press, 1948), 32.
17. Paul Tillich, *Political Expectation*, ed. James Luther Adams (Macon, GA: Mercer University Press, 1981), 179.

Eschatos can then be understood as the sense of time against which the dialectic of kairos and chronos is to be judged: it is what Ted Peters calls an *adventus* (a teleological aim of history that draws us from the future) instead of a mere *futurum* (the future characterized as the upcoming series of events in chronos time).[18] Eschatos should not be understood as being removed from that dialectic of kairos and chronos, but rather serves as a proleptic anticipation of realizing the fullness of the unconditional made manifest in the kairos moment, thereby continually drawing the time of chronos toward this hope.

This drawing is accomplished by co-presence: where an eschatological moment is distinct but non-separable in its relation to a moment in our current experience. The eschatologically significant, proleptic event is co-present to every moment in our daily experience (i.e. it subtends all of chronos time). A kairos moment is one where this co-presence of the eschatological is available to our awareness; it makes some new understanding of the dynamic force of God's presence to history possible. Herein the dynamic co-presence of the eschatos entangles with our present experience, which then conditions what we experience as the future possibilities of chronos time.

If we adopt this framework of kairos, chronos and eschatos, there is an interesting resonance with liminality. The experience of liminality is a kairos event. It is a moment where the entangled co-presence of the divine as eschatos reveals itself through the betweenness of the liminal event. In short, the liminal reveals a divine hope for realizing our fundamental relationality that is so often covered over in our everyday experiences. This kairotic break of the liminal into the structure of chronos then draws us toward a transformed future.

Cyborg Bodies as Exemplars of Being-With

One example of theology and science research that engages with the liminal domain is the cyborg body, set between our inherited categories. The

---

18. There are a number of theoretical constructs I am employing here from proleptic approaches to eschatology in Christian theology. The most important would include: Jürgen Moltmann, *God in Creation*, trans. Margaret Kohl (Minneapolis: Fortress Press, 1993), chap. 5; Ted Peters, *God, the World's Future: Systematic Theology for a New Era*, 2nd ed. (Minneapolis: Fortress Press, 2000), 319-21; Robert John Russell, *Time in Eternity: Pannenberg, Physics, and Eschatology in Creative Mutual Interaction* (Notre Dame, IN: University of Notre Dame Press, 2012), chaps. 2 & 3. Russell's account of co-presence as a means of integrating time *into* eternity is the most critical insight because it gives a specific way of integrating kairos and eschatos.

stable, fixed notion of a "natural" body separate from its world, bounding what is legitimately me (subject) as distinct from everything else (object), is antiquated in light of the posthuman.[19]

The cyborg body makes this clear insofar as it blatantly blurs these boundaries of subject and object, specifically the boundary between organism and machine. Succinctly, a cyborg body is one in which the activity and interplay between human beings and technology affects individual agency. In the cyborg body there is a technological amendment of the body that opens up new freedoms and manifestations of agency.[20]

When most of us think of cyborgs, it is the wild imagination of science-fiction that comes to mind. Perhaps we imagine the Borg from *Star Trek*, hacked bodies from *Deus Ex*, artificial intelligence becoming human in *Electric Dreams*, or superheroes like the Atom whose powers come from drastic technological development. Given the definition I have offered above, however, cyborgs need not be so fanciful. In fact, a cyborg could be living next door to you without you even realizing it. For instance, my daughter seems a little like a cyborg based on this definition. She recently learned to swing a baseball bat. At first, the bat was foreign to her, an object in the world that stood against her body. Gradually, with practice and time, she has come to swing the bat more naturally – to experience it as an extension of her arms and hands in hitting a baseball. Even more simply, we could claim the regular use of shoes might make each of us into cyborgs. Shoes are basic technology whose interplay with our bodies opens up new freedoms (an ability to walk over different terrains more easily for longer periods of time) and possibilities for our relationship to the world.

In both cases, a bodily attunement between self and worldly technology blurs the border between my sense of "me" and "not-me." It is important to emphasize that, even in this radically intimate action of incorporation, the cyborg body is not simply contiguous with the wider environment. There is not a merger but a hybridity: throwing askew our well-bounded concepts of what constitutes the self as distinct from the wider environment or "nature" in which a cyborg body is situated. Yet, in this proximity of hybridity there remains a separation – a distance (what Buber would have called *Urdistanz*) without which the proximity would not be possible and

19. My work is making use of a critical distinction between posthumanist and transhumanist accounts of cyborg hybridity and only deals with the posthumanist account. See Jeanine Thweatt-Bates, *Cyborg Selves: A Theological Anthropology of the Posthuman*, Ashgate Science and Religion (Farnham, Surrey and Burlington, VT: Ashgate, 2012). Parts of this section of the paper also appear in a different format in Adam Pryor, *Body of Christ Incarnate for You: Conceptualizing God's Desire for the Flesh*, Studies in Body and Religion Series (Lanham, MD: Lexington 2016), chap. 7.

20. Thweatt-Bates, *Cyborg Selves*, 19.

only fusion would occur. Instead, posthumanist accounts of the cyborg affirm an understanding of technologies as tricky agents with which our bodies reveal tentative and shifting relationships that are formative both of ourselves and the world we inhabit.

This experience of bodily extension and incorporation of the world reveals a liminal "betweenness." The single individual is not a solitary ego standing against the world as a series of objects that threatens to dissociate any sense of distinctive self. [21] Instead, in these liminal instances of bodily extension and incorporation there is a recognition of the flexibility of our bodily boundaries. We experience ourselves in terms of a lived wholeness of self and technology characteristic of Buber's I-Thou relation instead of an I-It relation. [22] The technology is no longer a tool enabling us to "travel over" or absorb the reality around us, persistently remaining at an objective distance from our sense of self; instead, it is experienced as something lived with, never appropriated, and complexifying the ways we can encounter the world. [23]

One may intuitively critique these two examples (swinging the bat and wearing shoes) as not being quite reflective of the cyborg. The cyborg forms an indelibly shaping relationship with technology that is highly somatic. [24] While my daughter may put down the bat when she is done

---

21. Martin Buber, *Die Frage an den Einzelnen*, Martin Buber Werke, vol. 1 (München: Kösel-Verlag, 1962), 221-25. Here Buber contrasts *der Einzige* as "the only one" associated with the radical egoism of Max Stirner as a characterization of the I-It relation, and *Die Einzelne* "the single individual" associated with Søren Kierkegaard as characterization of the I-Thou relation.

22. To claim an I-Thou relationship with technology does not violate the spirit of Buber's argument, which gives numerous examples of I-Thou relationships with various non-conscious living things. This may require the "lively" quality of technology. Addressing this issue goes beyond the scope of this chapter, but it has been well theorized by others such as Anne Kull in her works, "The Cyborg as an Interpretation of Culture-Nature," *Zygon* 36, no. 1 (March 2001), 49-56, and "Speaking Cyborg: Technoculture and Technonature," *Zygon* 37, no. 2 (June 2002), 279-87.

23. I am relying here on a distinction in German that Buber employs but is not necessarily clear in English translation. To describe the experience of the I-It relationship, Buber uses *Erfahrung*. However, to describe the experience of the I-Thou relationship, Buber uses *Erlebnis*. There is a rich distinction between these two terms in various German philosophical traditions. See Buber, *Ich Und Du*, Martin Buber Werke, vol. 1 (München: Kösel-Verlag, 1962), 80-91.

24. Thweatt-Bates, *Cyborg Selves*, 142-49. Her reconfiguring of Wesley Wildman's metaphor for human beings as "walking, thinking ecologies" is particularly apt (146). See also Wildman, "Distributed Identity: Human Beings as Walking, Thinking, Ecologies in the Microbial World," in *Human Identity at the Intersection of Science, Technology and Religion*, eds Nancey Murphy and Christopher C. Knight (Burlington, VT: Ashgate, 2010), 165-66.

playing baseball, or I can take of my shoes when I come in the house, the cyborg bodily attunement is more permanent. To quote Jeanine Thweatt-Bates: "This reconfiguration of human subjectivity through the increasing integration of self and environment makes this technological-biological merger an ontological, not merely practical, matter."[25]

Medical cyborgs, or human beings with self-regulating machine systems, are perhaps a better example to consider because of the more permanent nature of their technological hybridity. Here are clear examples of how blurring the boundary between organism and machine has opened new freedom and agency. Speech devices for patients with amyotrophic lateral sclerosis (ALS) are an easy example because they are so visible, personalizable (Stephen Hawking copyrighted his voice), and the effect they have is quite dramatic (enabling communication which before would have been impossible or far more difficult). However, the blurring of the machine/human boundary occurs in more subtle ways as well.

Permanent surgical mesh used in hernia repair is a good example. The permanent mesh fuses with the body, offering otherwise unimagined freedoms by enabling enhanced mobility and faster recovery. However, a fundamental dependence on the mesh as a visceral incorporation of a technology cannot be denied. The widening use of insulin pumps is a good example as well: a machine regulates the regular release of a synthetic hormone that allows diabetics increased freedom in their daily lives.

What the cyborg body can reveal in terms of liminality is put well in the question that Donna Haraway asks so provocatively in her "Cyborg Manifesto:" "Why should our bodies end at the skin or include at best other beings encapsulated by skin?"[26] Thinking with cyborg bodies calls for recognizing an "attunement" whereby the body incorporates the world around it in a permanent or semi-permanent fashion such that thinking of our bodies in terms of a fixed, dermal boundary is made more notably arbitrary. This resonates with Haraway's further insight that all incarnation, the shape of our bodily space in the world, is prosthetic.[27] We construct our sense of body betwixt and between the blurry borders of self and world; cyborg bodies just make this construction more noticeable.

The bodily attunement of the cyborg is a liminal phenomenon that can be kairotic, opening us to a new way of relating in the world that can otherwise remain latent or hidden. The technological enhancement of cyborg

25. Thweatt-Bates, *Cyborg Selves*, 21.
26. Donna Haraway, "A Cyborg Manifesto: Science, Technology, and Socialist-Feminism in the Late Twentieth Century," in *Simians, Cyborgs, and Women: The Reinvention of Nature* (New York: Routledge, 1991), 178.
27. Ibid., 180.

bodies implies a wider breakdown of traditional boundaries (indicative of its liminality), reconfiguring conceptions of human subjectivity and environment. The incorporation of technologies to the cyborg body is fundamentally an experience of liminality that re-enchants our sense of the world by calling us to pay careful attention to the porous border between self and world that is our body. This makes us aware of a fundamental relationality that prevents any simple objectification of self and world into distinctive categories.

More specifically, the cyborg body opens us to a subtending power of being-with the technologies of the world, that makes these technologies into more than a tool for our use as subjects. In the cyborg body, technology is not governed by the pattern of I-It relations, but of a liminal I-Thou encounter. This subtending power of being-with manifest in liminality is also eschatologically significant as a form of co-presence. It expresses a hoped-for, proleptic, unconditional respect of authentic and freeing encounters that is itself a manifestation of divine encounter without becoming mired in the objectification of the I-It relation. Taken this way, the betweenness of the cyborg body is kairotic, making us aware of this subtending eschatos where our sense of being-with is no longer threatening to the integrity of our selfhood. Recognition of this minimal ontological premise can then transform our experience of chronos time. As symbol, the liminal body of the cyborg represents a norm for our continued engagement with technology in terms of I-Thou relationships. It encourages the pursuit of a future that frees us to recognize the depth of our mutual interdependence with the world in increasingly complex ways.

There is an important caveat to all of this, though. The attunements of the cyborg body must not be pursued in service of realizing a mythical, natural wholeness. The prosthetic incarnation of Haraway must give way to what Sharon Betcher calls "prosthetic erratics:" a stitching together of body and machine unconstrained by unspoken normativity.[28] In this regard, disability theology is a critical dialogue partner. It looks to those who take up prostheses, thereby incorporating technology into their bodily spaces, each day. Taking the experience of bodily attunement in disability theology seriously draws the cyborg futurist back from any transcendent dream of enhancing the body towards the realization of some (mythical) perfect body.[29]

Nancy Eiesland expresses this need for disability theology well: "Unless the notion of embodiment is deliberately deconstructed, the cultural norms of 'body as natural' seep into the subtext;" we can lose sight of "the 'mixed blessing' of the body in the real, lived experience of people with disabilities" who help us imagine how to "explicitly deconstruct any norms which are

---

28. Sharon V. Betcher, *Spirit and the Politics of Disablement* (Minneapolis: Fortress Press, 2007), 102ff.
29. Thweatt-Bates, *Cyborg Selves*, 155ff.

part of the unexpressed agenda of 'normal embodiment.'"[30] Eiesland's examination of the narratives of Dianne DeVries and Nancy Mairs is then helpful in pursuing this end.[31] For both DeVries and Mairs the presentation of their body space includes devices and technologies that confound any sense of a normalizing body pattern.

For DeVries this took the shape of persistently rejecting prosthetic devices from childhood that facilitated the "normalcy" of bipedal, upright movement in favor of functional devices. As Eiesland aptly notes, DeVries is truly subversive with her subtle linguistic shifts: referring to the battery pack for her wheelchair as her legs or moving her wheelchair as walking.[32] For Mairs, this incorporation is slightly different and she describes it developmentally, which matches the progressive changes to her body space that accompany the onset of multiple sclerosis. Her account says not so much about adaption and linguistic subversion of normalizing body patterns, but concentrates on what is revealed about human experience through the lived experience of her own body as it incorporates "insensate" technologies. Here too, though, the bodily awareness is tied to functional adaptation – physical and social adaptation.[33]

These examples further reveal that the body is mutable; it is not well described by a natural wholeness or senses of normativity. The skin is not a divisive barrier, cordoning us off from the environment and technologies around us. Instead, the body is cyborg; its incarnation is prosthetic as it incorporates technologies that augment functionality in the world around it. However, appreciating the importance of this hybridity, and thereby also the kairotic potential of this liminal phenomena, requires a shift in beliefs about the incorporation of technology in order to embrace the idea of cyborg existence.

---

30. Nancy L. Eiesland, *The Disabled God: Toward a Liberatory Theology of Disability* (Nashville: Abingdon Press, 1994), 22.

31. Ibid., 47: "[T]he narratives highlight an alternative understanding of embodiment, recognizing it as an intricate interweaving of physical sensations and emotional attachments, irrespective of socially constructed notions of 'normal' bodies or 'appropriate' relations. DeVries and Mairs include as integral parts of their bodies braces and wheelchairs. Both rely on close relationships to increase their own sense of body. Their experiences reveal painstaking processes of putting themselves together using whatever resources that are available. In contrast to romantic notions of 'natural' embodiment, both discuss embodying technology. Some devices, for example, wheelchairs and braces, are integrated into their body awareness, while other appliances that frustrate their sense of body are rejected."

32. Ibid., 37-38; referencing Geyla Frank, "On Embodiment: A Case Study of Congenital Limb Deficiency in American Culture," in *Women with Disabilities*, ed. M. Fine and A. Asch (Philadelphia: Temple University Press, 1988), 51.

33. Eiesland, *The Disabled God*, 43-44; referencing Nancy Mairs, *Carnal Acts* (New York: Harper Collins, 1990), 111, and *Ordinary Time: Cycles in Marriage, Faith and Renewal* (Boston: Beacon Press, 1993), 167-68.

In this regard, the critical critique Sharon Betcher offers of the cyborg is invaluable. Speaking from her own experience with leg prostheses, she observes the body patterns that are too often reinforced by the cyborg. As she eloquently puts it:

> That this unveiling (of the donut hole of my limb loss), rather than the curious, cosmetically covered endoskeletal structure standing in for my leg, should throw off the light switch of desire is a clue for me that Haraway's analysis may be slightly off course. When considering inclusion among the human community, the cyborg's machine/human interface seems not to be as troubling as a prosthetically unprosthelytized body – a disabled body refusing social comeliness or seemliness.[34]

If the prosthetic limb covers over a social disgust and discomfort, then Betcher fears that thinking about the cyborg inadvertently re-inscribes a sense of bodily holism and wholesomeness. Betcher admits that this is certainly not an organic wholeness, but rightfully fears that the fusion of organism and machine covers, instead of (dis)covers, the somatic realities and discourses of real bodies using prosthetics most akin to the cyborg.[35] Betcher's critique is crucial to keep in mind because the hybridity of the cyborg will be lost if the technology with which we are fused is merely passive: if nature and technology are even remotely thought of as tools to approximate a prevenient wholeness, or even a means of enhancing a natural wholeness, then we simply return to a social problematic about the use of these tools and what counts as natural. When this sense of hybridity is lost, the cyborg body is not experienced in its liminality, thus silencing the potential it opens as a kairotic event expressing an eschatological co-presence of the divine.

The cyborg body is but one example of the many liminal spaces between theology and science that have yet to be explored. Emergence theory, studies of mutualism, astrobiology, deep ecology, and environmental ethics all provide rich areas of theology and science research where boundaries are being blurred and liminality may become an exceptionally helpful conceptual category. Connecting liminality to a theological understanding of kairos clarifies the value of this concept for theology and science research. In the liminal intersections between theology and science, kairos moments may emerge that transform ordinary time into something quite extraordinary, re-enchanting the world and revealing our sense of absolute dependence on being-with one another.

---

34. Betcher, *Spirit and the Politics of Disablement*, 97.
35. Betcher, *Spirit and the Politics of Disablement*, 99.

13
Inside the Russian Nesting Doll
Debra Jarvis

I have spent the last thirty years as a hospice and hospital chaplain. My last gig was at a cancer center where I had the dubious distinction of having my mother diagnosed with breast cancer and then a week later being diagnosed with the same cancer myself. This gave me a unique perspective, as I was suddenly a professional, a patient's family member, and a patient all at the same time.

Because I worked on an oncology floor and was familiar with breast cancer, its stages, and various treatments, I was not, like many people, seized with a paralyzing fear. Since I was able to continue my work as a chaplain while receiving treatment, my life did not change as drastically as the lives of many of my patients. I received my chemo on the same floor where I worked from the same nurses with whom I worked all day. The biggest change was that Thursday afternoons I knocked off an hour early so I could climb into a bed or chair and receive my chemo.

Pre-liminal or
"Everything Was Going Great Until . . . "

Because my experience was different from most cancer patients, I am sharing the experience of one my patients who had a more liminal experience than I did.

I had just spent a year in Malawi running a clinical trial. And then I was offered a job at a prestigious scientific institution in the U.K. My dreams were coming true. As a Ph.D. I had planned my career carefully. I connected with the right people. I worked hard. I was successful. And with this job offer I was on my way. For my

U.K. visa I had to get a chest X-ray to screen for tuberculosis. No problemo! The X-ray came back negative for tuberculosis – but positive for lung cancer. How could this be? I had never smoked a day in my life. My whole world collapsed.

Cancer is the quintessential liminal experience as it includes all the stages – pre-liminal, liminal, reintegration – and all the classic elements of the liminal journey: end of one way of life, loss of identity and status, bewilderment, confusion, ambiguity, reversal of hierarchy, uncertainty. Patients are between life as they once knew it and an uncertain future. They may go back to life with no more treatment, life with ongoing treatment or – no more life at all.

Within the liminal cancer experience is a subset of liminality – a regular Russian nesting doll of liminal experiences. After the initial diagnosis, patients wait for scans and pathology reports to come back. No test results? No treatment plan.

This is like taking a trip abroad without knowing your mode of transportation – car, train, plane, or boat? How do you know what to pack? How long will it be? Will the journey be enjoyable or intolerable? The cancer journey offers chemotherapy, surgery, radiation or any combination of the three. You cannot really prepare until you know your treatment. So, you simply have to wait.

At this point, fielding phone calls is excruciating. You find yourself saying, "I don't really know," over and over again. This uncertainty is disturbing. Well-intentioned friends and family will keep asking you what is going to happen, and instead of making you feel loved, it just makes you feel angry.

Receiving a treatment plan can give a false sense of certainty. It is like deciding, okay, we are going by car. However, what if the car breaks down or does not work? You may have to get a new car or even switch modes of transportation.

Is this the right chemotherapy? Did the radiation make a difference? Sometimes it is unclear whether the treatment is working or not, so you just have to wait and see – another nesting doll of liminality. A treatment switch means another period of liminality until you know that that particular treatment is working.

For most people, getting a cancer diagnosis brings their busy lives to a screeching halt. Instead of a day filled with work, family, and leisure activities, the day is filled with blood tests, X-rays, ultrasounds, MRIs and CT scans. They no longer watch cute cat videos but instead surf the Internet for information on their cancer. Where once a person may have been leading, teaching, explaining, he or she is now routinely bewildered and confused by the onslaught of information in an unfamiliar language.

Separation, or "Where Did Everybody Go?"

People actually avoided talking to me. I was furious. Lung cancer is not contagious, you know. I didn't know what to do about my new job because I didn't know how long I'd be in treatment. I didn't know if I could even be cured. My doctor friends kept saying how lucky I was that they found it early. That pissed me off. I didn't feel lucky about any of this.

Getting a cancer diagnosis marks you, it separates you. People avoid you because they think cancer equals death and we hate thinking or talking about death. Talking to you will cause others to think about death – yours and, even worse, theirs.

So, people avoid you because, first, they are uncomfortable with death and, second, they do not know what to say and how to behave. They forget you are their friend/relative/neighbor with a disease and instead see you as disease with a person attached.

You have cancer and you may look the same today as you did yesterday. However, you do not feel the same and will never be the same. Everything has changed. Here is the contradiction: outwardly – the same; inwardly – a mass of confusing emotions.

The Cancer Bill of Rites

At last they came up with a treatment plan: chemotherapy. But I still felt like I was in a holding pattern. I wanted my old life back or a new life that was anything but this. This just seemed like hell to me.

Once you get your treatment plan, the journey through liminality continues, and, as with other liminal experiences, it is disorienting, paradoxical, and ambiguous. Nevertheless, at least it gets you out of the No-Clue Zone. You have a few clues – but not many.

Now is when you enter into liminal ritual. A liminal ritual is described as that which follows a prescribed sequence where each person involved knows exactly what to do and how to do it. Everything must also be done under someone who is considered to be the authoritative master. Welcome to the chemo suite, your nurses, and your oncologist.

Ritual #1: Checking In

At the desk they will ask your name and birth date and whether you still live at your address. They ask you this every time. Then they make a plastic band and fasten it around your wrist. You are now officially a Patient.

Ritual #2: The Calling

You then sit and wait in the waiting area. Patients have described this experience to me in many ways.

"It's like waiting for your father to come home after your mother has already spanked you."

"It's like waiting outside the principal's office."

"It's like being on Death Row."

Nobody likes it.

Finally, you are called from the waiting room into the chemo suite itself. You know other people are watching you because you can feel the Pity Rays emanating from their eyes.

Ritual #3: The Placement

You may be in an upholstered chemo chair or you may be in a bed. Either one is the Holiest of Holies. All must perform a mandatory purification ritual. As they enter and exit, everyone washes his or her hands with soap and water at the sink or makes a pilgrimage to the wall for sanitizing hand gel.

Wacky and Witless and Weird, Oh My!

Many rules are different in this Chemo Underworld. You must leave your shoes on while lying on the clean white sheets. Wearing shoes in bed – it goes against everything your mother taught you. The rationale for shoe-wearing is that you might just hop out of bed in your stocking feet and step on something objectionable or run to the bathroom barefoot, the thought of which, is unspeakable.

It's a world of opposites. When your nurses ask about you, they do not want the usual, "Fine, thank you, and you?" Medical care providers will have none of it. They want details – your energy level, the intensity of your pain, the state of your fingernails, how you are sleeping, what you are eating, your bowel movements – if, when, and how often you have them. They ask you this – every time.

Good King Status Loss

Social status means little or nothing when you are in the chemo suite – unless you are an Arab prince. Seriously. We had one in for a stem cell transplant and the clinic was crawling with bodyguards and private nurses. Most of the time, however, you would not know a laborer from a lawyer.

I felt as if I were a child again – being told what to do, where to go and being too tired to protest. I was used to being the expert, giving presentations, teaching, knowing. But all that was gone. One day, while waiting for a procedure, they sent me into a small waiting room where three other people were waiting – all of us bald and in gowns. We could have been the Queen of England, Jesus Christ, Einstein, and Cher – but you wouldn't have known it.

Tombstone Territory

The constant uncertainty, disorientation, confusion, and ambiguity cause many to question their deepest beliefs. It is disturbing, depressing, uncomfortable – and it is great because this is where the transformation happens.

> I wasn't raised in a church but just figured there was a God and, if I was good, then I would have a good life. I believed that preparation is the key to success and happiness. I was thoughtful about where I trained and worked and taught. Everything was going just as I planned. Of course, I knew that shit happens. I just didn't think it would happen to me. I questioned everything I ever believed about my life, myself and my death.

It is precisely this surrender that precedes a breakthrough to a new kind of thinking. For most of us, a personal cancer diagnosis is the first time we think seriously about death – our own deaths. It is no longer an abstract idea, something that happens to others or happens when we are old. It is real, and it is now, and it can be paralyzing.

Dealing with cancer may be the first time we reflect on our spiritual beliefs and think about what gives our lives meaning, how we view life, what values hold our lives together.

Being in a liminal space requires a different kind of thinking in which we are willing to explore new ideas even though they may seem ridiculous, crazy or just plain wrong.

> I was furious all the time. I always got my sense of self-worth from how much I knew, what I could do, what I could achieve. What value did I have lying on a couch all day? Then one day my five-year-old niece crawled into my lap and said, "I like you better now. You're more here." It was the first time I wasn't angry about my cancer and I started to question who I was.

Life is not a nice, neat mathematical equation where everything adds up every time. We say we know this and yet we are shocked and furious when life does not present the way we expected it to. Being in a liminal place is like free falling through outer space: there is nothing to hang onto, not even a horizon we can use to orient ourselves. What a great time to question everything we have ever believed about life and death and ourselves.

If we replace dread with curiosity, the experience becomes interesting and not frightening. When we move forward with the questions, "I wonder what this will be like? Who shall I become? How will this affect my family?" it is no longer a march to the gallows but an existential expedition.

This is where "both/and" thinking comes into play. If we think that cancer is nothing but a horrible, painful experience with nothing of value, then that is what we will experience. However, it will be completely different if we can hold a creative tension between both/and and say: "Yes, this sucks *and* I will find something in this for me. There is some kind of insight, some kind of wisdom to be gained." This is deep spiritual work.

This confusing, uncomfortable liminal place is often described as a place of darkness. This is the tomb that contains not only the remains of our former selves, but also the nascent beginnings of our new selves. How do we know, however, that the walls are not going to collapse and crush us to death? The deeper we go, the scarier it gets, and we want to run toward that stone and claw at it until our fingers bleed. Nevertheless, going in is the only way out.

When we get comfortable in the dark and are inwardly still and alert, the eyes of our hearts adjust, and we can see there is something for us here. But what? We want to know. And we want to know *now*. There is, however, no rushing transformation. It is like demanding Christmas when it is only July.

This is what Rilke was talking about in his *Letters to a Young Poet:*

> Be patient toward all that is unsolved in your heart and try to love the questions themselves, like locked rooms and like books that are now written in a very foreign tongue. Do not now seek the answers, which cannot be given you because you would not be able to live them. And the point is, to live everything. Live the questions now. Perhaps you will then gradually, without noticing it, live along some distant day into the answer.[1]

His words have even greater impact now, a hundred years later, where to be uncertain is unthinkable. Where in social gatherings, "Google it!" is said more often than "Please," or "Thank you." We want to know, and we want to know now – and often we can.

Our discomfort with uncertainty is not a personal failing; we are hard-wired to avoid it. It is a survival tool. We have to be certain we can kill that animal, eat that plant, drink that water. We have to be certain our cave is safe.

---

1. Rainer Maria Rilke, *Letters to a Young Poet* (New York: W.W. Norton, 1993).

Researchers at the California Institute of Technology and the University of Iowa Medical School have carried out experiments measuring amygdala activity.[2] The amygdala is a tiny almond-shaped structure deep in our brains which is responsible for memory, survival instincts and emotions – especially fear. The researchers divided their subjects into two groups: one group was given a lot of information, one group just a small amount. Then they asked them to make decisions. The group making decisions with little information (more uncertainty) showed greater electrical activity in their amygdalas – greater fear and distress. So, it is no wonder we dislike uncertainty and lack of control.

Spiritual uncertainty is rarely appreciated. Most people do not realize that it is a pregnancy of the spirit. Something transcendent is growing inside us that we cannot yet name, we cannot yet appreciate. We want to rush to certainty, but this could be the death of that which is developing within us. Like many pregnancies it is uncomfortable. We have to allow uncertainty to gestate until we birth something sacred and amazing within ourselves.

Learning to sit with any uncomfortable feelings – uncertainty, sadness, regret, anger – can be painful but profound. We want to rush to process – emotions be gone! However, we need to welcome them all. This is what the thirteenth-century poet Jellaludin Rumi encourages us to do.

The Guest House

This being human is a guest house.
Every morning a new arrival.

A joy, a depression, a meanness,
some momentary awareness comes
as an unexpected visitor.

Welcome and entertain them all!
Even if they are a crowd of sorrows,
who violently sweep your house
empty of its furniture,
still, treat each guest honorably.
He may be clearing you out
for some new delight.

The dark thought, the shame, the malice,
meet them at the door laughing and invite them in.

---

2. Ming Hsu, Meghana Bhatt, Ralh Adolphs, Daniel Traell, and Colin F. Camerer, "Neural Systems Responding to Degrees of Uncertainty in Human Decision-Making," *Science* (9 December 2005), 1680.

Be grateful for whatever comes.
because each has been sent
as a guide from beyond.[3]

Just as we welcome a guest into our home, we must welcome every
emotion – even the painful ones. Just as we would with a guest, we invite
our emotions in, ask them to sit down, offer them a cup of tea or coffee
and ask, "So, what brings you here?" Then – and this is the difficult and
important part – we sit back and listen.

The two emotions that I encountered most in oncology patients were
anger and sadness. Initially the anger was displaced: patients were angry
with their doctors, their nurses, their spouses, me. When we got down to
the bottom of it, however, it was always anger that they had cancer at all,
that it had interrupted their lives, that it had happened to them.

I was happy being present with this anger (even when it was directed at me)
because I knew that beyond the anger was a sadness rich with possibilities.
However, sadness is a hard sell in this culture. Anger is respected because it
signifies power, might, and strength. Sadness is for the weak.

No one ever says: "See what you find in your sadness. What's there for
you?" We are unaccustomed to allowing ourselves to feel sad. We eat, drink,
drug or sex it away as quickly as possible and abort what is growing in us
waiting to be born.

Rilke assures us:

So you must not be frightened . . . if a sadness rises up before you
larger than any you have ever seen; if a restiveness, like light and
cloud-shadows, passes over your hands and over all you do. You
must think that something is happening with you, that life has not
forgotten you, that it holds you in its hand; it will not let you fall.
Why do you want to shut out of your life any agitation, any pain,
any melancholy, since you really do not know what these states are
working upon you?[4]

It is painful and often exhausting to examine our deepest held beliefs
about life and realize that perhaps, just maybe, they are not working. When
our beliefs are threatened, it is as if our very selves are threatened.

I had so much time on my hands. I tried to read or work on the
computer, but I couldn't focus. So I would just think. Imagine
that! I believed that there was something – not God exactly – but

---

3. *Jalal al-Din Rumi, Rumi: Selected Poems*, trans Coleman Barks with John Moynce,
     A.J. Arberry, and Reynold Nicholson (New York: Harper One Books, 2004), 109.
4. Rilke, *Letters to a Young Poet.*

something greater than myself. This scared me. I'm a scientist. I need proof. I wanted to talk with someone but couldn't go to my colleagues or my atheist family. I needed someone with whom I could sort out all these ideas and thoughts.

A conversation about theology – this is catnip to chaplains. It does not matter to me if there is no "theo" to the "logy," because it is a conversation about things that matter: meaning, love, life, and death. I do not have to trot out an explanation of systematic theology or explain the spirituality of Thomas Merton – it is much harder than that. I have to listen. I have to hold a safe space where the other person can question, doubt, reflect, ponder, reject, reframe. When he or she feels as if the walls of the tomb are crushing him/her, I help hold that person up. I make this place of transformation as hospitable as possible.

Let us switch metaphors for a moment. How about Noah's Ark? If that is not a place of liminality, what is? The Ark: oppressive, dark, and smelly. Up the ramp into the Ark, going inside to save your life but, once you are there, it feels like death. What happens in there before the dove appears and tells Noah it is okay to come out? The same thing that happens in the tomb: a mystical transformation. You have done the work and you have survived – welcome to your new life.

Roll Away the Stone, Pass Around the Rock

The clinic or hospital recognizes the magnitude of the last day of treatment. It is an end to the liminal experience of cancer and the beginning of re-entry into the patient's former world. Usually we approach it with good humor and a spirit of celebration. We place a crown on the patient's head, sing a good-bye song and blow bubbles.

However, sometimes we know the patient will probably never again get the care and attention he or she received while in treatment. We know the return to that person's former life may be more difficult than becoming a patient. So that is why for some patients we do the Rock Ritual.

Everyone who has been involved in the patient's care gathers around the bed. We take a smooth, polished rock – the kind that fits nicely in the palm of your hand – and we pass it around. As we each receive the rock we put our own particular strength into it: courage, optimism, patience, humor, love. We each say a few words about that and pass it on. And then we give it to the patient who in just a few moments will not be a chemo patient anymore.

That outward status will end but the change that has begun within will keep going. After six months or more of weekly visits, there are tears from both patients and care providers. The patient never wants to come

back as a patient again. And yet – he or she will miss us. Both/and, again.
We have become familiar and known during a time of deep uncertainty
and strangeness. As happy as that person is to complete treatment, it is a
bittersweet moment.

Imagine crawling out of a dark tomb into the blinding sunlight. You can
hardly stand it at first. Ironically, after all this time wanting to be out, you
crave to be in again. People welcome you back as if you are hero and have
no idea about this ongoing inward journey you are on.

It is as if you are a baby bird who has been pushed out of the nest. Some
are transformed and that informs their eventual take-off. Others attempt to
fly using old methods and they never get off the ground.

Cancer Camaraderie

Even though everyone's diagnosis, treatment, and response to treatment
is different, a special bond develops between patients. There is the
commiserating, the advising, the confiding, and the connecting. You can
do all these things in a college dorm, but facing a life-threatening illness
creates a different kind of bond between people because the stakes are
higher – the highest: life and death.

During treatment, distinctions between economic class, gender, and
race are blurred and sometimes erased completely. That is why you could
have the Queen of England, Einstein, Jesus, and Cher in the same room
and not know who is who. But once people meet in the "outside world,"
things are different. What they once had in common – nausea, nail fungus,
neuropathy and hair loss – is thankfully gone. Then they find they have
nothing else in common and the relationship gradually dies out. Other
patients cherish the friendship but want to go back to a life that does not
include any reminders of cancer, so that relationship dies of starvation.

Sometimes friendships between patients last forever and that is usually
because they already had more in common than their disease and its
treatment. And sometimes in spite of having nothing in common, they just
connect in a way that is strong and deep. What about friendships between
patients and providers, however?

Early in my chaplain career I learned that it was nearly impossible for me to
have a real friendship with a patient. Many patients wanted to keep in touch
with me because, hey, how great is it to have a friend that listens so closely to
you? The problem is that in a real friendship, there is a give-and-take, a mutual
sharing. So, the challenge is for both parties to make a switch. I tried, I really did.

I accepted a lunch invitation from a patient I always enjoyed seeing. It
never even felt like work when I met with her. So over Caesar salads and

Chardonnay my patient/friend and I started talking – that is, she started talking. We had a fine time until I began sharing things about my life. She looked stunned. Picking up on something I said, she quickly turned the conversation back to her life. All my attempts to talk about my life were thwarted. I had another glass of wine and realized we would never be friends. Reintegration is not easy – for anyone.

Turn and Re-Turn

Here is the last Russian nesting doll: reintegration is a kind of liminality within the last part of the liminal cancer experience.

If the treatment works, most patients realize that, even if we are considered "NED" – No Evidence of Disease, we cannot go back to our old lives. It is as if we made a big turn and, even by retracing our steps, we cannot go back to who we were. We are not the same and we continue to grow. So, we find new identities, make changes in relationships, and question our values.

> I hold everything lightly and gently now. My beliefs about how the world works, who I am, what's important – well, I'm constantly evaluating, shifting, rethinking those beliefs. And I was lucky – I met others with lung cancer who didn't make it because they found it too late. But don't ever tell anyone with cancer they are lucky.

After my own treatment I felt an even stronger urgency about life. I deeply appreciated both the strength and the fragility of my body. I wanted to scream at smokers and obese people: "Don't you know you're increasing your chance of cancer? Don't you know you have to care for this tender, animal body of yours?"

I was not the same person. I knew that once you had cancer you could easily have a recurrence. This understanding made me impatient – for example, with what I considered bureaucratic nonsense in my job. It was as if my internal editor was on a leave of absence, so I said whatever I felt or thought. I was slow to keep my opinions to myself. Why did everyone not realize that life could end at any moment? Why are we not training staff to talk about death?

This was terrible for those around me because, while I had a tinge of this before my diagnosis, after my treatment I was insufferable. For the most part, though, people were gentle and understanding.

This is all part of the reintegration process. We come back to our old lives as new persons. Not everyone becomes a bigger pain-in-the-ass as I did. Some of us return to our lives kinder and gentler. Almost always, however, we are clearer about what is important and we rarely forget that.

I personally know only one patient who realized, but then forgot, what is important. She was a chemo patient who was really having a rough time with side effects. They could not get her nausea and diarrhea under control. She was miserable. The only light in her life was her daughter who was pregnant at the time. All this patient could talk about was how she wanted to live to see this baby.

"I want to be involved," she said. "I want to take care of that baby and be sure that he knows who his Grammy is."

She went on to say how she had wakened up to the fact that she was not going to live forever and how now she really appreciated life and she was not going to work so damn much.

She said, "And I'm going to start gardening again. I want to dig in the dirt and feel the earth between my fingers. And I'm not going to be so critical and judgmental."

And I thought, wow, good for you! Because those are profound insights.

About three years later I ran into her at the grocery store. I wish I could say I was in the organic produce section, but, no, I was standing at the cheese case, holding a wheel of Brie in one hand and wheel of Camembert in the other and trying to remember the difference between them.

And a voice behind me said, "That'll chunk up your thighs!"

Them's fightin' words! I whipped around and there she was, looking fabulous and totally put together. Perfect hair, great jewelry, beautiful manicure.

I said, "Oh, my gosh, you look terrific! How are you? How is your grandson? You must be having such fun with him."

She said, "He's a little monster. Thank God they put him in daycare."

And I said, "Oh. Well, how's your garden?"

She thrust out her hands, "Oh, honey, look at these nails. You think I want to wreck these nails? I'm too busy anyway. I'm back in real estate and it's hard work right now – the market's flat."

And I thought, "Oh, no, you forgot."

I wanted to remind her how much she wanted to see her grandson and be in the garden and feel the earth in her hands and how she was not going to work so damn much or be so judgmental and critical.

So, I'm thinking all this with the Camembert in one hand and the Brie in the other and, before I could say anything, she said, "I'm telling you, you eat that cheese and you'll pack on the pounds, and you can't afford that."

I just smiled at her and put them both in my basket.

All of us who come through a liminal experience are changed in some way – some for the better and some not. Sometimes we forever carry the gifts we received and other times we drop them along the way. We are happy to be out of the tomb, and yet we remember that being in the tomb was the greatest gift of all.

14

I Was in Prison and You Visited Me

Jacob Davis

When I was eighteen years old I killed a man. He was my rival, and the murder was a crime of passion. When I pulled that trigger, two people fell. The first and most terrible was the victim of the bullet. I took the most precious thing any human being can take from another – life. However, a second life ended at that very same moment. Life, as I had known it, came to a jarring and sudden halt. My former life was over.

I grew up in a stable home and I had no experience of the criminal justice system. I was so naïve that I somehow assumed that criminal justice would resemble punishment at home – punishment with a purpose, discipline with the goal of correction and molding the child's character. As individual family members grow, that change strengthens the whole family. Estrangement needs to be overcome by reconciliation. Thus, I believed that punishment by the State would follow the same contours – signaling deterrence, correcting the individual, providing some opportunity for repentance, and, ultimately, reconciling and bringing everyone back together. I assumed that the process involved redemption.

What I have experienced for over twenty years is exactly the opposite of that assumption. In an era of mass incarceration, public policy is based on the assumption that people cannot change. Warehouse-model imprisonment disavows any interest in the prisoner's redemption or reconciliation with society. The only thing that matters in our current state of affairs is removal of the person from society for as long as possible. While that may be justified for those who mock the rule of law, the present blanket policy does more harm by denying the transformation that is possible for so many.

When I crossed the threshold into the strange world of incarceration, I was ushered into a state of permanent liminality, a time and space between the past and some seemingly unobtainable future. My life was stuck in a time between the times, a place between the spaces. Unlike van Gennep's *Rites of Passage*, however, there was no design for movement, for transformation in the liminal passage.

There are, however, two different views of this permanent liminality. From the outside, prisoners appear to be in a state of suspended animation, frozen in time and place. However, on the inside of the experience are things invisible to those on the outside, realms of the heart that are fluid. For prisoners serving long sentences like mine, the process of human development does unfold following that initial period of loss and acclimation to an entirely different context. After our horizons are rearranged by incarceration, we go on living like anyone else.

Because present criminal justice policy disregards the idea of redemption, it also rejects approaches in which prisoners are rehabilitated. In an earlier time, prisoners were given opportunities to change their thoughts and behavior with the hope of eventual reintegration into the communities that would receive them upon release. That view is non-existent today. The incarcerated are viewed as inherently unredeemable, guilty not only of crimes but of possessing permanently flawed natures. Such people cannot or do not deserve to be part of the fabric of community. Yet the vast majority of prisoners eventually return to their communities of origin.

To understand the current disinterest in rehabilitation, we need to look at the evolution of incarceration in the United States. In the earliest times, the crime I committed might have been prosecuted by throwing a rope over a tree branch and stringing me up while townspeople looked on. Beyond that vigilante justice developed the designs of the first prisons in early America and they all revolved around redeeming the prisoner.

Christian discourse of repentance and renewal figured heavily in this formula. Prison was conceived as a liminal space between the old individual and the new. In prison a person would be stripped down, disciplined, and given time to reflect until a new, moral and industrious individual emerged. The root of the word penitentiary is penitence. This understanding of justice balanced the good of society with the good of the individual; and it recognized the divinely endowed worth of each person.

This understanding of rehabilitation continued until the 1970s and the rise of mass incarceration. What supplanted the earlier narrative was a new ideology, namely, to remove people from their communities for as long as possible. In the age of warehouse imprisonment, the State does not care how the prisoner's time is occupied so long as he or she does not threaten the security of the institution. The prisoner's actions lack any redemptive dimension. If, in previous times, prisoners who showed contrition and a willingness to correct the harm they had caused were given new chances, today's ideal prisoner resembles an object on a shelf.

One of the hallmark punishments of prison is separation from all meaningful contact with society. The removal of this freedom of contact and movement is central. However, today's hallmark of prison includes a new layer: the creation of despair. It induces despair by consistently sending the message that prisoners are flawed, hopeless, and worthless.

While today's commentators often appeal to the shocking financial statistics of mass incarceration, a national annual price tag of over eighty billion dollars per year, they seldom speak of the loss of the former corrections discourse of development and redemption. It is as if the nation suddenly stopped believing that people can change; as if the nation became overwhelmed with the possibility of recovering the person from the crime.

Viewing incarceration through the lens of liminality places us in an unavoidable conflict, a tension between views of the human being. One view, the earlier view, holds the possibility for redemption. The opposing view of our time forever defines a person by a crime they once committed. We insiders know from experience that the system defines us solely as perpetrators of harm, rather than human beings that struggle, dream, and pray. That is our great challenge in the liminal domain: the tearing of our souls between authorities who say we are incapable of being redeemed and our own dignity, hope, and faith that remains.

Warehouse imprisonment is often justified by the argument that dangerous people need to be removed from society so they can do no more harm. I do not disagree with that necessity. Society has a responsibility to prevent foreseeable harm. We need to exercise that protection, however, without causing more harm than we prevent. I believe that the scales have now tipped toward a net harm rather than a net good and here is why: incarceration is vastly overused. Many people have their lives destroyed by imprisonment when they should never have seen the inside of a cell. Others who once needed restraint are held long past the point when they do. Mass imprisonment without regard for repentance, growth, forgiveness, and reconciliation is not justice. It is a wholesale devaluation of life and denies the potential for transformation that may come out of the liminal passage.

The New David

When one of my oldest friends went back to his home town to appear in court, it was as though no time had passed since the crime was originally committed. The townspeople regarded my friend exactly as he was the many years ago when the crime was committed. One woman said she could not comprehend how that angry, abused, mentally ill juvenile had become a middle-aged man in his forties. Her life had continued. However, the last thing she expected was for him also to change. The opinion expressed in court that day confirmed it: in their eyes he would remain a child monster forever.

What is important to note is the remarkable transformation my friend evidenced in his life. It has created a remarkable dissonance between the man he is now and the treatment he received when he returned to the town frozen in his past time.

I met David in prison when we were both in our early twenties and struggling to adjust to a radically different and often hostile environment. We hit it off quickly and formed a close friendship along with another young friend serving a life sentence. Around us blossomed a transitory community of like-experienced souls. This little community, one which still exists today, would become a haven for us as we dealt with the trauma of losing our former lives and adjusting to prison. Each of us felt out of place, not just because prison initially alienates everyone, but because our natures and our interests clashed so strongly with the culture of prison. A criminal lifestyle had not led us to prison and did not appeal to any of us once inside.

As we matured into men who shared a liminal space, we did everything together. We went to church together, wrote and played music together, worked at the same shop where we refurbished old PCs, and hung out together in the units where we lived. Our straight-edge counterculture circle constituted a home away from home that provided the comfort and safety of intentional community. We navigated the prison system with a mutually understood determination not to allow this environment to deform us. After fifteen years I was unwillingly parted from the rest. Nonetheless, the bond we created through this shared experience persists today and constitutes an example of what Victor Turner called communitas.

What is remarkable about David is that, by the time I met him, he had already changed to such a degree that it was almost impossible to believe he had committed a violent crime. When he experienced the horror of realizing his guilt, his heart broke and that fundamentally altered his internal landscape. The angry, disturbed young man became a thoughtful, kind, devout, and humble human being. David holds a special place in the hearts of many who have known him since his incarceration and I am proud to call him my lifelong friend.

When we first met, David stood out as a person of exceptional purity and steadfastness. David seemed unflappable. He never acted out, never cracked or changed under pressure. When I said something about him to a mutual friend of ours, he said simply that David was evidence of what happens when a heart really changes. All my youthful arrogance melted into admiration for David that has never waned. He is a model I still try and fail to emulate.

His transformation is evidence of what can happen when a young person is allowed to live. Just knowing David makes it clear that even horrible mistakes may give rise to miracles of growth. Yet, under the new ideology of our justice system, David's contrite heart and renewed life go entirely unrecognized.

David is not irredeemable; he is a precious child of God whose purity of heart shines in the lives of everyone who knows him now. David stands for what miracles are possible when the broken heart opens to the divine. The State's position is not simply mistaken; it is hostile to the possibility of David's human capacities. Even though the people of David's community and the officers of the court almost certainly embrace Christianity and its proclamation of repentance and rebirth, they still place David outside that grace. In fact, in an absolute denial of grace, they intentionally keep him in a state of involuntary permanent liminality.

For those of us who love David, it is very hard to witness his humanity being harshly and falsely denied. The system operates in willful ignorance of the truth about the man. David's example brings into clear focus the difference between the human potential of every prisoner and every attempt to define people solely by the crime they committed.

The Service Dogs

I presently work in a program that trains canines to become service animals. Our dogs can perform dozens of complex tasks upon request. They open and close doors, turn lights on and off, and retrieve items from shelves or the refrigerator. They can even alert a diabetic when their sugar level is off or warn an epileptic of an impending seizure. For us, the job is incredibly rewarding. Not only do the dogs go on to improve lives but for eighteen months each dog becomes part of the tapestry of our world. With the exception of when the dogs go out on trips to get acclimated to the world, they live right in our cells with us. The only truly difficult thing about the program is letting the dogs go when they find a home with a recipient who needs them. I am now halfway through the education process with my second puppy, a white Lab named Max.

Last spring, in a different part of the prison, a highly publicized incident took place in which prisoners took hostages to protest against their conditions. To distract the public from this story, the agency brought the newspaper and broadcast media into the prison and highlighted our canine program. We were proud to have our amazing dogs recognized. Because of our help, the puppy grows into a life-changing companion. Men with long sentences enjoy an opportunity to do something truly meaningful with their time. Opportunities like these are rare these days. Those who have hurt people in the past have the chance to actually help in the present.

Though our dog trainers would have been proud to appear with their dogs for this public moment, news media made sure there would be no public recognition. No identification of any prisoner was allowed. The prison authorities explained this by saying that such an appearance would "re-victimize" anyone associated with a crime. The irony of this situation was that only a few weeks earlier the agency and news media had no qualms about identifying the men who had taken hostages. Every prisoner involved in that incident appeared with their Department of Corrections numbers and photos on the news for days. For that event there was no great concern to protect people from "re-victimization."

The difference between these very selective portrayals of prisoners is this: humanizing facts are to be hidden and condemning facts are to be revealed. This is the confirmation of bias and reinforcement of the revisionist understanding of the human being in corrections. It is not enough today to remove the body from plain view. Criminal justice today is dominated by political forces and narratives that reject the ideas of redemption, reconciliation, and forgiveness. As a result, the prisoner's existence is never considered more than a threat, and hope of redemption is further distanced by the push for longer and longer sentences.

What Is a Life Sentence?

In Tennessee a life sentence with parole requires service of fifty-one calendar years before release eligibility. Prior to 1995 and the legislative action that increased it, a life sentence required twenty-five years before eligibility. Life without parole was still an option. However, this new law insures a hopelessness that denies redemption. The new life sentence officially annihilates any former regard our justice system might have had for a person's potential, their value, and their divinely endowed possibilities. Even if a jury sees that potential, as they did in my case, this law nullifies their choice.

Like many who have received this sentence, I heard the message clearly. It's not just that I forfeited freedom through my violation of the law. I was thrust into an existential dilemma. What the State is saying to me is that I am a no-thing with no hope of becoming some-thing. If my life means nothing, then why am I left to live? How am I more than a body on life support? If there is no redemptive dimension to my choices, is there some non-redemptive reason for leaving me alive? Does my suffering have some therapeutic value to others who have been harmed? Do I need to suffer to balance the cosmic scales of pain? Is my example a true deterrent? Is hopeless severity a demonstration of the rule of law over chaos? Is it mercy that keeps me alive or is it cruelty?

Even though my inner changes are unrecognized, I must, nevertheless, resist the vacuum of meaning. I have grown on the path of repentance regardless of the State. I long for reconciliation regardless of present laws. I refuse to collapse into the same pit of hopelessness that has claimed so many after hearing that they do not matter. Drug abuse, despair, violence, indolence, all manner of vices and afflictions are fostered when people are told they have no hope and are not wanted.

Though the pull of despair has at times torn my soul into pieces, friends, family, and my community of the in-between has formed around me. Though the fabric of human relationships is one of the targets of the violence of imprisonment, it is also and at the same time the one resilient saving grace that lifts me above the worst possibilities. Within community, within communitas, I have harvested a wealth of rich experiences that have made my life and my struggle meaningful to me. These riches have sustained me during my time of imposed permanent liminality.

Like my friend David, my broken heart has led me to an ongoing transformation, a humbling miracle of continuous soul expansion. Also like him, I am now a man approaching forty years old who carries the natural dignity of that experience. My development is real even if it disappears behind prison walls.

The most torturous dimension is my inability actually to connect with the people I hurt where my crime occurred, participate in reconciliation and restorative justice, and make amends. That I cannot do from here. I cannot participate in experiences of redemption in a concrete way. In fact, from a remote distance, the reality of the other can only be an abstraction and, like David, frozen in time. If there is a paradox, it is this: I cannot take responsibility for what I have done to the people I have harmed because of a system that is holding me responsible.

* * *

People with long sentences – like David, me, and the men in the dog program – endure the soul-wrenching challenges of permanent liminality. However, even people with short sentences find the liminal condition following them to the outside, there where they never quite belong again, the mark of the felon following them wherever they go.

When a system is structured to construct reality in this way, to create and maintain permanent liminality, to reinforce the idea that certain people are fundamentally unfit for freedom, this is the result. It has captured millions and will not let them go. They are treated with suspicion forever.

Today, anyone guilty of a crime is defined as dangerous and then imprisoned for as long as possible. The concepts of repentance, personal development, and redemption have been cynically tossed aside. The result is a system that interrupts a full cycle of conflict and healing. Absent are plans to recover the one who is punished. Sorrow and remorse are rendered irrelevant. Regardless of the sentence, the real punishment is a ritual transformation into a lifelong pariah. What could have been a liminal passage of transformation with reclamation of a person by the community at the end has become an unending purgatory.

At the beginning of the American republic, we slowly moved from barbaric punishments toward an enlightened protection of society and preservation of life. This move was in no small part informed by religious understanding of human reform and redemption. When repentance, reconciliation, forgiveness, restoration, and transformation become possible, the whole community is healed and renewed.

However, then came the rising phenomenon of mass incarceration and it plunged us into the other direction, toward an anti-redemption ideology. It methodically warehouses people who are defined as permanently flawed, whose condition can only be addressed with longer and longer sentences. With hope effectively eliminated and destroyed, with personhood denied, the only expectation is compliant despair. Such a system can only be called immoral.

Is there a way forward that respects the rule of law, protects citizens, and separates those who might harm from those who could be harmed? Is there a way forward that recognizes the human potential to change, repent, make amends, and forgive? Is there a way forward that assesses each prisoner individually, taking note of real healing and transformation?

Today, we do not hang people behind the courthouse while the ink dries on the judgment sheet, but we do consign people to something that can be even worse, a hopeless dungeon that denies the possibility of reform and restoration.

If we move toward a more humane and effective stewardship of community resources, if we re-evaluate incarceration for what and how long, and if we allow for restorative justice and reconciliation with actual communities in which people have been wronged, our prisoners will not be the only ones who are ushered into some new light of grace. This will impact our entire society, our whole people, and set us free from this form of ideologically-driven permanent liminality that harms us all.

15

Post-Apartheid South Africa and *Ubuntu*

John Eliastam

In April 2015, the world was shocked by graphic footage of Mozambican Emmanuel Sithole being hacked and beaten to death by a xenophobic mob on a Johannesburg street.[1] The images echoed the 2008 immolation of another Mozambican migrant, Ernesto Nhamuave, in the wave of xenophobic violence that swept South Africa. In April 2017, two white farmers were accused of the murder of a black teenager they claim was guilty of stealing sunflowers.[2] In 2016 two white farmers kidnapped a black man they claimed was trespassing on their land, forced him into a coffin, and threatened to douse him with petrol and burn him alive. They were recently convicted and sentenced to long jail terms.[3] In January 2016, government employee Velaphi Khumalo posted a number of times on social media saying that he wanted to cleanse the country of white people and calling for white South Africans to be killed in the same way that Hitler killed the Jews.[4] While these are somewhat isolated incidents,

1. "Butchered in the Street as He Begged for Mercy: Savage Last Moments of Mozambican Man Who Bled to Death in a Johannesburg Gutter after Becoming Latest Victim of South Africa's Anti-immigrant Violence," *Mail Online*, 20 April 2015, accessed 15 February 2018, http://www.dailymail.co.uk/news/article-3046924/Butchered-street-begged-mercy-Savage-moments-Mozambican-man-bled-death-gutter-victim-South-African-anti-immigrant-violence.html#ixzz57FbPEBKZ.
2. "Coligny: Where a Handful of Stolen Seeds Can Cost You Your Life," *Mail & Guardian*, 12 May 2017, accessed 15 February 2018, https://mg.co.za/article/2017-05-12-00-coligny-where-a-handful-of-stolen-seeds-can-cost-you-your-life.
3. "South Africa Coffin Case: White Farmers Convicted," BBC, 25 August 2017, accessed 15 February 2018, http://www.bbc.com/news/world-africa-41052626.
4. "Whites Deserve to Be Hacked and Killed Like Jews," *Politicsweb*, 6 January 2016, accessed 15 February 2018, http://www.politicsweb.co.za/news-and-analysis/whites-deserve-to-be-hacked-and-killed-like-jews--.

they reflect attitudes that lurk beneath the surface of many South African social contexts. What happened to the New South Africa, the reconciled, non-racial "Rainbow Nation" that was the dream of leaders like Nelson Mandela and Desmond Tutu?

A Hope Derailed

The birth of the new South Africa in 1994 generated hope for healing and transformation in a country torn apart by apartheid. The leadership of Nelson Mandela was an example and an inspiration that gave impetus towards forgiveness and reconciliation. Desmond Tutu spoke of a "Rainbow Nation," a phrase that encapsulated a vision for the future of South Africa that was full of possibility and hope. It is perhaps not surprising that, with the joy of liberation, there arose an optimism that the country would be able to make a smooth transition to a future in which all of its people would experience freedom and dignity. However, such changes seldom occur in a simple, linear fashion. Today, South Africa finds itself in-between stories. It seems that this vision, and the hope that accompanied it, has been significantly eroded.

The 1994 transition to a democratic and non-racial South Africa signaled a break with the country's past. From 1948 until 1994, South Africa was shaped by a dominant narrative of apartheid and separate development for different races. Racist government policies were highly oppressive to black South Africans. They were deprived of land, and influx-control policies pushed them to the often inhospitable peripheries of cities and towns where access to transport and other infrastructure was poor. They were provided with low-quality education and other state services. Job reservation policies favored whites, and black South Africans had very limited access to capital and economic opportunities. During the last two decades of apartheid, South Africa increasingly became a police state, in which the police and the military became instruments of violent oppression.

Twenty-four years after the laws that created this immoral system were dismantled, post-apartheid South Africa remains a context characterized by massive inequality, systemic poverty, endemic unemployment, and huge challenges in the areas of health and education. It is also a context with a long history of violence. From the violent dispossession of colonialism and apartheid, to the violence of the struggle against it and the violent repression of that struggle, to the violent crime and interpersonal violence that is recorded daily, violence is endemic to South African society and its history.

Poverty is a defining feature of life for many South Africans – often a bleak, hopeless poverty. The social engineering of apartheid, given impetus by the full power of the state, was highly effective in creating a country that was ordered along racial lines and characterized by profound inequality.[5] In 2009 South Africa's Gini coefficient (the most commonly used measurement of wealth distribution) was 0.632, making it one of the most unequal societies in the world.[6]

Within this context of appalling inequality, multiple problems affect the lives of many South Africans. There is a growing crisis in education that is reflected in Spaull's comments, "with the exception of a wealthy minority – most South African pupils cannot read, write and compute at grade-appropriate levels, with large proportions being functionally illiterate and innumerate."[7] Cronje notes that in 2012 only 39 percent of adults had completed high school and only 6.5 percent had any tertiary education. Cronje also notes that the quality of school education in South Africa was ranked 146th out of 148 countries by the World Economic Forum.[8] There are more South Africans living with HIV and AIDS than in any other country in the world.[9] On top of this, public healthcare is crumbling; facilities are under pressure, and their ability to provide services is hampered by mismanagement and corruption.

The dysfunctionality of local government structures, along with poor performance from elected representatives has resulted in many communities experiencing poor service delivery. Corruption, nepotism, and wasteful expenditure have undermined the capacity of government to deliver services and improve the lives of the poor.[10] Since the middle of the 2000s South Africa has experienced an increasing number of localized, and often violent, community protests about a lack of service delivery from the state, in what Alexander calls a "massive rebellion of the poor."[11] Corruption has

5. Jeremy Seekings, "Race, Discrimination and Diversity in South Africa," *CSSR Working Paper no. 194*. (Cape Town: University of Cape Town, Centre for Social Science Research, 2007), 2; Jeremy Seekings, "Poverty and Inequality after Apartheid," *CSSR Working Paper no. 200* (Cape Town: University of Cape Town, Centre for Social Science Research, 2007), 20.

6. Frans Cronje, *A Time-Traveller's Guide to Our Next Ten Years* (Cape Town: Tafelberg, 2014), 55.

7. Nicholas Spaull, *South Africa's Education Crisis: The Quality of Education in South Africa 1994-2011*. Report Commissioned by the Centre for Development and Enterprise, October 2013, 3.

8. Cronje, *A Time-Traveller's Guide*, 59.

9. Russell, *Time in Eternity*, 203.

10. Ivor Chipkin, "Whither the State? Corruption, Institutions and State-Building in South Africa," *Politikon* 40, no. 2 (2013), 211-31; Daniel W. Gingerich, "Yesterday's Heroes, Today's Villains: Ideology, Corruption, and Democratic Performance," *Journal of Theoretical Politics* 26, no. 2 (April 2014), 249-82.

11. Peter Alexander, "Rebellion of the Poor: South Africa's Service Delivery Protests – A Preliminary Analysis," *Review of African Political Economy* 37, no. 123 (2010), 25-40.

become endemic in South Africa, with massive corruption scandals exposed by the press and civil society. Despite the creation of robust legislation, state integrity frameworks, and strong oversight mechanisms, corruption has flourished in the public sector, sustained by networks of patronage. Evidence has emerged of what has been termed "State Capture," in which outside parties effectively gained control over former President Jacob Zuma and certain cabinet ministers in order to plunder state-owned enterprises, with billions of rands being looted from public coffers.[12] The inaction of political appointees at the highest level of the National Prosecuting Authority has created the perception that many individuals in government are being shielded from accountability and prosecution.

South Africa has been labelled the "world capital of crime,"[13] and the prevalence of crime is compounded by the brutal violence that often accompanies it. The newspapers contain daily reports of car hijackings, violent rapes, farm murders, lynching by mobs, cash-in-transit robberies, and more. While it is difficult to get accurate crime statistics, South Africa's murder rate consistently ranks in the top two or three countries in the world. Altbeker[14] argues that "socio-economic conditions in South Africa, though always likely to produce crime, cannot tell us why South African crime is as violent and pervasive as it is."

The dream of the "Rainbow Nation" has not been realized, and, despite the repeal of segregation and discriminatory laws, there has been little social integration. Only 17.8 percent of South Africans socialize regularly with people of other races, 21.6 percent do this occasionally, and the majority 56.6 percent rarely or never socialize across racial lines.[15] While a desire to build a unified country still exists, it is accompanied by doubts that this can be accomplished in a context of such inequality.[16]

In some ways South Africa has broken free of the apartheid narrative that defined it. However, while that threshold has been breached, the envisaged progress to a non-racial, democratic South Africa has stalled. Apartheid seems to have left an indelible imprint on the social and economic fabric of South Africa. It has scarred her psyche. The proposed new narratives

---

12. Thuli Madonsela, *State of Capture,* Report by the Public Protector of South Africa, accessed 17 January 2018, https://cdn.24.co.za/files/Cms/General/d/4666/3f63a8 b78d2b495d88f10ed060997f76.pdf.

13. Antony Altbeker, *A Country at War with Itself: South Africa's Crisis of Crime* (Johannesburg: Jonathan Ball, 2007), 33.

14. Ibid., 130.

15. Kate Lefko-Everett, "Ticking Time Bomb or Demographic Dividend? Youth and Reconciliation in South Africa," in *SA Reconciliation Barometer Survey: 2012 Report* (Cape Town: Institute for Justice and Reconciliation, 2012), 43.

16. Ibid., 49.

of reconciliation and the "Rainbow Nation" ring hollow. They have been disrupted by a lived reality that contradicts them. South Africa finds itself in a kind of liminal limbo. In this liminal space, multiple Discourses compete for dominance, as South Africans try to make sense of their lives.

The Discursive Lens

From a social constructionist perspective, people produce, maintain, and change meaning as they interact and use language – thereby producing our social world. Language does not reflect reality; it constructs it.[17] The various ways that meaning is expressed in society are reflected in Discourses, which describe aspects of the world in certain ways.[18] Alvesson and Kärreman describe two senses in which the notion of discourse is used. The term "discourse" (little "d") is used to describe talk and text in ordinary social practice, while "Discourse" (big "D") is used to describe broader, enduring systems of ideas within a historically situated context.[19] Discourses simultaneously construct our world and claim to be the truth about this constructed world. These Discourses are socially negotiated systems of thought that function as linguistic resources for people when they communicate. They provide certain terminology, metaphors, habitual forms of argument, and narratives that seek to make sense of life.[20]

Identity is therefore preceded by language and constructed through grammars, logics, and metaphors that already exist in language,[21] and these are the products of history and culture.[22] Furthermore, one's identity is embedded in social relationships and communities that use language to create meaning and knowledge. The consequence of this social and linguistic positioning of the self is that we are surrounded by and immersed within multiple Discourses that construct our identities and our reality through their descriptions of the world. To have an identity is to take up a position in one or more Discourses (e.g. white, male, and middle class are

---

17. Glynis M. Breakwell, Sean Hammond, and Chris Fife-Schaw, *Research Methods in Psychology*, 2nd ed. (London: Sage Publications, 2000).
18. Ian Parker, "Discursive Psychology," in *Critical Psychology: An Introduction*, eds Dennis Fox and Isaac Prilleltensky (London: Sage Publications, 1997), 285.
19. Mats Alvesson, and Dan Kärreman, "Varieties of Discourse: On the Study of Organizations Through Discourse Analysis," *Human Relations* 53 (2000), 1125-49.
20. Jonathan Potter, Margaret Wetherell, Rosalind Gill, and Derek Edwards, "Discourse: Noun, Verb or Social Practice?" *Philosophical Psychology* 3, nos 2 and 3 (1990), 205-17.
21. Vivien Burr, *An Introduction to Social Constructionism* (London: Routledge, 1995).
22. Michael White, *Narrative Practice and the Unpacking of Identity Conclusions*, accessed 3 December 2017, http://www.dulwichcentre.com.au./narrativepractice.htm, 6.

all stories about a certain way of being in society – with certain privileges
and rules – before they are descriptors for the self). As we take up subject
positions within Discourses, our identities are socially constructed. The self
is therefore a social and literary product rather than a metaphysical essence.

The subjectivity that arises from this discursive positioning provides a
sense of identity and shapes the narratives we use to think and talk about
ourselves and the world around us.[23] Discourses provide us with the resources
that we use to make sense of our lives and interpret the circumstances in
which we find ourselves. These shape the possibilities for future action that
are either desirable or open to them.

South Africa's liminal state is one existing between stories, as much a crisis
of identity, individual and communal, as it is a failure of post-apartheid
narratives to bring about the transformation they promised.

Discourses, Hegemony, and Dislocation

The poststructuralist political theory of Ernesto Laclau and Chantal Mouffe
provides a lens through which this liminal space in-between stories may be
understood. It is an appealing lens because of its sensitivity to conflict and
struggle over meaning, identity, and power within society.[24]

Laclau and Mouffe's original work, *Hegemony and Socialist Strategy,* arose
from their observation that conventional Marxist theory, which privileged
the working class and class struggle, was unable to account for the growth
of multiple social movements and struggles during the 1980s, whether
these were for women's rights, the environment, gay rights, or the rights
of ethnic minorities. They abandon the Marxist notion of core economic
identities in favor of identities that are the product of Discourse. Political
identities are not things that exist in and of themselves; they are constituted
and molded by conflict within society. They emerge as people mobilize
themselves around Discourses that are presented in society as metaphors
or tropes. They temporarily position social identities and meaning in a
relational system of signification. [25] While Discourses make meaning
possible, they are always undermined by the multiple possibilities that exist
for interpretation. As a result, they are always contingent and can never
achieve complete closure.

23. Elaine Graham, *Transforming Practice: Pastoral Theology in an Age of Uncertainty*
    (London: Mowbray, 1996), 30.
24. Bronwyn Boon, "Engaging with a Laclau and Mouffe Informed Discourse Analysis:
    A Proposed Framework," *Qualitative Research in Organizations and Management:
    An International Journal* 9, no. 4 (2014), 351-70.
25. Ernesto Laclau and Chantal Mouffe, *Hegemony and Socialist Strategy: Towards a
    Radical Democratic Politics* (London: Verso, 1985).

This openness to destabilization is important for Laclau and Mouffe. They describe the destabilization or failure of a discursive structure as its dislocation.[26] Dislocation occurs when a prevailing discursive formation cannot accommodate or make sense of new events or experiences, precipitating a crisis of meaning. Discourses are challenged by the articulation of other Discourses that call prevailing understandings into question and offer alternative interpretations of the world.

When Discourses experience dislocation, they are reorganized by social processes which Laclau and Mouffe call hegemonic struggles. These are articulatory practices that attempt to build a new Discourse by offering new signifiers and positioning them within a Discourse so that they have a unifying effect that brings multiple Discourses together in a new hegemonic Discourse. Such Discourses are created and organized around a nodal point that represents some social ideal. Constructed ideals such as "justice," "prosperity," "equality," or "greatness" function as anchors; they temporarily stabilize a Discourse, and in so doing they also temporarily stabilize other units of meaning in relation to that Discourse.[27] These nodal points consist of what Laclau terms empty signifiers or empty universals. These are signifiers that represent vague but powerful social ideals that have normative appeal despite their equivocal meaning.[28] Empty universals hold populist appeal because of their promise to "fill the gap" between the experience of dislocation, and its crisis of meaning, and the need for a unified and fulfilled identity.[29] Empty universals derive their authority because they represent opposition and resistance towards current, negative circumstances in a particular society. However, the positive meaning of an empty universal is elusive and it is more easily understood in relation to what it opposes.

The articulation of any Discourse takes place within a context of competing Discourses, with the result that the claims of a potentially hegemonic Discourse are premised on the simultaneous exclusion of meanings that are opposed to the empty signifier. Hegemony is created by the construction of a threat. The "constitutive outside" is the force that stabilizes the hegemonic Discourse.[30] It is the presence of a threatening "Other" that gives a hegemonic Discourse

26. Ernesto Laclau, *New Reflections on the Revolution of Our Time* (London: Verso, 1990), 39-45.

27. Laclau and Mouffe, *Hegemony and Socialist Strategy*, 135-42.

28. Judith Renner, "The Local Roots of the Global Politics of Reconciliation: The Articulation of 'Reconciliation' as an Empty Universal in the South African Transition to Democracy," *Millennium: Journal of International Studies* 42, no. 2 (2014), 263-85.

29. Ernesto Laclau, *Emancipation(s)* (London: Verso, 1996).

30. Laclau and Mouffe, *Hegemony and Socialist Strategy*; Lasse Thomassen, "Antagonism, Hegemony, and Ideology after Heterogeneity," *Journal of Political Ideologies* 10, no. 3 (2005), 289-309.

stability, while at the same time preventing its ultimate closure.[31] Hegemonic struggles create a frontier between the two groups; in Herschinger's words, they separate "a discursive space into two antagonistic camps: the good vs. the bad, the Self vs. the Other."[32]

Apartheid Discourse was organized around an ideal of purity, often formulated with reference to the Bible, and stabilized by reference to the "Swart gevaar" or the "Rooi gevaar."[33] Renner argues that the term "reconciliation" emerged as an empty signifier during South Africa's transition from apartheid. It was "a vague yet powerful social ideal that could be embraced by the antagonistic parties of the ANC and NP not because of any intrinsic value, but rather because of its vagueness and semantic flexibility."[34] It produced a contingent reconciliation Discourse, based on the claims of the various political protagonists, that was then stabilized by the Truth and Reconciliation Commission and its attempt to avoid retribution. In a similar way, Discourses of the "Rainbow Nation"[35] emerged in opposition to the racial division of apartheid, and a Discourse of "a better life for all"[36] was promulgated by the ANC as a counter to the racialized social development of apartheid that created massive inequality between black and white South Africans.

These post-1994 Discourses have become inadequate for making sense of life in South Africa. They have experienced profound dislocation as a result of the economic and social problems described earlier in this chapter. The result of this dislocation is seen in hegemonic struggles between these Discourses and new Discourses that have emerged as a consequence of this crisis of meaning.

The experience of dislocation creates the need to rearrange the social around new empty signifiers, thereby making social change possible.[37] It generates: "a set of new possibilities for historical action which are the

31. Jacob Torfing, "Discourse Theory: Achievements, Arguments and Challenges," in *Discourse Theory in European Politics: Identity, Policy and Governance*, eds David Howarth and Jacob Torfing (Hampshire: Palgrave Macmillan, 2005), 15.
32. Eva Herschinger, *Constructing Global Enemies: Hegemony and Identity in Global Discourses on Terrorism and Drug Prohibition* (Abingdon: Routledge, 2011), 23.
33. Afrikaans terms used in apartheid era propaganda to describe a "black peril" or a "red/communist peril."
34. Renner, "The Local Roots of the Global Politics of Reconciliation," 263.
35. Steven D. Gish, *Desmond Tutu: A Biography* (Westport, CT: Greenwood Press, 2004).
36. *African National Congress 1999 Election Manifesto*, accessed 3 July 2017, http://www.anc.org.za/show.php?id=2543; *African National Congress 2004 Election Manifesto*, accessed 3 July 2017, http://www.anc.org.za/elections/2004/manifesto/manifesto.html; *African National Congress 2009 Election Manifesto*, accessed 3 July 2017, http://www.anc.org.za/docs/manifesto/2009/manifesto.pdf.
37. Renner, "The Local Roots of the Global Politics of Reconciliation," 263-85.

direct result of structural dislocation. The world is less 'given' and must be increasingly constructed."[38] Liminality can therefore be understood as a space of hegemonic struggle, following dislocation, characterized by multiple discourses. These competing meanings attempt to gain dominance as the catalyst for a new state of homeostasis. New meanings bring with them possibilities for new action and for change.

Competing Discourses in South Africa

Following the dislocation of the hegemonic Discourse of apartheid, and the subsequent dislocation of the reconciliation and "Rainbow Nation" Discourses that followed it, the South African discursive space is characterized by a number of Discourses, some competing and some complementary. These include Discourses that focus on economic freedom and the return of the land, nationalistic/nativist Discourses, nostalgic reconstructions of apartheid, narratives about the collapse of the country, and intertwined Discourses of white victimhood and white supremacy.

Freedom Discourse

A Discourse of "total" or "complete" freedom was articulated in the 1999, 2004, and 2009 ANC election manifestos.[39] This encompassed political, economic, and social freedom. Housing, the provision of services, education, and social grants are argued to constitute social freedom. The ANC has consistently framed freedom in this way and promised to deliver it to people.[40] However, for the majority of South Africans, this ideal of freedom remains elusive. This has resulted in a re-shaping of the freedom Discourse to focus on economic freedom. There is an emerging post-apartheid Discourse in which freedom is constructed as a certain level of economic status and consumption.

Posel points out that modern consumption has always been linked to race in South Africa. Colonial rulers allowed natives a degree of upward social mobility if they adopted European dress and manners. Thus, a certain kind of consumption came to be a marker of social respectability. Modern consumption refers to acquiring and using things, the context in which this occurs, and its cultural, political and psychological effects. Posel lists the defining elements of this as the consumption of commodities, the manner

---

38. Laclau, *New Reflections*, 40.
39. ANC *Election Manifesto*, 1999, 2004, and 2009.
40. Teboho P. Bojabotseha and Kholeka C. Moloi, "Discursive Constructions of the African National Congress (ANC) and Its Discourse of Freedom: A Critical Analysis," *Academic Journal of Interdisciplinary Studies* 3, no. 4 (2014), 98-99.

in which these processes of consumption are a source of psychological social value as well as economic value, and the emergence of mass markets across class lines, and the mass aspirations and desire to consume. These aspirations to consume are part of the construction and performance of selfhood.[41] Consumption is a critical dimension of the exercise of power, because modes of consumption are fundamental to a person's sense of who they are and their place in society.[42]

This idea of freedom as economic consumption or freedom as affluence represents a shift from earlier freedom discourse within liberation movements in South Africa. Mngxitama argues that, unlike the Zimbabwean liberation struggle that was essentially about the land, the South African struggle focused on freedom as equality.[43] In that sense it was a political struggle before it was an economic struggle, and the economic benefits of equality were almost an assumed corollary to political freedom. The discourse has shifted towards a focus on economic freedom, benchmarked against white affluence, and which is seen as attainable through "radical economic transformation" that includes the nationalization of key industries, expropriation of land from white South Africans without compensation, and the redistribution of land and other resources.

Nativist Nationalist Discourse

Anderson's analysis of the rise and spread of nationalism in early modern Europe provides insights into nationalistic Discourses in South Africa. Anderson explored nationalism in terms of personal identity and sense of belonging and described nations as socially constructed "imagined communities," imagined, "because the members of even the smallest nation will never know most of their fellow-members, meet them, or even hear of them, yet in the minds of each lives the image of their communion."[44] In spite of this, members of a nation form deep attachments to each other and to the nation. For Anderson, the notion of a state involves the construction of various boundaries that determine inclusion or exclusion. Anderson describes this imagined community as a political community with a

---

41. Deborah Posel, "Races to Consume: Revisiting South Africa's History of Race, Consumption and the Struggle for Freedom," *Ethnic and Racial Studies* 33, no. 2 (2010), 161.

42. John L. Comaroff and Jean Comaroff, *Of Revelation and Revolution, Volume Two: The Dialectics of Modernity on a South African Frontier* (Chicago: University of Chicago Press, 1997), 219.

43. Andile Mngxitama, "South Africa: Land Reform Blocked," *Green Left Weekly* 406, accessed 1 November 2017, https://www.greenleft.org.au/node/22276.

44. Benedict Anderson, *Imagined Communities: Reflections on the Origin and Spread of Nationalism* (London: Verso, 1983), 15.

common origin, historical experience, and destiny. This in turn creates a community of shared interests. Nations become imagined communities of solidarity, with clear territorial boundaries. Within these boundaries, certain collective goods belong to members of the nation, particularly political, social, and economic rights.

Within nationalistic Discourse in South Africa there is an increased tendency towards an autochthonous understanding of what constitutes a nation.[45] The notion of autochthony refers to the concern about who or what is indigenous to a place or nation, and therefore who or what has a legitimate claim to exist in that place or nation.[46] Comaroff and Comaroff identify two parallel discourses in South Africa — a negative discourse in relation to migrants, and a negative discourse in relation to non-indigenous plants. They juxtapose these discourses in developing their theory about the alien in South Africa. According to the Comaroffs, aliens, whether they are people or plants, symbolize contradictions of belonging and boundedness. The language of the alien offers new ways of expressing discrimination in a civil rights culture.[47] Their analysis of these discourses suggests that there is movement towards nativist thinking, in terms of which only that which is indigenous to South Africa belongs in South Africa. Mbembe also makes a strong case for a powerful nativist Discourse that is gaining credence in South Africa,[48] as does Neocosmos.[49]

Foreigners are the Problem

The most visible expression of nativist Discourse has been ongoing xenophobic violence against foreign migrants from other African countries. Foreign migrants started to arrive in South Africa after 1994. Their number increased in the late 1990s around the time of the passing of the Refugees Act in 1998, and again around 2005 with the collapse of the Zimbabwean

---

45. Noor Nieftagodien, "Xenophobia in Alexandra," in *Go Home or Die Here: Violence, Xenophobia and the Reinvention of Difference in South Africa*, eds Shireen Hassim, Eric Worby, and Tawana Kupe (Johannesburg: Wits University Press, 2008); Tamlyn Monson, "Everyday Politics and Collective Mobilisation against Foreigners in a South African Shack Settlement," *Africa: The Journal of the International African Institute* 85, no. 1 (2015), 131-52.

46. Peter Geschiere, *The Perils of Belonging: Autochthony, Citizenship, and Exclusion in Africa and Europe* (Chicago: University of Chicago Press), 2009.

47. John L. Comaroff and Jean Comaroff, "Naturing the Nation: Aliens, Apocalypse and the Postcolonial State," *Journal of Southern African Studies* 27 (2001), 627-51.

48. Archibald Mbembe, "South Africa's Second Coming: The Nongqawuse Syndrome," *Open Democracy*, 2006, accessed 4 December 2017, https://www.opendemocracy.net/democracy-Africa_democracy/southafrica_succession_3649.jsp.

49. Michael Neocosmos, *From Foreign Natives to Native Foreigners: Explaining Xenophobia in Post-Apartheid South Africa* (Dakar: CODESRIA, 2010).

economy. Census data from 2011 shows a dramatic increase in the number of foreign migrants living in informal settlements since 2001.[50] This influx resulted in South Africa being the primary host of new asylum seekers in the world between 2006 and 2011.[51] According to the South African Department of Home Affairs there were 889,943 documented foreign migrants living in South Africa between 2010 and 2015.[52] It is impossible to get accurate figures for the number of undocumented migrants living in South Africa, with estimates ranging from 200,000 to eight million. The Southern African Migration Programme argue that South Africans show levels of hostility and intolerance to foreign migrants that are virtually unparalleled elsewhere in the world. Foreign migrants were perceived to be involved in crime, taking economic opportunities from South Africans, and placing an undue strain on government resources.[53]

The scapegoating of foreign migrants resulted in outbreaks of violence in 2008 against African migrants living in townships and informal settlements around South Africa. While such incidents were not new, the intensity and pervasive nature of the 2008 violence was unprecedented. In the period between 11 and 26 May, sixty-two foreign nationals were killed, around 700 injured, and an estimated 35,000 foreigners were driven from their homes. Misago, Landau and Monson provide a detailed account of the May 2008 violence.[54]

There was a decline in anti-foreigner sentiment between 2008 and 2010, but ongoing incidents of violence against foreign migrants were documented between 2008 and 2013.[55] Violence against foreigners continued to smolder in settlements across South Africa in 2013 and 2014, sometimes escalating into organized attempts to force foreign migrants to leave communities, often by attacking their businesses or taking their possessions from them. Violence against foreigners increased in 2015, particularly after a speech given by the

50. Monson, "Everyday Politics and Collective Mobilisation," 131-52.
51. United Nations High Commissioner for Refugees, *Global Trends 2012 – Displacement: The New 20th Century Challenge* (Geneva: UNHCR, 2012).
52. Rebecca Davis, "Lawmakers Crunch Xenophobia Numbers," *Eye Witness News*, 29 April 2015, accessed 19 December 2017, http://ewn.co.za/2015/04/29/ OPINION-Rebecca-Davis-Lawmakers-crunch-some-xenophobia-numbers.
53. Jonathan Crush, *The Perfect Storm: The Realities of Xenophobia in Contemporary South Africa*, Southern African Migration Programme (Cape Town: IDAS, 2008).
54. Jean Pierre Misago, Loren B. Landau, and Tamlyn Monson, *Towards Tolerance, Law and Dignity: Addressing Violence Against Foreign Nationals in South Africa*, Report for the International Organisation of Migration (Pretoria: International Organisation of Migration, 2009).
55. Jonathan Crush, Sujata Ramachandran, and Wade Pendleton, *Soft Targets: Xenophobia, Public Violence and Changing Attitudes to Migrants After May 2008*, Southern African Migration Programme (Cape Town: Bronwen Dachs Muller, 2013).

Zulu king, Goodwill Zwelethini, in which he was understood to instruct people to take action to deal with the "problem" of foreigners. The government has tried to counter the xenophobic violence with the narrative that "We are all Africans," but this has not addressed the issues that underlie the conflict.

Since 2012 attention has increasingly turned towards white South Africans. Despite the fact that many have been in the country for generations, they are being described as foreigners, who must give back the land they stole and to return to Europe. Whether a white South African is entitled to call themselves African, with its implications of belonging, is contested.[56]

While the narratives described above are compelling for many black South Africans, the dominant narratives among many white South Africans are markedly different.

Maintaining Privilege: Narratives of Whiteness

Although race remains a primary constituent of identity in South Africa, whiteness is not about race. Rather, it is about power and privilege – and maintaining these.[57] White people in South Africa still find themselves in a position of privilege, while the majority of black people remain poor and marginalized.[58] Whiteness describes the way in which white identity is viewed in almost non-racial terms, compared to a racialized other. White culture, norms, and values are then viewed as natural and normative standards, against which other groups and individuals are measured.

Studies have explored how ongoing white privilege and the persistence of whiteness is produced by the discursive performance of whiteness in what has been described as "white talk." In white talk, certain Discourses are deployed by white people as they create new narratives to make sense of their circumstances and negotiate new social identities within post-apartheid South Africa.[59] Nakayama and Krizek have also described white talk as

---

56. Sally Matthews, "Shifting White Identities in South Africa: White Africanness and the Struggle for Racial Justice," *Phronimon* 16, no. 2 (2015), 112-29.

57. Natasha Distiller and Melissa E. Steyn, eds, "Introduction: Under Construction," in *Under Construction: "Race" and Identity in South Africa Today* (Sandton: Heinemann, 2004), 1-11; Cornel Verwey and Michael Quayle, "Whiteness, Racism and Afrikaner Identity in Post-Apartheid South Africa," *African Affairs* 111, No. 445 (2012), 551-75.

58. Jo Beall, Stephen Gelb, and Shireen Hassim, "Fragile Stability: State and Society in Democratic South Africa," *Journal of Southern Africa Studies* 31, no. 4 (2005), 683.

59. Anoop Nayak, "After Race: Ethnography, Race and Post-Race Theory," *Ethnic and Racial Studies* 29, no. 3 (2006), 411-30; Claire Scott, "*Die Antwoord* and a Delegitimised South African Whiteness: A Potential Counter-Narrative?" *Critical Arts* 26, no. 5 (2012), 745-61.

"strategic rhetoric" because it serves to evade any critical interrogation of its privilege and history, while at the same time framing whiteness positively, thereby maintaining its centrality, power and superiority.[60]

Discourses of reconciliation and equality have become problematic in this context because they are deployed to maintain the status quo. The "Rainbow Nation" Discourse is seen to foster a colour-blindness that protects privilege and maintains racial inequality. Similarly discourse about "forgetting the past" and "moving on" because apartheid ended nearly twenty-five years ago tend to be deployed by groups that were most advantaged by apartheid.

Verwey and Quayle explore white Afrikaner discourse in private conversations. They note that, while certain visible aspects of Afrikaner identity have been discarded, these have been replaced by the notion of whiteness as central to Afrikaner identity. This is accompanied by a "recycling" of apartheid ideology that depicts black people as incompetent and white people as under threat. This is often accompanied by narratives of white supremacy that argue that white people have a benevolent history because they built the roads, harbors, hospitals, schools, and other infrastructure in the country.

Narratives of Nostalgia for the "Good Old Days"

There are narratives expressed by some South Africans that depict the country's apartheid past as some kind of "golden age" in which everything functioned, the government delivered, and economy flourished. This is contrasted with the current social, economic, and political climate which is characterized with exaggerated descriptions of backwardness, crime, and decay.[61] Verwey and Quayle describe the narrative of one of their research participants, who looks back on the good old days when: "'we' were in charge and the country was 'right.' Now that whites are no longer in power," he argues, "South Africa can 'only go backwards' and 'can never come right again'".[62]

Steyn examines white Afrikaner discourse in letter to newspapers. She notes nostalgic discourses, in which people look back to the "good old days" when you could sleep with your windows and doors open because there was no crime, and people lived without fear.[63] Steyn describes this as a "blend

---

60. Thomas K. Nakayama and Robert L. Krizek, "Whiteness: A Strategic Rhetoric," *Quarterly Journal of Speech* 81, no. 3 (1995), 291-309.
61. Thomas Blaser, "Looking at the Heart of Whiteness in South Africa Today," *The Journal of South African and American Studies* 9, no. 1 (2008), 81-96; Verwey and Quayle, "Whiteness, Racism and Afrikaner Identity."
62. Ibid., 570.
63. Melissa Steyn, "Rehabilitating a Whiteness Disgraced: Afrikaner White Talk in Post-Apartheid South Africa," *Communication Quarterly* 52 (2004), 143-69, 152.

of nostalgia, confusion, self-pity, racism, self-delusion, self-righteousness, and tenacious faith in a discredited worldview."[64] While these narratives of nostalgia for life under apartheid are typical of certain white South African social contexts, what is interesting is that some black South Africans have expressed similar sentiments.[65]

The Country Is Falling Apart

Many South Africans express concern at falling standards in education, healthcare, the deterioration of infrastructure, and the high levels of violent crime, such as rapes, murders, and violent robberies, and hijackings. Some white South Africans view these failures of government through a racial (and racist) lens, describing the perpetrators as savages and barbarians, articulated in discourses that argue that "they" are destroying the country. They argue that crime points to a need for more severe treatment of "them."[66] Narratives about crime, corruption, and the deterioration of infrastructure coalesce to portray the state of affairs in South Africa as a farce. This is accompanied by stories of being excluded from the job market and the economy, marginalized in the spheres of culture and sport, and forced out of the country by crime.[67] There is an increasing anxiety among white South Africans that South Africa will experience economic collapse in the same way as its neighbor Zimbabwe did, when that country implemented populist policies in which land was expropriated from white citizens without compensation.

Narratives of White Victimhood

Steyn observes that there is a tendency among white South Africans to see themselves as victims.[68] Many feel as though they are under threat, particularly from a black "other."[69] For many, this is expressed with unhappiness about affirmative action and Black Economic Empowerment (BEE) policies, and racial quotas that have been imposed on sports teams.

---

64. Ibid., 153.
65. Jacob Dlamini, *Native Nostalgia*, (Auckland Park, Johannesburg: Jacana, 2009); Amber R. Reed, "Nostalgia in the Post-Apartheid State," *Anthropology Southern Africa* 39, no. 2 (2016), 97-109.
66. Steyn, "Rehabilitating a Whiteness Disgraced," 155.
67. Nadine Dolby, "White Fright: The Politics of White Youth Identity in South Africa," *British Journal of Sociology of Education* 22, no. 1 (2001), 5-17; Melissa Steyn and Don Foster, "Repertoires for Talking White: Resistant Whiteness in Post-Apartheid South Africa," *Ethnic and Racial Studies* 31 (2008), 25-51.
68. Steyn, "Rehabilitating a Whiteness Disgraced."
69. Melissa Steyn, *Whiteness Just Isn't What It Used to Be: White Identity in a Changing South Africa* (Albany, NY: State University of New York Press, 2001).

Discussions about these issues draw from a "reverse apartheid" narrative that claims institutionalized discrimination against white people, some of whom had no responsibility for apartheid.[70]

Perhaps the most visible depiction of the demise of privilege for some whites has been the emergence of white people living in squatter camps.[71] In these shanty towns, euphemistically described as "informal settlements" by the government, people live in conditions of squalor and extreme deprivation. Until these white settlements emerged, it was only black South Africans who experienced the harshness of living in such conditions.

The "White Genocide" Narrative

The most extreme examples of a narrative of white victimhood are claims of a genocide against white South Africans, particularly farmers.[72] Suidlanders, the website of the alt-right civil defense organization of the same name, has repeatedly disseminated claims of an impending genocide against white people. Simon Roche, the head of Suidlanders recently told United States alt-right news site Infowars that certain South African leaders have threatened "the slaughter of all whites, and the removal of all whites within five years," prompting Suidlanders to prepare for a civil war which it believes is imminent. Other alt-right websites have carried similar stories, along with claims of a media conspiracy to engage in a cover-up of the genocide that they claim is taking place. Claims of genocide continue to surface; for example, in October 2017, a small independent television website quoted a Breitbart source, claiming that "White genocide continues in South Africa."[73]

In reality, white people are far less likely to be murdered than any other group in South Africa, although there is a disproportionately high murder rate for farmers. Stories of white genocide may have their origins in a 2013 tweet made by Afrikaans activist, Sunette Bridges that 70,000 white South

---

70. Vije Franchi, "The Racialization of Affirmative Action in Organizational Discourses: A Case Study of Symbolic Racism in Post-Apartheid South Africa," *International Journal of Intercultural Relations* 27 (2003), 157-87.
71. Thomas Burrows, "The 'WHITE Squatter Camps' of South Africa: Shanty Towns Built after the Fall of Apartheid Are Now Home to Hundreds of Families," *Mail Online*, 2016, accessed 7 January 2018, http://www.dailymail.co.uk/news/article-3462336/The-white-squatter-camps-South-Africa-home-hundreds-families-enduring-terrible-poverty-blame-fall-Apartheid.html.
72. Verwey and Quayle, "Whiteness, Racism and Afrikaner Identity," 574.
73. "White Genocide Continues in South Africa," *Red Ice News*, 17 October 2017, accessed 27 September 2018, https://redice.tv/news/white-genocide-continues-in-south-africa.

Africans had been murdered since 1994, which would equate to over ten white people murdered a day. There were 361,015 murders in South Africa between 1994 and March 2012, and there were estimated to be 1,544 murders on farms between 1990 and March 2012, although as many as 187 of the victims were black.[74] The actual murder rate of white people in South Africa is 3.4 per 100,000, which is well below the global average of 6.9 per 100,000, and similar to the 3.5 per 100,000 murder rate in Europe. Since South Africa's overall murder rate is a shocking 34.2 per 100,000, it indicates that black South Africans are ten times more likely to be killed than white South Africans.[75]

This description of the South African discursive space is by no means exhaustive, but it illustrates how polarized much South African social discourse has become. There is also a range of social discourse that is positive, and that seeks to overcome the effects of South Africa's past and find means of redress for inequality. However, these voices tend to get lost in the no-man's-land between opposing discourses that point the finger of blame at the other group.

Reflections from a Liminal Space

These multiple, sometimes conflicting and sometimes congruent Discourses reflect the tensions and the contested meanings that are characteristic of South Africa's current liminal state. According to Laclau and Mouffe's theory, for one of the Discourses to achieve hegemony, it would need to broadly reflect the needs and aspirations of the majority of South Africans, and then generate and sustain antagonism against an "other." Hegemony is premised on antagonism and the creation of an "other." In order for a "we" to be constructed, a frontier must be established that separates us from "them," thereby constituting "them" as an enemy.[76] Antagonism is: "'the presence of the Other [that] prevents me from being totally myself. The relation arises not from full totalities, but from the impossibility of their constitution.' To the extent that antagonism exists, 'I cannot be a full presence for myself.'"[77] Antagonism is not opposition that arises from differences of opinion. Antagonism has "an *ontological* [author's italics]

74. Nechama Brodie, "Are SA Whites Really Being Killed 'Like Flies'?" *Africa Check*, 24 June 2013, accessed 9 January 2018, https://africacheck.org/reports/are-white-afrikaners-really-being-killed-like-flies/.

75. Jonathan Jansen, "Even in Death South Africans Are Divided," *Times Live*, 2 November 2017, https://www.timeslive.co.za/ideas/2017-11-02-even-in-death-south-africans-are-racially-divided/.

76. Chantal Mouffe, *The Return of the Political* (London: Verso, 1993), 69.

77. Ibid.,125.

dimension: it imposes a limit on intrinsically polysemic social identities, furnishing them, however temporarily, with a sense of objectivity and potential coherence."[78] The "Other" simultaneously threatens us and creates a sense of unity for "us" as it draws various Discourses together and aligns them against the "Other" through a "logic of equivalence" based on unmet political demands.[79]

The question is whether hegemonic struggle, with its inescapable antagonism, is the only pathway to political identity as Laclau and Mouffe claim, or whether the crisis of identity that is precipitated by dislocation can be resolved in another way. The "us" versus "them" of hegemonic struggle inevitably produces a win-lose (or lose-lose) zero-sum conflict that at best offers temporary resolution. In a world that is increasingly characterized by the dislocation precipitated by continuous and often disruptive change, it would seem prudent to explore alternative pathways to resolution and stability.

"Transversality" may offer such a pathway, particularly as a mode of dialogue. Schrag applies the mathematical notion of transversality to philosophy and explains that it refers to the point of intersection between one line and a system of other lines or surfaces.[80] Transversal rationality is therefore an intersecting of different Discourses, it is as a lying across, an extending over and linking together. It is a place of convergence in space and time where multiple beliefs, practices, habits of thought and assessments come together.[81] Müller borrows the concept of an ecotone, a transition area between neighboring but different communities of plants or animals, as a metaphor for the kind of space created by transversality.[82] In an ecotone, two communities meet and integrate, but there is also a wider variety of species found in this transitional zone in what is called the "edge effect." Instead of hegemonic struggle and antagonism, transversality facilitates a coming together – an exploring of points of intersection and difference. It is in the transversal arrangement of narratives that new meanings emerge, particularly at the points of intersection, which oftenrepresent shared needs and concerns.

---

78. Torfing, "Discourse Theory," 146.
79. Laclau and Mouffe, *Hegemony and Socialist Strategy*; Mark A. Wenman, "Laclau or Mouffe? Splitting the Difference," *Philosophy & Social Criticism* 29, no. 50 (2003), 581-606.
80. Calvin O. Schrag, *The Resources of Rationality: A Response to the Postmodern Challenge* (Bloomington, IA: Indiana University Press, 1992).
81. J. Wentzel van Huyssteen, *The Shaping of Rationality: Toward Interdisciplinarity in Theology and Science* (Grand Rapids, MI: Eerdmans Publishing Co., 1999), 135.
82. Julian C. Müller, "Postfoundational Practical Theology for a Time of Transition," *HTS Theological Studies* 67, no. 1 (2011), 1-5.

As I complete the writing of this chapter, Jacob Zuma has been forced to resign as president by pressure from his own party and threats of impeachment from the opposition. He leaves behind him an undisputed legacy of maladministration, nepotism, and corruption. However, both the problems created by Zuma and the problems created by apartheid are not problems that belong to an "other." They are our problems. When the focus is on finding resolution through the satisfaction of "our" demands, whatever metaphor we choose to represent them, we shut ourselves off from "them," and, more importantly, we neglect the rich terrain of shared interests and concerns. The stories that we tell to make sense of our world and our lives simultaneously open up certain possibilities for action and close others off. They define and limit the options we think exist. The danger is that we become so enamored with our own narrative that we shut ourselves off from the narratives of the "other." What if each of us needs both the presence and the narratives of the other to navigate the ambiguities of liminality?

Rather than trying to force what is good for "us," perhaps liminality offers unique opportunities to listen to "them" and co-create a future that takes into account "our" needs and the concerns of them, as well as us, and is ultimately better for all of us. Like the edge effect described earlier, the multiplicity and diversity in the liminal space create a discursive ecotone. Within this space, transversality makes it possible for new meanings to arise. The task of leadership is to facilitate transversal dialogue. Such dialogue, and the deconstruction and critique of our own narratives that it offers, could facilitate the emergence of deeper understanding, more accurate descriptions, and transformative action in the contexts to which it is applied. The homogenized binaries constructed by identity politics in turn construct political identities that are rigid and adversarial, locking "us" and "them" into seemingly perpetual antagonistic struggle. Transversality makes it possible for new meanings to emerge, for different ways of knowing, different ways of being with those who are different to us, and new ways of solving social problems and eliminating oppression and injustice. New narratives are made possible that not only have the potential to create new identities, but are able to create new communities and new cultures. The narratives that define who we are and what we think is possible can be deconstructed and renegotiated.

An African ideal that captures this is the notion of *ubuntu*. *Ubuntu* articulates the worldview that is reflected in the Zulu proverb "*umuntu ngumuntu ngabanye abantu*" ("a person is a person through other persons"). A person's humanity is realized and expressed within and through their relationships with other people.

Ubuntu has been translated in a variety of ways: as "humanity;"[83] "African humanness;"[84] "humanism or humaneness;"[85] or "the process of becoming an ethical human being."[86] Mkhize further proposes that *ubuntu*, "incorporates ideas of social justice, righteousness, care, empathy for others and respect."[87] Mnyaka and Motlhabi write that *ubuntu*, "is best realised in deeds of kindness, compassion, caring, sharing, solidarity and sacrifice."[88] For Tutu, the importance of *ubuntu* is that: "'a person is a person through other people.' It is not 'I think therefore I am.' It says rather: 'I am human because I belong.' I participate, I share."[89] The notion of *ubuntu* points to the interconnectedness of human beings, with the implication that people should treat each other as though we are all members of an extended family.[90] Ackermann captures the implications of *ubuntu* in the following statement:

> In this boundless human web I acquire my humanity as something
> which comes to me as a gift . . . shaped and nurtured in and through
> the humanity of others. I can only exercise my humanity by being
> in relationship with others and there is no growth, happiness or
> fulfillment for me apart from other human beings.[91]

For a country whose transition has stalled and become stuck in a liminal space, *ubuntu* offers an ecotone that arises from our shared humanity. While black South Africans demonstrated *ubuntu* in the post-apartheid years, there was a distinct lack of reciprocation from their white counterparts. Can white South Africans take the initiative and embrace *ubuntu* as an underlying principle for addressing the endemic poverty and inequality that exists along racial lines in South Africa?

---

83. Augustine Shutte, *Philosophy for Africa* (Cape Town: University of Cape Town Press, 1993).

84. Johann Broodryk, *Ubuntu: Life Lessons from Africa* (Pretoria: Ubuntu School of Philosophy, 2002), 13.

85. Mluleki Mnyaka and Mokgethi Motlhabi, "Ubuntu and Its Socio-Moral Significance," in *African Ethics: An Anthology of Comparative and Applied Ethics*, ed. Munyaradzi F. Murove (Scottsville, Pietermaritzburg: University of KwaZulu-Natal Press, 2009), 63.

86. Nhlanhla Mkhize, "Ubuntu and Harmony: An African Approach to Morality and Ethics," in *Persons in Community: African Ethics in a Global Culture*, ed. Ronald Nicolson (Scottsville, Pietermaritzburg: University of KwaZulu-Natal Press, 2008), 35.

87. Ibid., 43.

88. Mnyaka and Motlhabi, "Ubuntu and Its Socio-Moral Significance," 74.

89. Desmond M. Tutu, *No Future without Forgiveness* (London: Rider, 1999), 34-35.

90. Gish, *Desmond Tutu*, 122.

91. Denise M. Ackermann, "Becoming Fully Human: An Ethic of Relationship in Difference and Otherness," *Journal of Theology for Southern Africa* 102 (1998), 19.

Michael Eze[92] makes a distinction between essentialist and performative notions of *ubuntu*. Essentialist *ubuntu*, like learned religion, looks to past traditions and dictates what should or must be in order to retain a pure version of *ubuntu* – based on the way that the past is imagined. Performative *ubuntu* is dynamic and involves confluence and dialogue with other cultures and Discourses. It is *ubuntu* as lived experience or way of life. Performative *ubuntu* looks to the past to make sense of the present and shape the future. The performance of *ubuntu* at multiple levels in the social and economic lives of South Africans might offer a pathway out of this stalemate. An *ubuntu* ecotone, particularly one that arises from concrete expressions of *ubuntu* by white South Africans, might lead South Africans to a future that is the best possible one, where we learn or are reminded that it is making space for the other in our lives that we experience our humanity in its most authentic form.

---

92. Michael O. Eze, "The History and Contemporary Frame of Botho/Ubuntu: Philosophical and Sociocultural Complexities," Paper presented at 2017 Mind and Life XXXII Conference, "Botho/Ubuntu: A Dialogue on Spirituality, Science and Humanity," Gaberone, Botswana, 17-19 August 2017.

16
Gender Benders and Communitas
Dianne Dentice and Michelle Dietert

Always be a little kinder than is necessary.

Sir J.M. Barrie

* * *

If liminal space is inhabited by anyone in contemporary societies such as the United States, it is by transgender individuals and other gender non-conformists.[1] The expression of alternative forms of gender identity is often met with disdain and, in some instances, violence in societies that do not recognize more than two genders. Individuals who refuse to conform in socially prescribed ways of gender expression often fall somewhere along a gender continuum between female and male. Others may not identify with either gender and assume an anti-gender stance. At least for a time, some gender variant individuals experience liminality as they transition from one gender identity to the other; however, not all transgender people elect to fully transition.

Some liminality is permanent in nature, the result of condition or social definition. But other forms of liminality are more transitional, and transformation is fostered through ritual processes and strong supportive communities. More permanent, socially imposed liminality may produce insecurity and/or vulnerability, especially for individuals who exhibit ambiguity in their gender presentation and may or may not be transsexual – which involves physical transformation of some type. These people are at higher-than-average risk for abuse and stigmatization. The persistence of gender panics, which occur especially with regard to stereotypical perceptions of transgender individuals, affects continued

---

1. Some people prefer the term gender variant but we use both terms interchangeably throughout this chapter.

progress for transgender rights.[2] If confusion of identity and the potential of transformation through transition characterizes the liminal person, the transgender experience adds even greater dimension in the tension between gender identity and biological sex determined at birth.

Transgender individuals represent an array of gender and sexual identities that transcend binary arrangements. Each day, they negotiate their daily lives with family, friends, co-workers, and strangers. They also navigate public spaces that include but are not limited to restrooms, workplaces, and educational institutions. Over the years many people have shared their stories with us. Christi, born female, identifies in various ways that include agender, multigender, and genderqueer: "I see myself somewhere between genders. I would say that I lean somewhere towards the female side of things but definitely in the middle somewhere. I just kind of feel like I'm multigendered or sometimes I've thought of myself as agendered because I certainly don't see myself as either male or female and I don't know how to really wrap my brain around the in-between."

Lucas identifies as a "genderqueer transguy" with feminist tendencies. Sherith's identity as genderqueer enables her to dive deeply into gender by playing different roles depending on her mood on any given day. Rather than denouncing gender all together, she performs gender in multiple ways regardless of her sex at birth which is female. Lee identifies on the male end of the gender spectrum although she does not plan on any type of physical transition and does not bind her breasts. The use of gender specific pronouns bothers her but she realizes that in our culture a gender-neutral pronoun shift will take decades – perhaps even longer.

The Changing World of Gender

The simplistic definition of gender as a binary construct is outdated; however, many societies still strictly adhere to the male/female dichotomy in which an individual (based on sex at birth) has one of two choices. This social constructionist approach attempts to maintain conformity and the gender status quo. Males are expected to exhibit specific traits associated with maleness. The same goes for females. People who fail to conform to these expectations assume a stigmatized identity based on rigid binary expectations imposed by broader social processes. Gender is one of the organizing principles of the social world in that it contextualizes individual identities and structures social interactions. Adherence to a strict binary, either female or male, affects how transgender people live their everyday lives.

---

2.   Kristen Schilt and Laurel Westbrook, "Bathroom Battlegrounds and Penis Panics," *Contexts* (20 August 2015), 27.

Foucault argued that highly disciplined institutional spaces fix individual social positions to ensure conformity.[3] This fact impedes the process of achieving gender freedom for those who desire to live their lives according to who they really are, despite sex assigned at birth. The argument for conformity begins early in the socialization process. Foucault referred to this as the surface of emergence. Parents control how their children do gender through physical presentation which is enhanced by proper clothing, encouraging play with gender appropriate toys, and reinforcing proper social roles based on biological sex. Extending his theory to the larger society, Foucault identified authorities of delimitation within social institutions that determine and perpetuate gender binary arrangements. Gender non-conformists become targets for stereotyping and institutionalized discrimination – especially if they present in ways that are not in line with classic binary thinking about gender.

In recent decades we have experienced a fundamental shift in how transgender people conceive of and express their gender identities. Contemporary transgender youth have unlimited access to information on the Internet and other social media outlets. Many colleges and universities offer courses in gender and women's studies that explore different ways of doing gender. There are also a growing number of transgender images in popular culture such as Caitlyn Jenner, Chaz Bono, and Laverne Cox, to name a few. In this environment, many transgender youth acknowledge and embrace their identities more quickly than ever before. Activists (many of whom are young trans persons) are pioneering the idea that there are many ways to be gendered and to sexually orient. They encourage everyone (not just other gender non-conformists) to question the concept of biological identity altogether. Within this contemporary liminal passage, a community of gender bending activists appears with new ways of defining who they are and why that is important.

A genderqueer mantra is to make your own choices rather than taking the easy way out by submitting to convenient gendered boxes in which one must conform to accepted gender ideals – not so easy for some transgender individuals. As was stated earlier, not all transgender people elect to transition with the aid of surgery and other methods. With a more flexible approach to gendering, they have permission to resist forced transition through surgical intervention and/or hormone therapy. One must wonder how Turner might react to this unique version of communitas, especially among young people who are engaged with the contemporary LGBTQ movement.

---

3. Michel Foucault, *Discipline and Punish: The Birth of the Prison*, trans. Alan Sheridan, 2nd ed. (New York: Vintage Books, 1991), 148.

"Suffering Makes Kinsmen of Us All"
Elbert Hubbard

Harold Garfinkel[4] hypothesized that societies exercising close controls over the sex composition of their populations tend to privilege persons who regard themselves as normally sexed. Historically, people in the LGBTQ community fall into Garfinkel's "prohibited" category of gender identity, which puts them at risk of abuse, especially at the hands of social control agents such as law enforcement and homophobic bosses. Expectations of gender roles emanate from deeply rooted socialization processes, gender stereotypes, and fear. Fundamentalist religious perspectives that demand adherence to strict heteronormative gender roles also prove troublesome for the entire LGBTQ community.

In June 2015, same-sex marriage became the law of the land thanks to a U.S. Supreme Court decision that made it possible for same-sex couples to marry. However, thirty-two states lack fundamental laws that fully protect LGBTQ people against discrimination in the workplace, housing, education, healthcare, and, most recently, public accommodations such as restrooms — especially for transgender and gender non-conforming individuals.[5] Although gays and lesbians can legally marry, some business owners refuse to make wedding cakes or provide flowers and other services in the name of religious freedom rooted in beliefs that define marriage as between one man and one woman. The religious right has aggressively supported religious freedom bills in some states where LGBTQ anti-discrimination laws are non-existent. For example, Republican governor Phil Bryant of Mississippi, a Baptist minister with ties to Christian fundamentalist leader Tony Perkins, signed Mississippi House Bill 1523 that became law in July 2016. Among other things, this bill states that gender is defined by anatomy at birth.

Under the law, there is a recusal process that allows clerks, magistrates, judges, and justices of the peace to refuse licensing marriages based on their religious beliefs. Medical professionals can refuse to participate in treatments, counseling and procedures related to gender confirmation for transgender citizens of the state. Employers and school administrators have the power to dictate access to bathroom and locker room facilities for transgender students. It also prevents state government officials or workers

---

4. Harold Garfinkel, *Studies in Ethnomethodology* (Englewood Cliffs, NJ: Prentice Hall, 1967), 117.
5. Brandon Lorenz, "Map: How Many States Still Lack Clear Non-Discrimination Protections?" He is quoting from the Human Rights Campaign Internet site at http://www.hrc.org/blog.

from taking steps to protect LGBTQ people from harm if the abuse is believed to be faith-based. This law conflicts with U.S. federal laws that protect LGBTQ people, including Title VII (covering employment), Title IX (covering federally funded education programs), and federal funding for a range of child welfare programs and services. The state of Mississippi has codified discriminatory practices aimed at the LGBTQ community in the name of religious freedom for a very narrow sector of the population.

"You Lose a Lot of Time, Hating People"
Marian Anderson

Religious beliefs about good and evil are reinforced by supernatural sources of social control such as the Christian Bible, the Jewish Torah, and the Islamic Koran. It is a powerful force for conformity in a given society. Social values are prescribed and institutionalized through rituals such as attending church services, praying, singing, and obeying God's commandments. Religion can provide many positive things for true believers. It may also provide the escape from reality that Marx referred to as "The Opium of the People."[6] Through symbols, rituals, and the promise of life after death, religion serves as a moral compass for people in search of a higher purpose. In trying to explain what has gone wrong with America, the Christian right argues that Americans have lost their way because they have strayed from a covenant with God.[7] The religious freedom laws such as the one enacted by the state of Mississippi are a last-ditch effort by the religious right to circumvent what they view as an assault on values established by the framers of the Constitution that include rules governing both marriage and gender roles.

Data collected by the National Coalition of Anti-Violence Programs indicates that police harassment of the entire LGBTQ community continues to be a problem in contemporary American society.[8] In collections of self-report surveys of the transgender community, researchers have found higher-than-average incidences of violence and other forms of abuse. One of the most documented types of violence against transgender people is

---

6. Karl Marx and Friedrich Engels, *On Religion* (Moscow: Progress Publications, 1957), 41.
7. Ross Douthat, *Bad Religion: How We Became a Nation of Heretics* (New York: Free Press, 2012), 2.
8. Emily Waters, Chai Jindasurat and Cecilia Wolfe, "Lesbian, Gay, Bisexual, Transgender, Queer, and HIV-Affected Hate Violence in 2015. NY: National Coalition of Anti-Violence Programs," NCAVP Report 2015, 13-15, accessed 1 October 2018, http://avp.org/wp-content/uploads/2017/04/ncavp_hvreport_2015_final.pdf.

sexual assault and rape with young gender non-conforming persons being at a higher risk. Victimization of trans folk occurs globally and includes domestic abuse as well as random acts of violence aimed at transgender people. Many gender non-conforming persons are also victimized by patriarchal value systems that dictate boundaries for gender identity and expression. Imposing arbitrary gender rules enables fathers, brothers, uncles, and even mothers to try and fix the errant family member. Unfortunately, hate crimes legislation in countries as diverse as Canada and Jamaica, among others, does not include gender identity as a protected category.[9]

"We've Got to Make Change Our National Pastime and Hold Protests More Regularly than Weekend Parties"
Rivera Sun

Gender identity refers to a deep sense of self. You know who you are in spite of the biological imperative. In societies that demand a strict binary interpretation of one's gender identity, markers are established for proper designation. They become part of one's legal identity based on sex assigned at birth. Cisgender describes a person whose gender identity matches the sex assigned at birth, although not all cisgender people conform to cultural expectations based on gendered norms. Agender persons do not identify as having a gender identity that can be categorized using binary terms. They may simply exist without being encumbered by a specific gender identity. These examples indicate that people express their gender identities in many different ways. Gender expression is informed by culture, age, social class, race and ethnicity, and religion. Gender identity is personal and gender variant individuals often find themselves in socially precarious situations that put their safety at risk.[10]

This brings us again to Victor Turner's concept of liminality, that suspension betwixt and between following symbolic death and preceding symbolic rebirth. He contrasted social structure (a more ordinary condition of hierarchies and dividedness) with anti-structure (a condition of flux, equality, and potential growth) contained in liminal conditions. If the liminal space between familiarity of structures or anti-structure is filled with flux and ambiguity, it is also filled with creative potential. A central byproduct of liminal time and space is the creation of communitas, the unique affiliation of those passing through the same intense experience. It provides a sense of common unity and solidarity as little else can. According to Turner:

9. Barbara Perry and D. R. Dyck, "I Don't Know Where it is Safe: Trans Women's Experiences of Violence," *Critical Criminology*, Vol. 22, 49.
10. Eli Green and Luca Maurer @ http://www.teachingtransgender.org/.

> I have used the term "anti-structure," . . . to describe both liminality
> and what I have called "communitas." I meant by it not a structural
> reversal . . . but the liberation of human capacities of cognition,
> affect, volition, creativity, etc., from the normative constraints
> incumbent upon occupying a sequence of social statuses.[11]

There is more than one distinction between structure and communitas:
the difference between secular and sacred. This sacred component is acquired
during rites of passage or the changing of positions and is achieved through
phases (moving from place to place), allowing subordinate groups to
eventually achieve a higher position within the social hierarchy in which they
reside. For many gender non-conforming individuals, the whole concept of
gender is turned upside down or inside out by their choice of ways to express
(overtly) who they are. They experience liminality as a group because of
their marginalized status, assigned by the more powerful, dominating social
institutions that dictate traditional gender norms. Petra Doan, a transgender
woman, referred to her closet as a sacred space prior to coming out and
beginning her transition.[12] Other trans people we have spoken with over the
years also talked about certain rituals that meant so much to them, some as
basic as getting a haircut or shopping for clothes of their preferred gender.

"There Can Be No Progress Without Head-on Confrontation"
Christopher Hitchens

Change happens when people connect in ways to accomplish a common
goal. In other words, out of the liminal experience social movements are
born. Examples are the Stonewall riots in New York City[13] and Harvey
Milk's[14] activism for gay rights in San Francisco. The Stonewall incident
occurred in 1969 when raids on gay bars were routine and frequent in
cities across the United States. The incident at Stonewall was different
because the gay and transgender community fought back. Protests and
disturbances continued with varying intensity for five days. In the wake of

---

11. Victor Turner, *From Ritual to Theatre: The Human Seriousness of Play* (New York: Performing Arts Journal Publications, 1982), 44.
12. Petra L. Doan, "The Tyranny of Gendered Spaces: Reflections from Beyond the Gender Dichotomy," *Gender, Place & Culture* 17, no.5 (2010),635-54,DOI:10.108 0/0966369X.2010.503121, 639-640.
13. Lionel Wright, "The Stonewall Riots 1969," *Socialist Alternative*, accessed 27 September 2018, https://www.socialistalternative.org/stonewall-riots-1969/.
14. Harvey Milk, "Biography," in *Encyclopedia of World Biography*, accessed 27 September 2018, http://www.notablebiographies.com/Ma-Mo/Milk-Harvey. html#ixzz4l8MneKOI.

the riots, intense discussions took place within the city's gay community and eventually the Gay Liberation Front (now defunct) was formed and the L(esbian) G(ay) B(isexual) part of the movement was born.

During the 1970s, San Francisco city politician Harvey Milk helped open the door for gays and lesbians in the United States by championing civil rights for homosexuals. However, he was not a one-issue politician. He battled for a wide range of social changes in education, public transportation, childcare, and low-income housing. As city supervisor, Milk was the driving force behind the passage of a gay rights law that prohibited discrimination in housing and employment based on sexual orientation. At his urging, the city announced a drive to hire more gay and lesbian police officers. He gained national attention for his role in defeating a state senate proposal that would have prohibited gays and lesbians from teaching in public schools in California. On 27 November 1978, Milk and San Francisco Mayor George Moscone were shot dead in City Hall by Dan White, a former city supervisor who had quit the board in protest at the passage of the city's gay rights law championed by Milk and supported by the mayor. While there have been huge advances in the struggle for LGBTQ rights since the Stonewall riots and the death of Harvey Milk, there is still a long way to go before we achieve full liberation for some of our most vulnerable citizens.

The term transgender has political connotations all of its own and is often associated with the continuing fight for social equality and justice for all gender non-conforming individuals. However, just as with the second wave of the American women's movement, people of color and others from lower socio-economic backgrounds may experience exclusion from the broader movement due to the fact that many activists come from middle- and upper-class backgrounds and have higher levels of education.[15] Matzner found that the term transgender did not personally resonate with some of the people he interviewed in an oral history project, and for this reason they preferred not to be identified by it.[16]

The complexities of gender identity are evident when examining narratives provided by gender non-conforming young people and their adult counterparts. Again, the term transgender does not always fit as the preferred label for everyone. In January 2017, *National Geographic* published a gender issue that illustrated the many facets of navigating the

---

15. Petra Doan acknowledges this fact in her biographical discussions about her activism in the LGBTQ movement.

16. Andrew Matzner, "Transgender, Queens, *Mahu*, Whatever: An Oral History from Hawai'i," accessed 27 September, http://intersections.anu.edu.au/issue6/matzner.html.

gender lens. Henig[17] interviewed a fourteen year-old called E., who was
born female but expressed hesitation at the label transgender to explain her
gender identity. She was still using her birth name and the pronoun "she"
at the time of the interview. At this point in her life she is not willing to say
that she was born in the wrong body even though she has always felt more
like a boy than a girl. Her solution includes some body modifications in
order to accommodate her self-described androgyny.

We are learning more about the biological components of gender,
especially for people who are gender non-conforming. Unfortunately, many
of the studies contain very few cases. They may also include people who
have already begun taking hormones to transition to the opposite gender,
affecting the researcher's ability to explain observed brain differences.
Then there is the intersex condition where a baby is born with a mix of
male and female chromosomes, testicular and ovarian tissue, genitals, and
other sexual characteristics. In advanced societies such as the United States,
parents of these babies, at least in the not-so-distant past, were counseled by
healthcare professionals to intervene with various procedures that included
surgery and hormone replacement. Other less developed cultures such as
Samoa, the Dominican Republic, and various countries in Africa have
historically accommodated the intersex condition and incorporated third
gender individuals into their communities as they mature into teenagers
and adults.

"Recognize Yourself in He and She
Who Are Not Like You and Me"
Carlos Fuentes

Thomas Laqueur developed a one-sex model theory using historical data
from European antiquity to the beginning of the Middle Ages. According
to sixteenth-century scientists, the vagina was really a penis and the uterus a
scrotum. The difference in perception regarding anatomy was not because
of the stupidity of the observers but because they had a different way of
conceptualizing sexuality as Laqueur illustrates in the following passage:

> The absence of a precise anatomical nomenclature for the female
> genitals, and for the reproductive system generally, is the linguistic
> equivalent of the propensity to see the female body as a version of
> the male. Both testify not to the blindness, inattention, or muddle-
> headedness of Renaissance anatomists, but to the absence of an

---

17. Robin Marantz Henig, "Rethinking Gender," *National Geographic*, January 2017,
    51.

imperative to create incommensurable categories of biological male and female through images or words. Language constrained the seeing of opposites and sustained the male body as the canonical human form. And, conversely, the fact that one saw only one sex made even words for female parts ultimately refer to male organs.[18]

For example, Aristotle viewed sexuality as an ascending ladder of perfection with females at the bottom, boys and adolescent males in the middle, and at the pinnacle were Greek aristocratic males. The earliest strain of creation stories in Hebrew scripture speaks of gender emerging from a shared common source; centuries of interpretation overlaid the text with hierarchy: women were derived from males.

Although Laqueur's one-sex model is not directly connected to the concept of liminality, one might be able to infer that being born female during the Renaissance era automatically resulted in liminal status. In essence, women were mere extensions of men or rather in a constant state of betwixt and between. Some twenty-first-century gender non-conformists embrace the idea of being both female and male or neither female nor male. They are pushing the gender envelope in response to the perceived problem of individuals who do not fit into either of the two sex/gender categories culturally prescribed and generally accepted as "normal." In some ways they have elevated the one-sex model to a new, more egalitarian concept. They may or may not prefer the label of transgender to describe their choice of gender self-expression.

Before the term transgender came into vogue, another term – transsexual – was invented to describe the phenomenon. American psychiatrist and sexologist Robert Stoller defined transsexualism as the conviction of a biologically "normal" person that he or she was a member of the opposite sex. His definition was accepted and widely used during the 1960s and 1970s. This definition denies any possibility of an alternative gender. Transsexuals were perceived as occupying a temporary, in-between sex status until they transitioned from one sex to the desired other. This sounds strikingly like Turner's theory of liminality directly applied to the transsexual experience.

Back in the day, transsexualism was understood as a discordance between anatomy and subjectively experienced gender. As Garfinkel wrote in his ethnography of Agnes, born male, her sex organs were a "trick of fate, a personal misfortune, an accident . . . that she had never accepted."[19] At

---

18. Thomas Laqueur, *Making Sex: Body and Gender from the Greeks to Freud* (Cambridge, MA: Harvard University Press, 1990), 96.

19. Harold Garfinkel, "Passing and the Managed Achievement of Sex Status in an Intersexed Person, Part 1," in *Studies in Ethnomethodology* (Cambridge: Polity Press, 1984), 131.

the time, a sex change operation was the way to relieve gender ambiguity while at the same time upholding the status quo of the binary sex/gender system. Definitions continue to change and new identities emerge within the LGBTQ community. In 2013 the American Psychiatric Association published the fifth edition of the *Diagnostic and Statistical Manual of Mental Disorders* (DSM) and added the diagnosis of Gender Dysphoria to replace Gender Identity Disorder. With that change in wording, a discussion began about hormonal and genetic components contributing to the diagnosis, as well as various medical treatments that included hormone therapy and gender confirmation surgery.

What has not changed is that transgender individuals continue to experience hostility and discrimination. As a group, their unemployment rates are twice those of the general population. They are four times more likely than the general population to have incomes of less than $10,000 a year. They suffer from housing instability and in some cases chronic homelessness. Transgender children, tweens, and teens report harassment by other students and teachers, including physical assault. College-age transgender students have documented denial of access to gender-appropriate housing.[20] These facts reveal continued evidence of transphobia and homophobia that characterize a segment of the population and its efforts to discredit and deny LGBTQ people basic civil rights protections.

"Our Problems Stem from Our Acceptance of this Filthy, Rotten System"
Dorothy Day

Since Christine Jorgensen made international headlines in the early 1950s for having a sex change operation, the dominant model of transgender identity development has involved individuals who recognize themselves at a young age as a gender different from their birth sex. Initially, many transgender people struggle to understand their feelings – especially if there is no family support. After years of shame, denial, anxiety, and abuse they begin to accept themselves. They may take hormones and have gender confirmation surgery to align their outward appearance with their inner sense of self. Others push the gender envelope by presenting in ways that do not involve any type of physical transformation or as in the case of E., minor adjustments to accommodate one's true identity.

---

20. Kevin M. Barry, Brian Farrell, Jennifer L. Levi, Neelima Vanguri, "A Bare Desire to Harm: Transgender People and the Equal Protection Clause," *Boston College Law Review* 57 (April 2016), 527, 551, 552.

Gender transformations do not occur without challenges for individuals undergoing the change, their friends, family members, and others in society who refuse to accept the individual's right to do so. Turner wrote that liminality is frequently likened to death, to being in the womb, to invisibility, to darkness, to gender ambiguity, to being in the wild, and to an eclipse of the sun or moon. In Petra Doan's[21] discussion about her transition, she spoke of the tyranny of gender or the oppression of individuals whose behavior, presentation, and expression fundamentally challenge socially accepted gender categories. She acknowledged the tendency of others to try to discipline and control people who violate gender norms in ways that continually marginalize transgender and other gender non-conforming people.

Doan alludes to communitas in her relationships with other transgender individuals. She notes that both activists and scholars are reclaiming their stories in order to describe their experiences in their own words. They often use narratives to reveal patterns of inequality from a first-person perspective. Gender transitions are never private affairs because they occur in public places with activists in the movement fighting against attempts by others to silence transgender individuals and their allies. Gender variant identities challenge accepted gender norms at significant social cost: loss of power, approval, and material benefits such as a paycheck or a place to live. Interestingly, in our years of research we found that, in some instances, trans men who successfully pass as male after full transition do not lose power, approval or material benefits. In fact, they end up benefiting from the dominant status of males in a patriarchal society – especially if they are white.

Does this successful transition for some trans men require a denial of their once-marginalized status on two counts? First of all, their sex at birth was female. Next, confronting their true gender identity most likely caused some conflicts along the way. To have a label, such as transgender, in a culture that demands gender conformity most certainly produces marginalization. Keeping gender transition a secret may allow some individuals to deny the label and avoid shame and stigmatization. But does this solve the broader problem of inequality and the social shaming of the entire LGBTQ community?

During the 1940s and 1950s, postwar reconstruction and the shift to consumerism resulted in promotion of the nuclear family stereotype. Anyone who stepped out of line by engaging in same-sex relationships was admonished and sanctioned. For that reason, many gays and lesbians lived their entire lives in the closet. Additionally, the acknowledgment of gender

21. Petra Doan is an American trans woman and university professor.

diversity by the general public was still in the distant future even though Christine Jorgenson helped move it along after her very public sex change hit the airwaves and newspapers. Then into the 1960s and 1970s, gay life continued to be marred by overtly homophobic policing and stereotyping by the general public. We have made some progress but, in today's world, transgender youth and adults have far higher rates of suicidal thoughts and suicide attempts than average. The suicide rate among transgender adults in a recent international study was roughly 800 per 100,000. In comparison, the suicide rate in the U.S. for all people is thirteen per 100,000.[22]

Members of the entire LGBTQ community share a common history of exploitation and abuse. There is no denying that we all live in a culture that is dominated by heteronormative values. We also know that some members of our society are both homophobic and transphobic and that they hide behind social institutions such as the churches, the military, and schools to justify their denial of basic human rights to socially marginalized groups like our transgender citizens and neighbors. Marx once said that overcoming obstacles is a liberating activity.[23] Communities help identify, support, and build connections between people. They can provide strategies to deal with attempts to destroy and subjugate their members. Our collective challenge for the future is to produce a society that accepts diversity, welcomes difference, and champions human rights for all its citizens. If accomplished, this might enable Turner's view of positive social change through community building actually to become reality. One can always remain hopeful.

22. Stacey Freedenthal @ http://www.speakingofsuicide.com/2015/01/02/transgender-suicide/.
23. Karl Marx, *Grundrisse* (Harmondsworth: Penguin Books, 1973), 611.

17

Three Spaces and an Excursus

Kenneth Krushel

The Refugee Camp

Think how strange it is to endure a childhood confined to a sliver within a city where you do not know the language of those on the other side of a "separation barrier," where you are a legal resident in a country whose symbols are not your symbols, where holidays are foreign, where posters of martyrs – often adolescents, sometimes your friends – are pasted along alleys and between heaps of garbage outside your home. You live in what is known as "the Holy City" and "the city of the Lord of Hosts" (Psalm 48:8).

This childhood within Jerusalem exists in the Shuafat Refugee Camp, the only Palestinian refugee camp in Jerusalem or any other Israeli-administered area. Most residents have a blue ID card, permitting limited entry to Israel through a checkpoint, but no citizenship, thus a vague legitimacy. Residents pay taxes to Israel even while their language is threatened. Currently, the Israeli government is proposing to revoke Arabic's "official language status."

This is a life in exile, living behind an obdurate concrete wall, a form of involuntary permanent liminality where lives teeter between ambiguity and disorientation, deconstructing one's self-definition.

For Shuafat's youth, among the choices – if there are choices given the seductive malignancies lurking all around – are to enlist in the blade intifada or "lone wolf" attacks using a knife or scissors to maim, even kill, and in exchange be killed or at least imprisoned. Or turn in a different direction: perform rap music.

In a small room within the Palestinian Child Center in Shuafat Refugee Camp, a twenty-year-old aspiring rap artist sits before his tools: a modest computer equipped with digital audio software, and assorted recording equipment. "Outside, it's a jungle," says the young man, Mohammed Hamouda.

Hamouda the Rapper, his performance name, is matter-of-fact in describing his refugee camp childhood: "To survive means to fight. To be a violent kid is the culture. Even at six or seven you know you have to hit back. I would fight other kids, showing the street that I wasn't afraid. You fight or be bullied."

Walking in the camp offers scant evidence of where one might experience childhood. There is little space to run. There is an ever-present stench of sewage, detritus clogs alleyways snaking between crumbling building facades, damaged cars are abandoned along narrow streets. A common street scene includes clusters of young men, their posture sunken, expressions sullen and resigned, yet also defiant.

The camp is unique, not for its warren of squalid structures and sense of nullity, but for its lack of definition. To many Israeli citizens, the Shuafat refugee camp is invisible. It is hidden behind a wall. To those aware of its existence, they see it best ignored as a Palestinian enclave resistant to Israeli sovereignty, and as a menace to a unified Jerusalem.

The Shuafat Refugee camp was created in 1965 by the Jordanian authorities and the United Nations Relief Works Agency (UNRWA) to house refugee families from Jerusalem's Old City. Within weeks following the 1967 war, Israel expanded the city's municipal boundaries, resulting in the camp's becoming part of Jerusalem. With Israel's completion of the separation barrier in 2011, the camp found itself planted within the West Bank, severed, though technically remaining within the city's municipal footprint.

Since the Palestinian Authority has no role here, the camp exists in a governance vacuum. Without clear lines of authority, municipal services are neglected: erratic access to clean water, frequent electrical outages, a malfunctioning sewage system, and irregular garbage collection contribute to an atmosphere of daily crisis. As an NGO official working in the camp noted, "What you see is a frenzy of mutual denial by anyone/everyone who has some responsibility for this."

With special refugee status assigned by the United Nations, UNRWA struggles to provide rudimentary support for the burgeoning population. The camp nurtures anger and alienation, and has been the source of frequent attacks on Israeli border control forces. Fueling a smoldering rage is the contempt youths feel not only for Israel, but for the Palestinian Authority, viewed as a tool of the Israeli government for maintaining the status quo.

In the spring of 2017, the Israeli Police Department opened its first post in the camp since 1967, whether to protect Israel or Shuafat is unclear, though the Jerusalem Police Chief, Yoram Halevy, claims the police station "will lead to strengthening mutual trust between police and residents."

After sunset, however, lawlessness asserts itself with criminal gangs flourishing in the no-man's-land. Unsurprisingly, the Israeli security service, Shin Bet, considers the camp an incubator of anti-Israeli violence and those who target Israeli soldiers. It is considered an enemy by Israel, and used rhetorically by the Arab world to condemn Israel's treatment of Palestinians.

Because there has been no official census, it is estimated that the refugee camp and surrounding neighborhood population is between sixty thousand and eighty thousand. According to the Association for Civil Rights in Israel (ACRI) over eighty percent of children live below what is considered the poverty line. For men under twenty-four, unemployment estimates range from thirty to fifty percent.

The director of the Palestinian Child Center, Khaled Al Sheikh, explains that the one safe playground with adult supervision in the refugee camp is within the confines of the Center, where there are also after-school academic classes and "peace education" activities supported by a German government organization, GIZ, and its Civil Peace Service (CPS) program, offering instruction in art, the traditional dance of *dabkah*, music, drama, and athletics, including "flag football" taught by a German social worker who loves the American sport.

Using the center's Internet access, Hamouda the Rapper discovered hip-hop, particularly Ice Cube's recording of "Gangsta Rap Made Me Do It." "Even if I only understood a little of Ice Cube's music, I knew it was me," Hamouda says.

YouTube was his English instructor. At first attracted to the music's driving rhythm, he studied rap language while withstanding outside pressures. Two brothers had been imprisoned, one for throwing stones at Israeli soldiers, such a commonality that the "stones to prison choreography" is a rite of passage.

"I didn't throw stones," Hamouda says, "First of all, I can't throw. Besides, throwing stones doesn't make anything."

Hamouda is large, American-high-school-football-player-large, and moves fluidly, having inherited from his father, a professional soccer player, an obvious athleticism. He can also be very still and silent and an attentive observer. When asked about his childhood, he weighs the question before responding: "Hell is traveling hours to sit across from your brother, thick glass separating you, speaking by prison phone. When you see your brothers and you can't touch them, it's a nightmare but you are awake."

Beginning in the late 1990s, rap music took root in the Palestinian community. Several groups became popular, including DAM (meaning "lasting forever" in Arabic, and "blood" in Hebrew) from Lod, and G-Town from Shuafat. An identification with African-American urban ghetto culture inspired a new form of self-expression, challenging stereotypes, replacing some of the energy of stone-throwing for rapping.

> I want to find the right way to translate my pain
> I hate terrorism and I love my religion
> I feel like I'm living alone, not a human being
> Because no one knows what's going on in my refugee camp
>
> I want you to live your childhood dream
> And imagine yourself to be superman
> And fly away with your dream
>
> It doesn't matter who failed before you
> Believe and struggle to achieve your dream
>
>   from "*Alhaya Amal*" ("Life is Hope")
>   by Mohammed Hamouda

"I loved to sing and wanted a piano even before rap," says Hamouda. "My father bought a keyboard for me and I taught myself to play 'Happy Birthday.' There really wasn't any place in Jerusalem for rap. I'd go home, read about it, work on my music, and then started performing."

Taking workshop classes in rap music at the Child Center, he participated in a young rapper project in Bethlehem. One of the members of G-Town heard Hamouda perform and became his teacher. Khaled Al Sheikh, who once had a music studio, donated equipment for a recording space which soon became Hamouda's proverbial second home.

Sitting in a restaurant in East Jerusalem, the young rapper is dressed like a kid you'd see at a suburban mall or Brooklyn café: flannel shirt, graphically busy t-shirt, ripped jeans, boots. An Israeli couple at a neighboring table hears the English language conversation and politely interrupts.

"Is it safe to go through the Damascus Gate?" they ask, referring to an Old City entrance and the site of a recent stabbing. Hamouda's posture changes, his face an arena of deliberation. He turns expressing a youthful kindness, yet something paternal as well.

"You'll be safe. What's the difference how you enter? Of course, you can go." But he understands there's a difference.

The youngest of nine children, Hamouda began to teach rap at the center when he was seventeen. "I had my eye on one kid who was about to get into trouble. I started with him. Now he's the best."

The center's director explains that Hamouda is popular and effective because, "He deals with the children on their level, the level of their thoughts, and he is dealing with them not as a teacher but as a friend."

He teaches three times each week: two days for boys, one day for girls. "I explain to them that rap is hard," Hamouda says. "It's more than just dressing like me. I teach them about lyrics. I tell them, you are artists. Think about things, think differently, you are different from everyone else. Watch differently, see differently."

> Me and my friend chill in the park
> We fly through the air and we don't see any haters
> Life put us together, who can hear us
> Even if life is tough we will stay together
> Even if nobody understands us.
>
> from "*Ishabi*" ("My Friend")
> by Nour, aged thirteen

"The kids, at first, had violent lyrics in mind," Hamouda says as he sits in the center's music room. "I wanted to reduce the violence. We talk a lot about feelings. Over time, the songs began to have something different. They learn that violence doesn't make things. Yes, violence is the culture. The kids know Facebook. They start to think in a crazy way. The violence creeps in."

"No one asked me to teach," Hamouda continues. "I asked myself. You see, I had a teacher, it was important, so I became a teacher. I started with an eleven year-old. Others followed. We hang together. The kids have dreams. They want to create music, and now they have someone who can help them."

More than a third of the Shuafat youths do not graduate high school. All of Hamouda's students are in school, some having dropped out and returned. The schools offer no classes in art or music, "nothing creative" according to Hamouda.

"I say to my students, what do you know about war?" Hamouda says. "Do you see war? Is that what you want? Go to school. There is a life, not just guns. I tell them there is not just red color everywhere like Syria. It's all about your imagination, and colors. I don't want to see just black and red, where everything then is destroyed and becomes gray. I want to see white, blue, green. I don't tell the kids to change. They change themselves. I explain: We are artists, not political actors."

> Believe in your dreams
> Even if it's just something simple
> Get on the road
> Keep the hope in your life.
>
> from "*Alhaya Amal*"
> by Mohammed Hamouda

Hamouda continues: "I know that we are all in danger. I am stronger teaching the children. They support me. They change. The kids start to see life with positive eyes even if we live in a refugee camp. Some of the kids already quit school, but now they started to study again. All of them want to keep doing music. That's what is most important for me."

One young man working with a dozen boys and girls, transforming chaos into nascent self-definition, is not the scalable model that will heal the profound despair present in Shuafat's alleys and the crevices of almost every refugee camp and walled-in West Bank community.

Hamouda himself realizes this, but explains that, rather than inhabiting a prison cell, there is a means for self-expression, taking what is budding existential rage, refining it into something other than hatred. A graffiti portrait on a wall facing the children's center captures the maelstrom of passion within the refugee camp, fueled by fear, trauma, and a pervasive sense of futility. By studying urban ghetto rap, the children are not just victims, but also participating in their own recovery, demonstrating a capacity for survival and hope, perhaps an act of redemption.

Hamouda is a liminal guide, shaping meaning and purpose within unrelenting chaos. His pupils experience creativity's transformative power; under Hamouda's tutelage they progress against crushing odds. And Hamouda? One can only wonder where, in addition to his artistic expression, he gains sustenance. Several times each week he passes through border gates, most literal and most real. Is crossing the threshold an attempt to understand whatever tumult plagues him?

There is danger here. Expose children to aspiration and self-expression, respond to their thirst and nurture a sense of possibility, help them navigate between dignity and disgrace, and you are taking a great risk: If the children become enraged by a sense of confinement, if their creative outlet is ultimately cauterized by something ferocious that swallows that very sense of possibility, the dream might descend into nightmares.

Following a visit with Hamouda at the Child Center, I walk to an awaiting bus that will pass through the checkpoint, returning to "my side" of Jerusalem. A few steps behind me are two children from the center. When I turn to look at them, they return my gaze, offering faint smiles, but not with an unbridled child's innocence. Puzzled, when I enter the bus I ask my seatmate, who knows the camp and its residents, why the two children stared at me and offered faint smiles. "They wanted you to be safe."

The Desert

This particular "No Trespassing" sign is a solitary sentinel in the Western Negev desert, its message emphatically clear: proceed and death is a distinct possibility. The sign's universal symbol – threatening skull and crossbones – prohibits entry to a weapons training zone, where unexploded munitions are as deadly as active shelling.

Skirting the fire zone is a path leading to Wadi Aricha, the "hidden Bedouin village." At the trailhead, turn one way and there is endless desert vista. Turn in the opposite direction and barbed wire obscures the view of the firing zone. Turn completely around and there is an asphalt road in the direction of Bahad 1, the Israeli Defense Force (IDF) officers' school, a facility held in such esteem that it attracts elite military units from the United States and NATO countries. Glimpses of the training program can be seen on YouTube. The IDF-sanctioned promotional video details the training's rigor and an essential teaching: an officer must love soldiers under one's command.

Tucked behind the outer border of the firing zone is Wadi Aricha. Like many Negev Bedouin villages, Wadi Aricha is "unrecognized" by the Israeli government. It is illegal. No official roads, no electricity, no water system, no building permits. It can be bulldozed at any time.

Salman Sadin, a Wadi Aricha elder, receives visitors in the shade of a tent, seated on a kilim carpet made from dyed sheep and camel wool, with embroidered pillows scattered about on which to recline as sweet tea, dates, and olives are served. His aged mother sits in a corner dressed in traditional black thobe, its neckline and sleeves intricately embellished with red and white traditional design. Salman is dressed in jeans and a thin sweatshirt. His face is the color of the desert sandstone, his age indeterminate. Large, dark eyes are enigmatic and weary as Salman patiently observes a visitor's every gesture. He is comfortable with silence. He offers more tea. Smaller tents and a lean-to providing uncertain shelter for vehicles in various states of collapse form a vague circle around the central tent, the reality of tenuous tenurial residence.

Entering the Western Negev, the most direct route to Wadi Aricha passes by Beersheba, the "well of oath" (Genesis 21:31) where Abraham and Abimelech settled a dispute over water. The ancient town served as part of the *Limes Arabicus*, the Roman Empire's defensive threshold delineating the Rubicon. A Bedouin encampment serving caravans then settled upon the ruins, but soon vanished as empires and nations – whether Byzantine, Muslim Caliphate, Crusaders, Ottoman, European colonialists, or the State of Israel – occluded evidence of indigenous peoples' heritage.

With the realization of the State of Israel in 1948, waves of immigrants settled in what was then a frontier town: Mizrahim, Sephardim, Beta Israel immigrants from Ethiopia and, with the demise of the Soviet Union, Russian-speaking émigrés who, among other influences, introduced crime syndicates and a culture nurturing more chess grandmasters per capita than any city in the world. Currently, Ben Gurion University serves as a magnet for cyber security investment: multinationals – for example, Deutsche Telecom, IBM, Oracle, numerous venture capitalists, and the Israeli Army – cluster in Beersheba to invent technology that will defeat digital intruders.

Thus commences the convoluted passage to the Western Negev and Wadi Aricha. From time immemorial this landscape has attracted those in search of the metaphysics of God's nature, the nature of divinity, of wisdom, of autonomy. Beginning in the third century AD – in the Nile Delta, a few hundred miles west across the Sinai – the desert fathers sought a liminal space from which to observe the passions defining human life and accompanying inner torments. They fled to the desert to avoid self-erasure and interior anarchy. The emergence of early Christian cosmology rose from these anchorites' isolation and piety.

Today there are real and severe boundaries for the Negev Bedouin. The government considers the Bedouin community "unrecognized" if citizenship cannot be indisputably proven, a challenge given the dearth of administrative records. The Wadi Aricha Bedouin are part of an "in-between" issue; the government has ideas and expectations, the Bedouin have "wishes" and aspirations; some vague general agreement goes in and out of focus.

For critics of the Israeli government, the Negev Bedouin are subject to a series of discriminatory policies and practices because of their ethnic and indigenous identity and itinerant way of life. Successive Israeli governments have expropriated Bedouin lands and attempted to concentrate Bedouin into specific planned townships in a small area of the northeast Negev.

For those Israelis who affirm a spiritual connection to the "land of Israel," any benign view of the Bedouin is misguided. National Zionists value every square centimeter of *ha'aretz* as Israel's soul incarnate, seeing the Bedouin not as indigenous people, but as migrants, fostering illegitimate claims to the land. There is also a suspicion that Bedouins are involved in criminal activity and have links with terrorist organizations, to which critics of the state respond that a policy of discrimination has created fertile ground for dispossession and sprouting radical ideology.

Philosopher Giorgio Agamben's study of the ancient Roman term *homo sacer* (Latin for "the sacred man" or "the accursed man") is a meditation upon the place of the individual struggling to exist between potentiality and surrounding social ethics that are losing religious, metaphysical and cultural anchorage.[1] His work is relevant to understanding Wadi Aricha and an "unrecognized" identity. The Bedouin endure a contemporary form of *homo sacer*: the right to private property abolished, human rights restricted, and confinement with or without physical barriers. The sovereign power constructs a political order sanctioning an exclusion of bare, human life, stripped of recognized, legal status, an existence of exception. The *homo sacer* is in continuous relationship to the power that banished him and exposes him to the ever-present threat of death.

There are three overriding issues that place the Negev Bedouin in involuntary permanent liminality. Israel rejects "foreign" historic title claims. Israel introduces its own overriding moral title. For the religious, there is also scriptural title. This three-tiered historical self-legitimization creates a national intransigence: my covenant trumps yours.

Not only is Wadi Aricha unrecognized, but there is a pre-emptive dismissal of Bedouin identity, as exemplified in comments by Israeli's iconic military leader, Moshe Dayan:

> We should transform Bedouins into urban proletariat. . . . This will be a radical move which means the Bedouin would not live on land with his herds but would become an urban person who comes home in the afternoon and puts his slippers on. His children will get used to a father who wears pants, without a dagger, and who does not pick out their nits in public. They will go to school, their hair combed and parted.[2]

Salam continues to sit with visitors, share food, and listen to travelers' stories of faraway places. He speaks Hebrew well, representing his village to the outside world. He is of the Azazmeh tribe, known for hospitality, which defines Salman's humility and faith. Ironically, out of the chaos of a shattered life Salman understands the mission inspired by the Hebrew prophets: probing deeper into one's heritage, protecting the collective history as a primordial covenant.

What aspect of liminality is a source of hope and determination when the government would prefer his village disappear? As a Negev guide, Hen Yannay, an Israeli who has befriended Salman, explains: "He often loses his hope. He gets support from many local Jewish friends. The desert and desert time sure helps."

---

1. Giorgio Agamben, *Homo Sacer: Sovereign Power and Bare Life* (Stanford, CA: Stanford University Press, 1998).
2. Moshe Dayan, Interview, published in *Haaretz*. 1963.

Hen has a sense that Salman, like Hen himself, inhabits the desert: "to avoid reality in its common sense. Less news, less politics, less interaction with authorities, more open spaces, and beautiful sunsets."

But the government is ever-present, supplying a surplus of negation and limitation, such as the deliberate deprivation demonstrated by refusing municipal services. Salman is the subject of dominion, prohibited from crossing a threshold (legal rights), prevented passage from bare, subsistence life into national life, expunged from society.

Suffering the indignities of the government, colliding with the spiritual and political needs of Israelis who, in their own uncertain world, desperately cling to their land, could lead the Bedouin to rage. But Salman, influenced perhaps by the desert's austerity, silence and unrelenting intensity, has reached for heightened meaning, seeing beyond the immediate threats to Wadi Aricha because of the claim that it is in a "closed military zone." The village replants olive trees and rebuilds structures. Salman continues to define his existence by offering hospitality. These acts are a form of coherence within the in-between as he reaches beyond his own context to others, such as the Sioux Nation, another indigenous people in exile, where familiar landmarks and claims to the land are plowed under. He has written to the protestors in Mandan, South Dakota, a world away, but also in exile.

October 18, 2016

Dear People of Standing Rock,

My name is Salman Sadin, I am a member of the Azazmeh tribe and live in the Bedouin village Wadi Aricha in Israel. Although we never meet in person, as a member of a traditional tribal society I feel connected to you, to your traditions and to your way of life. After hearing your story, I feel we have much in common. I believe I share with you some of your challenges, struggles and dilemmas. Both of us face the challenge of maintaining our traditional way of life, which I believe has a very important role in the world, even in a technologically developed society.

The refusal of the authorities to acknowledge the importance of your lands and of your social needs is familiar to me from my struggles here at home.

I wish to send my support. I stand with you, my brothers and sisters of Standing Rock, and hope to strengthen your spirit. Your courage inspires communities around the world.

Allah Ma'akum, God is with you

Salman

An NGO worker at the site of the Standing Rock confrontation writes that Salman's pictures and stories are shared at campfires among the Standing Rock protestors. He says that Salman's voice extends from afar and provides a sense of ascendance, much like the sacred wolf's howl or the diaphanous threads of the Northern Lights extending from the horizon to the furthest reaches of the celestial vault. Lakota Indians wish to meet Salman directly if the travel restrictions can be worked through. If not, they will come to him in the unrecognized village in the Negev.

The Classroom

"The course of study," she explains, "is like an earthquake. The land you are standing on is shaking." She is not by nature bombastic, but earnest, restless, and seeking to help her students define, each in her or his own way, the nature of truth. When first entering her class, the students might carry a rudimentary interest in civil society, but when crossing this academic threshold nothing in their education, nothing in their lives has prepared them for what will follow.

The course intentionally comprises Israeli Palestinians, Israeli Jews, and Palestinian residents of East Jerusalem. These distinctions are important, for this is how these women and men have learned to define themselves: borders circumvent their lives and those of "the other". Before attending the university, their respective curricula have asserted that "the other" is a potential enemy; these young lives are taught to carry entrenched ideological narratives, viewing discourse as troubled territory. Now they sit before one another in a seminar room, a locale and situation entirely foreign to them.

The professor, Daphna Golan, is a liminal guide creating a transformative space where students shape meaning, stepping beyond their world of mutual recrimination, fractured ambiguity, and dislocation. They will, often for the first time in their memory, freely converse with those they have seen on campus, or silently sit next to in a university classroom where they are strangers to one another, not invisible but peripheral and anonymous.

"The class was the first time I had a connection with someone who otherwise lives so close. I had never realized how difficult it was to be a Palestinian student. There is generally no formal framework to discuss issues. I had not truly heard Palestinians talk. They generally remain quiet. Learning with them in this class is a privilege. I am now going to study Arabic," said Michal, Israeli Jew, now a lawyer, and studying Arabic.

For the past seventeen years students have been coming to Daphna Golan's Human Rights Fellows Program, under the aegis of the Minerva Center for Human Rights at the Hebrew University of Jerusalem. Unbeknownst to them they will soon realize the difference in mistaking knowledge from knowing. They may carry basic information about Jews or Arabs, but what they know has reverberated only in echo chambers. These students are intellectually gifted, curious, aware of inequalities, but have not come upon a haven in this conflicted society where "the other" can be safely acknowledged. What they have experienced since childhood is an acquired fear in speaking aloud about the distrust and prejudice they sense in the other, or sense within themselves.

"I am not a matchmaker, I'm not making friends. This is a learning process. We meet, we talk, we discover ambiguities, and sometimes we are more confused at the end," Daphna says. "High school curricula don't discuss the Arab presence. This class is one of the few places that provides safe shelter. I was motivated to create this class after the second intifada. There was no framework, no place to ask, 'What do you think?' It was assumed talk doesn't work."

For students, to participate in the course is not a perfunctory exercise.

"At first, I distanced myself, but Daphna's class opens space. I saw that the Israelis are so highly educated but ignorant about Palestinians, just seeing us as bad. In this class we discuss what is taboo. For example, I have several identities. When I travel abroad I am of Jordanian nationality, though in Israel I have Israeli travel documents and East Jerusalem residency. Who and what am I related to? In this class Daphna makes all of us feel important, that we matter." (Sarah, East Jerusalem Palestinian)

In listening to the students' language there is generally an absence of narcissism, less interest in "I," more attention invested in "we," for there is a collective sense of misapprehension, of struggle. What is liminal here? That students discover not only the stranger across the seminar table, but that one's "official" identity is a stranger to one's self.

Students talk about conflict, about their family and community, about the intolerance they experience, and the accompanying sense of displacement. They question, argue, castigate, show anger, apologize, sometimes laugh, and as one student said hesitantly, "We learn to love each other."

"I have never been in such a diverse learning situation. It is not comfortable. The Israeli students may be anticipating equality, but there is no equality just sitting in the same room. Daphna is not looking for closure. We are delivered into the incongruity of insight. The class can be like a support group. We sometimes have a collective catharsis." (Suf, Israeli Jew)

Depending upon one's ancestry, religion, address, and how the government assigns identification classifications, Israeli and non-Israeli citizenry follow elementary and secondary school curricula that are not only disparate, but seek to invalidate the other's historical narrative. For example, the Israelis study of Independence Day is not only a celebration of a political aspiration, but of a spiritual quest. For Arabs, the date commemorates *al-Nakba*, "the catastrophe," the Palestinian term for the events of 1948 when hundreds of thousands of Palestinians were displaced by the creation of the new State of Israel. Joy for one is despair for the other.

Jewish students are likely to be ignorant about what *al-Nakba* means. Palestinian students may be entirely unaware of the holocaust.

"There is no equality between Arabs and Jews, in or outside the university. The government does not support equality. Friendship can exist outside the campus, but there is always a barrier reminding you of limits. But here in this class we go beyond barriers." (Fairouz, East Jerusalem Palestinian)

Mordechai Kremnitzer, among the foremost authorities on Israeli education, having served as chairperson of numerous ministry committees assessing curriculum and "education of good citizenship," comments on the institutionalized barriers: "The curricula division is not only between Jewish and Arab schools. There are also splinters in the Muslim, Christian, Jewish, public and private schools. Within Jewish schools there are decided separations: between the secular, public and private, national religious, religious, and branches of the Haredim (ultra-Orthodox).

"Arab schools in Israel have no autonomy. They do what the Education Ministry tells them. There is no principal government-authorized curriculum. Mainly, the material reflects the basic Zionist narrative taught in Jewish schools. Israel's national religious party (or Jewish Homeland) has full autonomy," Kremnitzer explains. "There is almost no study of civic values and even the top-tier secular schools are being steered in a national religious direction."

Kremnitzer says that the curriculum preference is squarely on Jewish values over democratic ones, without any "Arab" consultation. The Arab language translation of the current Israeli civics textbook presents Israeli Arabs as hostile to Israel. In describing the "Israeli Jewish nation" the Palestinian minority is excluded. In turn, many Palestinian schools outside Education Ministry influence use a curriculum emphasizing Israel's illegitimacy.

To make the curriculum issue even more unsettled, Palestinian residents of East Jerusalem are often taught according to a Jordanian curriculum. As might be expected from Palestinians seeing themselves under occupation, their education does not nurture a climate to depict Israelis in an objective, neutral or friendly way.

"I knew the course would deal with human rights, but I did not expect we would so openly discuss the Israeli-Palestinian conflict. Many things have changed inside of me. I didn't know that Israeli Jews are so uninformed about 'the other side.' They didn't even know why I wear a *hijab*, seeing it as a threat. It is not in their background because in fact neither 'side' is free to cross over to know one another. There is a fundamental neglect and misunderstanding. Now I try to find opportunities to stand, to communicate what I am, what we are." (Hiba, the first student from East Jerusalem to attend an Israeli medical school)

The Program includes two year-long components – an academic course, Human Rights and Israeli Society, and weekly volunteer work at a human rights civil society organization of the student's choice under Daphna's supervision. Students do not receive credit for the volunteer work, but it is a requirement of the Program in order to expose the students to on-the-ground human rights work.

"We put a great deal of emphasis on choosing a diverse group in terms of ethnicity, gender, previous experience in the field, geographical background, academic field, etc. – We want the group dynamic and course discussions to be stimulating and challenging," according to Danny Evron, the Minerva Center's executive director.

"There are stereotypical ideas controlling the minds on both sides. Some Israelis think Palestinians are terrorists and can only stand in the street and stab them. When I first started the volunteer work, I was scared of the Israeli NGO. I thought I would be attacked, but my experience opened my eyes. There are Israeli Jews who are willing to work for Palestinian rights. But I carry little hope because in this country you cannot be overly optimistic. We have been in occupation for all of my life." (Rulah, Palestinian citizen of Israel)

"Before this class, everything at Hebrew University was fine. But now there is another layer of meaning. I grew up in an Orthodox family, completely surrounded by right wing, completely. Daphna is really hard on us: you realize you know nothing, you think you are smart, but then see the reality. My family's response is awful, claiming I am creating tension." (Moriya, Israeli Jew) Moriya and Rulah are now best friends.

The class exists in a political environment where those who self-identify as national Zionists or religious orthodox question open and free classroom discussion, suggesting that it is unwise to encourage questioning of bias and misconceptions. Who knows where it would lead?

However, the course at Minerva is all about acknowledging the other, even requiring students to go outside of the classroom and to volunteer with civil society organizations. According to Evron, the class and volunteer work allow each "side" to see "that there are good, sensitive, caring people on the other side."

The initial class meetings of Daphna's students veer around sensitivities, avoiding such subjects as violent conflict, distrust, prejudice. They are hesitant for they do not, at first, know how to recognize a safe space for such dialogue. Nevertheless, with Daphna's stewardship, they make their way across the great divide and begin to challenge the knowledge they have accumulated since childhood, considering what it is to "know" the other, to "know" oneself in relation to the other.

Observing the students interact, a quote from Saint Augustine serves to illuminate: "*Mihi quaestio factus sum.*" ("I have become a question to myself.") (*Confessions* X, 35:50)

Excursus

(a) The word resists easy embrace. And making earnest sense of "the liminal" may too easily become a pursuit of meticulous definition which anaesthetizes the reader with empty language about ambiguity and faith.

The rap singer, the Negev Bedouin elder, the teacher guiding a classroom of Israeli Jews and Palestinians and East Jerusalem students: all experience a sense of being "outside," standing before a threshold, embarking on, well, embarking on what precisely?

Agamben explains in *The Coming Community* that the notion of the "outside" is, in numerous European languages, a word derived from "threshold" and "at the door". In Greek, *"thyrathen"* means "at the threshold" or "from outside". In Latin *"foris"* is the door of a house and as an adverb, "outside" or "outdoors". Outside is not something beyond, but rather a passage.[3] In other words the threshold is not something other than the limit, but rather the experience of the limit itself, being within an outside.

(b) A setting sun radiates a gentle mutation of light, a permeable membrane of color, connecting the material world outside the body with the immaterial world of the mind.

Recognizing that there is a strong inclination to anchor this seemingly liminal moment of sheer wonder into something other than fleeting, something unified, where can sustained meaning be realized beyond disparate fragments, a hearing of what is not said? Do we challenge the language we whisper to ourselves? Do we work to introduce fresh language

---

3. Georgio Agamben, *The Coming Community* (University of Minnesota Press, 1993).

to support clarity and purpose, as if the pedestrian life we live is defined by a meagre vocabulary where we are incapable of definition, save for the manifest meanings of anything beyond the very little?

Is the liminal uplifting, suggesting what is sublime, exalted, inviolate and inspired? Or is it closely related to subliminal, what is underneath and concealed? Is this fresh language, or pretense? Is there anything more to share than questions?

The light lingers on Northwestern Connecticut's Taconic plane, a presence honest and beautiful, an axis of dignity, unlimited in terms of solace, enhancement and joy. It seems here the liminal is a deliverance: to cajole the ability to try to understand existence, to try to comprehend the wonder and responsibility of one's own existence, to arrive at an inner cessation before an annihilating ambiguity, false starts, and darkness which crowds our coherence.

Some small animal scuttles beneath the floorboards and in the turning to see what is directly aside or beneath, sublime or subliminal, the wonder is how the animal is not to be cheated out of its potentials. Above the horizon, the blinking light of a jet airplane migrates across the sky, too remote to be heard or clearly seen. The distant flashing beacon and the nearby animal's rustling dangle essences of barely perceptible anguishes and joys: there is a sensing of the incontrovertible glimpse of the incredible.

Is this liminality, that which is and has always been, like the Sirens, deceptive and murderous, or is the liminal the source and guide of all hope and cure, rarely encountered but when encountered reminding us of origins? After all, the Ancient Greek word *"thura"* also means door as well as the conditions which must be present in order to be received into some notion of the Kingdom of God. Why so rarified, this liminality, this condition? For the liminal is not a convenience, cannot be experienced as a "full and authentic purification" unless, as Thomas Merton writes, "we first pass through the dread, anguish, trouble and fear that necessarily accompany the inner crisis of 'spiritual death.'"

I do not know what the key is to the essence of the word and efforts at understanding it progress slowly. If there is too practiced an insight, grasped in order not to flee, the words become a recitation. The meaning doesn't pass through, but withers. To examine the liminal, where it may reside, are we well advised to avoid the paved road where, by following the markers, we do arrive, but it just may be a camouflaged dead end?

In considering the liminal we are pointed toward an intensification of self-consciousness, even without a clear, consistent idea what it means, because when traveling beyond the words, suddenly touching the unveiled meaning, all chaos arrives. Is this so abstract as to fall from sense, becoming a vaudeville routine, and yet competing with a wish that on another, as yet unverified level, life might not be "unrecognized" and ludicrous?

Is there a liminal realm, an unrecognized, vaguely ephemeral, indeterminate and even illegitimate space, where we are confronted with questions not directly related to day-to-day preoccupations, but rather with the latent, unanswered questions of one's life that force us to wrestle with our essential humanness? The rap singer, the Bedouin elder, and the teacher reveal there is threshold and passage, something authentic to see beyond drifting constructs, as what is customarily opaque becomes unfolding discovery.

Conclusion
Timothy Carson

We have seen the highest circle of spiraling powers.
We have named this circle God.
We might have given it any other name we wished:
Abyss, Mystery, Absolute Darkness, Absolute Light,
Matter, Spirit, Ultimate Hope, Ultimate Despair, Silence.

Nikos Kazantzakis, *The Rock Garden*

* * *

Years ago, when I first took a deep dive into liminality studies, I had a conversation with a friend who was a postdoctoral fellow in cell biology. After describing the outlines of liminality, I asked him a simple question: "Where do you find this in your research?"

After staring into an invisible world beneath the floor, he began describing the process of cellular mitosis. After sketching out the process of cell division in its several phases – how the chromosomes make a copy of themselves in the cell nucleus and the envelope of the nucleus dissolves, releasing the organelles into the cellular space and proteins move them into place – he smiled and drew an analogy with line dancing: "All these strands of chromosomes called kinetochores line up across from one another in preparation for the dance to commence. They bow to their partner and wait for the music to begin. But it appears that the fiddler has broken a string and the band can't begin. The dancers just stand there, waiting. In the process of mitosis, it appears this is the moment when everything is being checked out – to see that every dancer has a partner on the other side and everyone is lined up correctly. But we can't tell exactly what is happening during this grand pause. And there is your liminal moment. This metaphase is the most mysterious and least understood moment in time, but holds the most raw potential for what is about to happen."

Liminality is the grand pause on the other side of life as we know it, the mysterious space that is entirely unfamiliar yet filled with extraordinary potential. It is found in the structures of nature, the unfolding of the individual psyche, realignments of society, collective rituals, voluntary and involuntary wilderness, and the surprising intersections between disparate ways of knowing. When shared with others passing through the same or parallel experience, liminality may create a special and lasting bond that may even transcend time.

Seen through the lens of quantum mechanics, on the one hand is the surface or appearance of reality, the presenting structure with which physicists of the past have been preoccupied. However, then, as the philosopher and physicist Bernard d'Espagnat reminded us, there are veiled aspects beneath what appears to be ordinary reality. On this side of the threshold, the liminal veil, we live with the appearance of structure, the ordinary and ongoing way of things that belong to the Newtonian domain. Once we lift that veil, however, we cross a threshold into mysterious quantum territory, a time and space that plays by its own rules, bizarre and unpredictable behavior that does not match what we normally observe above the surface. Beyond everyday appearance is a whole other invisible world that actually determines the visible one.[1]

This is parallel to what the mystics of most world religions have intuited and shared for as long as human beings have gazed into the wonder and mystery of the universe. Spiritual seers have always peered behind the veil of appearance to find that which is determinative, beyond the structure of the ordinary to what informs it, into the mysterious spaces where other worlds are known and experienced. They did not speak the language of science or quantum reality or think of the world in those terms. Nevertheless, they did presume unseen powers on the other side of the dark interval of perception. Their sacramental world regarded outward appearance as a window to an inward and invisible reality. They embraced an enchanted world, one eventually dismissed by the materialism of modernity, but later reclaimed – in non-doctrinal form – by the new science.

It may very well be that the most baffling challenges of this time – the hardened polarization, the resistant barriers to the next breakthrough – will require exploring something approximate to liminal time and space in order to discover the answers. Every liminal quandary requires an equally liminal solution.

1. Bernard d'Espagnat, *Veiled Reality*, (New York: Basic Books, 1995).

As the Persian poet Rumi portended in his verse, "Out beyond ideas of wrong-doing and right-doing there is a field. I'll meet you there." Out beyond the structure of what is known and presumed, beyond the hardened silo of my absolutist position, we must cross boundaries and thresholds into the unknown field. Only a new and different sense of time and space may take us to the new landscapes where the impossible may become possible.

This means that all disciplines will be required to search at their own edges, in the margins, the intervals between the known and unknown. Even more, interdisciplinary exploration may take place in the field between sometimes strikingly different worldviews, searching for the larger truth that exists between them. The most revolutionary answers of the future may be found in ideas, strategies and technologies that function in the gaps, much as Blockchain is now attempting to bridge human consciousness with artificial intelligence.

In the meantime, the classic arc of liminality will continue to act in ways that challenge, inform, and even transform us. Human communities will practice rites of passage to transport themselves from one state of being to another. We will be thrust into permanent liminal states we did not seek but that end up defining us. The inner life of individuals will continue to be shaped by powerful passages, shifts, and rebirths, and, for those who share these dramatic transitional states, they may experience a bond and affiliation stronger than stone.

Of the many aspects that the great world myths hold in common, it is perhaps the necessity of the protagonist crossing uncharted seas and threatening terrain on the way to rebirth that is most universal. Once the happiness of life's former structure is left behind and the threshold toward the abyss crossed, the greatest threat and opportunity for transformation emerge. We encounter many strange creatures, guides, and tasks along that dangerous path. In the locale farthest from what has been known with certainty, a new light slowly dawns and, in the middle of that passage, the emptiness slowly becomes full, a mysterious realization of something that has always been present in that baffling liminal time and space.

Bibliography

Abani, Chris. "Ethics and Narrative: The Human and Other." *Witness* 22, no. 1 (2009).

Ackermann, Denise M. "Becoming Fully Human: An Ethic of Relationship in Difference and Otherness." *Journal of Theology for Southern Africa* 102 (1998).

African National Congress 1999 Election Manifesto. Accessed 3 July 2017. http://www.anc.org.za/show.php?id=2543.

African National Congress 2004 Election Manifesto. Accessed 3 July 2017. http://www.anc.org.za/elections/2004/manifesto/manifesto.html.

African National Congress 2009 Election Manifesto. Accessed 3 July 2017. http://www.anc.org.za/docs/manifesto/2009/manifesto.pdf.

Agamben, Giorgio. *The Coming Community.* Minneapolis: University of Minnesota Press, 1993.

———. *Homo Sacer: Sovereign Power and Bare Life.* Stanford, CA: Stanford University Press, 1998.

Alexander, Peter. "Rebellion of the Poor: South Africa's Service Delivery Protests – A Preliminary Analysis." *Review of African Political Economy* 37, no. 123 (2010), 25-40.

Altbeker, Antony. *A Country at War with Itself: South Africa's Crisis of Crime.* Johannesburg: Jonathan Ball, 2007.

Alvesson, Mats, and Dan Kärreman. "Varieties of Discourse: On the Study of Organizations Through Discourse Analysis." *Human Relations* 53 (2000), 1125-49.

American Adoption Congress. "State Adoption Legislation." https://americanadoptioncongress.org/state.php.

Anderson, Benedict. *Imagined Communities: Reflections on the Origin and Spread of Nationalism.* London: Verso, 1983.

Aquili, Eugene d', and Andrew Newberg. "Liminality, Trance, and Unitary States in Ritual and Meditation." *Studia Liturgica* 23, no. 1 (1993), 2-34.

Athanasius. *The Life of Anthony and the Letter to Marcellinus.* Translated by Robert Gregg. New York: Paulist Press, 1980.

Australian Public Service Commission. "Tackling Wicked Problems: A Public Policy Perspective." 31 May 2012. Accessed 26 February 2018. http://www.apsc.gov.au/publications-and-media/archive/publications-archive/tackling-wicked-problems.

Barry, Kevin M., Brian Farrell, Jennifer L. Levi, and Neelima Vanguri. "A Bare Desire to Harm: Transgender People and the Equal Protection Clause." *Boston College Law Review,* 57 (April 2016), 507-82.

Bauman, Whitney. "Meaning-Making Practices and Environmental History: Toward an Ecotonal Theology." In *Routledge Companion to Religion and Science.* Edited by James Haag, Gregory Peterson, and Michael Spezio. Malden, MA: Routledge, 2014.

Beall, Jo, Stephen Gelb, and Shireen Hassim. "Fragile Stability: State and Society in Democratic South Africa." *Journal of Southern Africa Studies* 31, no. 4 (2005), 681-700.

Berry, Thomas. *The Sacred Universe: Earth, Spirituality, and Religion in the Twenty-First Century.* New York: Columbia University Press, 2009.

Betcher, Sharon V. *Spirit and the Politics of Disablement.* Minneapolis: Fortress Press, 2007.

Björk. "Who Is It?" In *Medulla.* London: One Little Indian, 2004.

Blaser, Thomas. "Looking at the Heart of Whiteness in South Africa Today." *The Journal of South African and American Studies* 9, no. 1 (2008), 81-96.

Bojabotseha, Teboho P., and Kholeka C. Moloi. "Discursive Constructions of the African National Congress (ANC) and Its Discourse of Freedom: A Critical Analysis." *Academic Journal of Interdisciplinary Studies* 3, no. 4 (2014), 93-101.

Boon, Bronwyn. "Engaging with a Laclau and Mouffe Informed Discourse Analysis: A Proposed Framework." *Qualitative Research in Organizations and Management: An International Journal* 9, no. 4 (2014), 351-70.

Brakke, David. *Athanasius and Asceticism.* Baltimore: Johns Hopkins University Press, 1998.

Bratton, Susan Power. *Christianity, Wildlife, and Wilderness: The Original Desert Solitaire.* Scranton, PA: University of Scranton Press, 1993.

Breakwell, Glynis M., Sean Hammond, and Chris Fife-Schaw. *Research Methods in Psychology.* Second edition. London: Sage Publications, 2000.

Brodie, Nechama. "Are SA Whites Really Being Killed 'Like Flies'?" *Africa Check,* 24 June 2013. Accessed 9 January 2018. https://africacheck.org/reports/are-white-afrikaners-really-being-killed-like-flies/.

Brodzinsky, David, and Susan Smith. "Post-Placement Adjustment and the Needs of Birthmothers Who Place an Infant for Adoption." *Adoption Quarterly* 17 (2014).

Broodryk, Johann. *Ubuntu: Life Lessons from Africa.* Pretoria: Ubuntu School of Philosophy, 2002.

Buber, Martin. *Die Frage an den Einzelnen.* Martin Buber Werke, Vol. 1. München: Kösel-Verlag, 1962.

———. *Ich und Du.* Martin Buber Werke, Vol. 1. München: Kösel-Verlag, 1962.

———. *I and Thou.* Translated by Walter Kaufmann. New York: Touchstone, 1971."number-of-pages":"192","source":"Amazon","event-place":"New York","abstract":"Martin Buber's I and Thou has long been acclaimed as a classic. Many prominent writers have acknowledged its influence on their work; students of intellectual history consider it a landmark; and the generation born since World War II considers Buber as one of its prophets. The need for a new English translation has been felt for many years. The old version was marred by many inaccuracies and misunderstandings, and its recurrent use of the archaic \"thou\"

was seriously misleading. Now Professor Walter Kaufmann, a distinguished writer and philosopher in his own right who was close to Buber, has retranslated the work at the request of Buber's family. He has added a wealth of informative footnotes to clarify obscurities and bring the reader closer to the original, and he has written a long \"Prologue\" that opens up new perspectives on the book and on Buber's thought. This volume should provide a new basis for all future discussions of Buber.","ISBN":"978-0-684-71725-8","language":"English","author":[{"family":"Buber","given":"Martin"}],"translator":[{"family":"Kaufmann","given":"Walter"}],"issued":{"date-parts":[["1971",2,1]]}}}],"schema":"https://github.com/citation-style-language/schema/raw/master/csl-citation.json"}

———. *Between Man and Man*. Mansfield Centre, CT: Martino Fine Books, 2014.

Buell, Frederick. *Apocalypse as a Way of Life: Environmental Crisis in the American Century*. New York: Routledge, 2004.

Burghardt, Walter. "Contemplation: A Long, Loving Look at the Real." *Church* (Winter 1989), 14-18.

Burr, Vivien. *An Introduction to Social Constructionism*. London: Routledge, 1995.

Burrows, Thomas. "The 'WHITE Squatter Camps' of South Africa: Shanty Towns Built after the Fall of Apartheid Are Now Home to Hundreds of Families." *Mail Online*, 2016. Accessed 7 January 2018. http://www.dailymail.co.uk/news/article-3462336/The-white-squatter-camps-South-Africa-home-hundreds-families-enduring-terrible-poverty-blame-fall-Apartheid.html.

Burton-Christie, Douglas. "The Place of the Heart: Geography and Spirituality in the *Life of Anthony*." In *Purity of Heart in Early Ascetic and Monastic Literature: Essays in Honor of Juana Raasch, O.S.B.* Edited by Harriet Luckman and Linda Kulzer. Collegeville, MN: The Liturgical Press, 1999.

"Butchered in the Street as He Begged for Mercy: Savage Last Moments of Mozambican Man Who Bled to Death in a Johannesburg Gutter after Becoming Latest Victim of South Africa's Anti-immigrant Violence." *Mail Online*, 20 April 2015. Accessed 15 February 2018. http://www.dailymail.co.uk/news/article-3046924/Butchered-street-begged-mercy-Savage-moments-Mozambican-man-bled-death-gutter-victim-South-African-anti-immigrant-violence.html#ixzz57FbPEBKZ.

Carson, Timothy. *Liminal Reality and Transformational Power: Transition, Renewal & Hope*. Revised edition. Cambridge: The Lutterworth Press, 2016.

Cassidy, Sheila. *Sharing the Darkness*. Maryknoll, NY: Orbis Books, 1991.

Celan, Paul. *Breathturn*. Translated by Pierre Joris. Los Angeles: Sun & Moon Press, 1995.

Chipkin, Ivor. "Whither the State? Corruption, Institutions and State-Building in South Africa." *Politikon* 40, no. 2 (2013), 211-31.

"Civil Defense Expert: White Genocide Imminent in South Africa." *Suidlanders*, 4 May 2017. https://www.suidlanders.co.za/civil-defense-expert-white-genocide-imminent-in-south-africa/.

Colaner, Colleen Warner. "Measuring Adoptive Identity: Validation of the Adoptive Identity Work Scale." *Adoption Quarterly* 17 (2014).

Colaner, Colleen Warner, and Haley Kranstuber. "'Forever Kind of Wondering:' Communicatively Managing Uncertainty in Adoptive Families." *Journal of Family Communication* 10 (2010).

Colaner, Colleen Warner, and Jordan Soliz. "A Communication-Based Approach to Adoptive Identity: Theoretical and Empirical Support." *Communication Research* (2015).

Colaner, Colleen Warner, and Kristina Scharp. "Maintaining Open Adoption Relationships: Practitioner Insights on Adoptive Parents' Regulation of Adoption Kinship Networks." *Communication Studies* 67 (2016).

Colaner, Colleen Warner, Danielle Halliwell, and Phillip Guignon. "'What Do You Say to Your Mother When Your Mother's Standing Beside You?' Birth and Adoptive Family Contributions to Adoptive Identity via Relational Identity and Relational-Relational Identity Gaps." *Communication Monographs* 81 (2014).

Colaner, Colleen Warner, Haley Kranstuber Horstman, and Christine Rittenour. "Negotiating Adoptive and Birth Shared Family Identity: A Social Identity Complexity Approach." *Western Journal of Communication* (2017).

"Coligny: Where a Handful of Stolen Seeds Can Cost You Your Life." *Mail & Guardian*, 12 May 2017. Accessed 15 February 2018. https://mg.co.za/article/2017-05-12-00-coligny-where-a-handful-of-stolen-seeds-can-cost-you-your-life.

Comaroff, John L., and Jean Comaroff. *Of Revelation and Revolution, Volume Two: The Dialectics of Modernity on a South African Frontier.* Chicago: University of Chicago Press, 1997.

———. "Naturing the Nation: Aliens, Apocalypse and the Postcolonial State." *Journal of Southern African Studies* 27 (2001), 627-51.

Cook, Jeanne. "A History of Placing-Out: The Orphan Trains." *Child Welfare* 74 (1995).

Coontz, Stephanie. "Revolution in Intimate Life and Relationships." *Journal of Family Theory & Review* 7 (2015).

Cronje, Frans. *A Time-Traveller's Guide to Our Next Ten Years.* Cape Town: Tafelberg, 2014.

Crush, Jonathan. *The Perfect Storm: The Realities of Xenophobia in Contemporary South Africa.* Southern African Migration Programme. Cape Town: IDAS, 2008.

Crush, Jonathan, Sujata Ramachandran, and Wade Pendleton. *Soft Targets: Xenophobia, Public Violence, and Changing Attitudes to Migrants After May 2008.* Southern African Migration Programme. Cape Town: Bronwen Dachs Muller, 2013.

Csikszentmihalyi, Mihaly. *Flow: The Psychology of Optimal Experience.* New York: Harper Perennial, 1990.

Culp, Kristine A. "Pilgrimage: Journey Toward the Holy." Cover story and photos in collaboration with Kay Bessler Northcutt. *The Disciple* 137, no. 1 (January/February 1999), 2-7.

———. "'A World Split Open?' Experience and Feminist Theologies." In *The Experience of God: A Postmodern Response.* Edited by Kevin Hart and Barbara Wall. New York: Fordham University Press, 2005.

———. *Vulnerability and Glory: A Theological Account.* Louisville, KY: Westminster John Knox Press, 2010.

Dahill, Lisa. "Addressing God with Names of Earth." *Currents in Theology and Mission* 43, no. 4 (July 2016).

Davies, Bronwyn. *A Body of Writing: 1990-1999.* Oxford: Altamira, 2000.

Davis, Rebecca. "Lawmakers Crunch Xenophobia Numbers." *Eye Witness News*, 29 April 2015. Accessed 19 December 2017. http://ewn.co.za/2015/04/29/ OPINION-Rebecca-Davis-Lawmakers-crunch-some-xenophobia-numbers.

Dayan, Moshe. Interview. *Haaretz*, 1963.

Deane-Drummond, Celia. *The Wisdom of the Liminal: Evolution and Other Animals in Human Becoming*. Grand Rapids, MI: Eerdmans Publishing Co., 2014.

Distiller, Natasha, and Melissa E. Steyn, eds. "Introduction: Under Construction." In *Under Construction: "Race" and Identity in South Africa Today*. Sandton: Heinemann, 2004.

Dlamini, Jacob. *Native Nostalgia*. Auckland Park, Johannesburg: Jacana, 2009.

Doan, Petra L. "The Tyranny of Gendered Spaces – Reflections from Beyond the Gender Dichotomy." *Gender, Place & Culture* 17, no.5 (2010),635-54,DOI:10.10 80/0966369X.2010.503121.

Docan-Morgan, Sara. "'They Don't Know What It's Like to Be in My Shoes.' Topic Avoidance About Race in Transracially Adoptive Families." *Journal of Social and Personal Relationships* 28 (2011).

Dolby, Nadine. "White Fright: The Politics of White Youth Identity in South Africa." *British Journal of Sociology of Education* 22, no. 1 (2001), 5-17.

Douglas, Mary. *Purity and Danger*. New York: Frederick A. Praeger, 1966.

Douthat, Ross. *Bad Religion: How We Became a Nation of Heretics*. New York: Free Press, 2012.

Downey, Dara, Ian Kinane, and Elizabeth Parker, eds. *Landscapes of Liminality: Between Space and Place*. London: Rowman & Littlefield International, 2016.

Dylan, Bob. "Ye Shall Be Changed." In *Bob Dylan: Lyrics 1961-2012*. New York: Simon & Shuster, 2016.

Eiesland, Nancy L. *The Disabled God: Toward a Liberatory Theology of Disability*. Nashville: Abingdon Press, 1994.

Eliade, Mircea. *Rites and Symbols of Initiation*. New York: Harper & Row, 1958.

Eliastam, John L.B. "Re-Storying Xenophobia in South Africa: A Postfoundational, Narrative Exploration of Ubuntu in the Eastern Cape." Ph.D. diss., University of Pretoria, 2015.

———. "Discursive Leadership and the Other." In *The Future of Lived Religious Leadership*. Edited by Rein Brouwer. Amsterdam: VU University Press, 2018.

Espagnat, Bernard d'. *Veiled Reality*. New York: Basic Books, 1995.

Evans, Delia. *Blue Guide Midi-Pyrénées: Albi, Toulouse, Conques, Moissac*. New York: W.W. Norton, 1995.

Eze, Michael O. "The History and Contemporary Frame of Botho/Ubuntu: Philosophical and Sociocultural Complexities." Paper presented at 2017 Mind and Life XXXII Conference, "Botho/Ubuntu: A Dialogue on Spirituality, Science and Humanity." Gaberone, Botswana, 17-19 August 2017.

Farley, Edward. *Deep Symbols: Their Postmodern Effacement and Reclamation*. Valley Forge, PA: Trinity Press International, 1996.

Felstiner, John. *Paul Celan: Poet, Survivor, Jew*. New Haven, CT: Yale University Press, 1995.

Finkel, Eli J., et al. "The Suffocation Model: Why Marriage in America Is Becoming an All-or-Nothing Institution." *Current Directions in Psychological Science* 24 (2015).

Foster, Kenny. "Hometown." 2011. https://kennyfoster.bandcamp.com/track/ hometown-single.

Foucault, Michel. *Discipline and Punish: The Birth of the Prison.* Translated by Alan Sheridan. Second edition. New York: Vintage Books, 1995.

Franchi, Vije. "The Racialization of Affirmative Action in Organizational Discourses: A Case Study of Symbolic Racism in Post-Apartheid South Africa." *International Journal of Intercultural Relations* 27 (2003), 157-87.

Frank, Geyla. "On Embodiment: A Case Study of Congenital Limb Deficiency in American Culture." In *Women with Disabilities.* Edited by M. Fine and A. Asch. Philadelphia: Temple University Press, 1988.

Freedenthal, Stacey. http://www.speakingofsuicide.com/2015/01/02/transgender-suicide/.

Friedman, Maurice. "The Interhuman and What Is Common to All: Martin Buber and Sociology." *Journal for the Theory of Social Behaviour* 29, no. 4 (1 December 1999), 403-17. https://doi.org/10.1111/1468-5914.00110.

Galvin, Kathleen. "Diversity's Impact on Defining the Family." In *The Family Communication Sourcebook.* Edited by L.H. Turner and R. West. Thousand Oaks, CA: Sage, 2006.

———. "International and Transracial Adoption: A Communication Research Agenda." *Journal of Family Communication* 3 (2003).

———. "The Family of the Future: What Do We Face?" In *The Handbook of Family Communication.* Edited by A.L. Vangelisti. Mahwah, NJ: Lawrence Erlbaum, 2013.

Galvin, Kathleen, and Colleen Warner Colaner. "Created through Law and Language: Communicative Complexities of Adoptive Families." In *Widening the Family Circle.* Edited by K. Floyd and M.T. Morman. Thousand Oaks, CA: Sage, 2013.

Garfinkel, Harold. *Studies in Ethnomethodology.* Englewood Cliffs, NJ: Prentice Hall, 1967.

———. "Passing and the Managed Achievement of Sex Status in an Intersexed Person, Part 1." In *Studies in Ethnomethodology.* Cambridge: Polity Press, 1984.

Geary, Patrick J. *Furta Sacra: Thefts of Relics in the Central Middle Ages.* Revised edition. Princeton, NJ: Princeton University Press, 1990.

Gennep, Arnold van. *Rites of Passage.* London: Routledge & Kegan Paul, 1960.

Geschiere, Peter. *The Perils of Belonging: Autochthony, Citizenship, and Exclusion in Africa and Europe.* Chicago: University of Chicago Press, 2009.

Gilbert, Elizabeth. https://www.facebook.com/GilbertLiz/posts/806653502750100:0.

Gingerich, Daniel W. "Yesterday's Heroes, Today's Villains: Ideology, Corruption, and Democratic Performance." *Journal of Theoretical Politics* 26, no. 2 (April 2014), 249-82.

Gish, Steven D. *Desmond Tutu: A Biography.* Westport, CT: Greenwood Press, 2004.

Glúingel, Amergin. "Song of Amergin." In *The Deer's Cry: A Treasury of Irish Religious Verse.* Edited by Patrick Murray. Blackrock, Co. Dublin: Four Courts Press, 1986.

Graham, Elaine. *Transforming Practice: Pastoral Theology in an Age of Uncertainty.* London: Mowbray, 1996.

Green, Eli, and Luca Maurer. http://www.teachingtransgender.org/.

Grof, Christina, and Stanislav Grof. *The Stormy Search for the Self: A Guide to Personal Growth Through Transformational Crisis.* New York: J.P. TarcherPerigee, 1992.

Grotevant, Harold, et al. "Adoptive Identity: How Contexts Within and Beyond the Family Shape Developmental Pathways." *Family Relations* 49 (2000).

Grotevant, Harold, et al. "Contact Between Adoptive and Birth Families: Perspectives from the Minnesota/Texas Adoption Research Project." *Child Development Perspectives* 7 (2013).

Haraway, Donna. "A Cyborg Manifesto: Science, Technology, and Socialist-Feminism in the Late Twentieth Century." In *Simians, Cyborgs, and Women: The Reinvention of Nature*. New York: Routledge, 1991.

————. *When Species Meet*. Minneapolis: University of Minnesota Press, 2008.

Harré, Rom E. "The Social Construction of Selves." In *Self & Identity: Psychosocial Perspectives*. Edited by Krysia Yardley and Terry Honess. New York: John Wiley & Sons, 1987.

Harris, Ruth. *Lourdes: Body and Spirit in the Secular Age*. London: Allen Lane, 1999.

Heidegger, Martin. *Being and Time*. Translated by John Macquarie and Edward Robinson. Reprint. New York: Harper Perennial Modern Classics, 2008, secs. 25-27.

Henig, Robin Marantz. "Rethinking Gender." *National Geographic*, January 2017, 48-70.

Herschinger, Eva. *Constructing Global Enemies: Hegemony and Identity in Global Discourses on Terrorism and Drug Prohibition*. Abingdon: Routledge, 2011.

Hirshfield, Jane. "Salt Heart." *Lives of the Heart*. New York: Harper Collins, 1997.

Hoge, Charles. *Once a Warrior, Always a Warrior*. Guilford, CT: Lyons Press, 2010.

Horvath, Agnes, Bjorn Thomassen, and Harald Wydra, eds. *Breaking Boundaries: Varieties of Liminality*. New York and Oxford: Berghahn Books, 2015.

Houston, Jeanne Wakatsuki, and James D. Houston. *Farewell to Manzanar*. New York: Ember, 1973.

Hsu, Ming, Meghana Bhatt, Ralh Adolphs, Daniel Traell, and Colin F. Camerer. "Neural Systems Responding to Degrees of Uncertainty in Human Decision-Making." *Science* (9 December 2005). https://brunel.rl.talis.com/items/FC0877AE-B134-D5B3-FD41-E1C2D991F889.html.

Huegel, Elena, trans. "*Con Esperanza y Valiente: Imágenes de la Naturaleza para la Sanidad de Traumas y el Desarrollo de la Resiliencia en Niños y Niñas*" ("With Hope and Bravery: Images from Nature for the Healing of Trauma and Development of Resilience in Children"). "Roots in the Ruins" program. Centro Shalom, Chile, 2014.

Huyssteen, J. Wentzel van. *The Shaping of Rationality: Toward Interdisciplinarity in Theology and Science*. Grand Rapids, MI: Eerdmans Publishing Co., 1999.

Inside Ex-Gay. http://insideexgay.org.

International Political Anthropology 2, no.1 (2009).

Jabes, Edmond. "The Commentary of Reb Zam." In *The Book of Questions: Volume 1*. Translated by Rosemarie Waldrop. Hanover, NH: Wesleyan University Press, 1991.

Jansen, Jonathan. "Even in Death South Africans Are Divided." *Times Live*, 2 November 2017. https://www.timeslive.co.za/ideas/2017-11-02-even-in-death-south-africans-are-racially-divided/.

Jenkins, Willis. "After Lynn White: Religious Ethics and Environmental Problems." *Journal of Religious Ethics* 37, no. 2 (2009).

Jennings, Chris. *Paradise Now: The Story of American Utopianism*. New York: Random House, 2016.

Joplin Globe, 12 August 2012.

Jung, C.G., and Aniela Jaffe. *C.G. Jung: Memories, Dreams, Reflections*. London: Routledge, 1963.

Kabat-Zinn, Jon. *Full Catastrophe Living: Using the Wisdom of Your Body and Mind to Face Stress, Pain, and Illness*. Second Edition. New York: Bantam/Random House, 2013.

Kanter, Robert K., MD, and David Abramson, Ph.D., MPH. "School Interventions After the Joplin Tornado." In *Prehospital and Disaster Medicine* 29, no. 2 (April 2014), 214-17.

Kim, Min-Sun. *Non-Western Perspectives on Human Communication*. Thousand Oaks, CA: Sage, 2002.

Kolbert, Elizabeth. *Field Notes from a Catastrophe: Man, Nature, and Climate Change*. New York: Bloomsbury, 2006.

Kraft, Heidi Squier. *Rule Number Two: Lessons Learned in a Combat Hospital*. New York: Back Bay Books, 2007.

Kull, Anne. "The Cyborg as an Interpretation of Culture-Nature." *Zygon* 36, no. 1 (March 2001), 49-56.

———. "Speaking Cyborg: Technoculture and Technonature." *Zygon* 37, no. 2 (June 2002), 279-87.

Laclau, Ernesto. *New Reflections on the Revolution of Our Time*. London: Verso, 1990.

———. *Emancipation(s)*. London: Verso, 1996.

Laclau, Ernesto, and Chantal Mouffe. *Hegemony and Socialist Strategy: Towards a Radical Democratic Politics*. London: Verso, 1985.

Lane, Belden. *The Solace of Fierce Landscapes: Exploring Desert and Mountain Spirituality*. New York: Oxford University Press, 1998.

Laqueur, Thomas. *Making Sex: Body and Gender from the Greeks to Freud*. Cambridge, MA: Harvard University Press, 1990.

Latour, Bruno. *Facing Gaia: Eight Lectures on the New Climatic Regime*. Translated by Catherine Porter. Cambridge: Polity Press, 2017.

Lee, Sang Hyun. *From a Liminal Place: An Asian American Theology*. Minneapolis: Fortress Press, 2010.

Lefko-Everett, Kate. "Ticking Time Bomb or Demographic Dividend? Youth and Reconciliation in South Africa." In *SA Reconciliation Barometer Survey: 2012 Report*. Cape Town: Institute for Justice and Reconciliation, 2012.

LeVasseur, Todd, and Anna Peterson, eds. *Religion and the Ecological Crisis: The "Lynn White Thesis" at Fifty*. New York: Routledge, 2017.

Lew, Alan. *Be Still and Get Going: A Jewish Meditation Practice for Real Life*. New York: Little Brown & Co., 2005.

Lewis, C.S. "A Grief Observed." Quoted in Sheila Cassidy. *Sharing the Darkness*. Maryknoll, NY: Orbis Books, 1991.

Lorenz, Brandon. "Map: How Many States Still Lack Clear Non-Discrimination Protections?" Human Rights Campaign. http://www.hrc.org/blog.

Louth, Andrew. *The Wilderness of God*. Nashville: Abingdon Press, 1991.

Luzzatto, Moses Hayyim. *Mesillat Yesharim: The Path of the Upright*. Introduction and commentary by Ira F. Stone. Translated by Mordecai M. Kaplan. Lincoln, NE: The Jewish Publication Society, University of Nebraska Press, 2010.

Macdonald, Helen. *H is for Hawk*. New York: Grove Press, 2016.

Madonsela, Thuli. *State of Capture*. Report by the Public Protector of South Africa. Accessed 17 January 2018. https://cdn.24.co.za/files/Cms/General/d/4666/3f63a 8b78d2b495d88f10ed060997f76.pdf.

Mairs, Nancy. *Carnal Acts*. New York: Harper Collins, 1990.

———. *Ordinary Time: Cycles in Marriage, Faith and Renewal*. Boston: Beacon Press, 1993.

Mamin, Mark. "Warrior Culture, Spirituality, and Prayer." In *Journal of Religion and Health* 52 (2013): 740-58.

Martell, Yann. *Life of Pi*. New York: Harcourt, 2001.

Martin, William. *The Parents' Tao Te Ching*. Philadelphia: Da Capo Press, 1999.

Marx, Karl, and Friedrich Engels. *On Religion*. Moscow: Progress Publications, 1957.

Marx, Karl. *Grundrisse*. London: Penguin Harmondsworth, 1973.

Matthews, Sally. "Shifting White Identities in South Africa: White Africanness and the Struggle for Racial Justice." *Phronimon* 16, no. 2 (2015), 112-29.

Matzner, Andrew. "Transgender, Queens, Mahu, Whatever: An Oral History from Hawai'i." *NCAVP Report*, 13-15. Accessed 29 September 2018. http://intersections.anu.edu.au/issue6/matzner.html.

Mbembe, Archibald. "South Africa's Second Coming: The Nongqawuse Syndrome." *Open Democracy* (2006). Accessed 4 December 2017. https://www.opendemocracy.net/democracy-Africa_democracy/southafrica_succession_3649.jsp.

McFague, Sallie. *A New Climate for Theology: God, the World, and Global Warming*. Minneapolis: Fortress Press, 2008.

McKibben, Bill. *Eaarth: Making a Life on a Tough New Planet*. New York: Henry Holt & Co., 2010.

McMillan, Sylvia. "Kierkegaard and a Pedagogy of Liminality." Brigham Young University, 2013. https://scholarsarchive.byu.edu/cgi/viewcontent.cgi?article=4623&context=etd.

Melczer, William, trans. "Introduction." In *The Pilgrim's Guide to Santiago de Compostela*. New York: Italica Press, 1993.

Merton, Thomas. *The Climate of Monastic Prayer*. Collegeville, MN: Liturgical Press, 2018.

Milk, Harvey. "Biography." In *Encyclopedia of World Biography*. Accessed 29 September 2018. http://www.notablebiographies.com/Ma-Mo/Milk-Harvey.html#ixzz4l8MneKOI.

Misago, Jean Pierre, Loren B. Landau, and Tamlyn Monson. *Towards Tolerance, Law, and Dignity: Addressing Violence Against Foreign Nationals in South Africa, Report for the International Organization of Migration*. Pretoria: International Organization of Migration, 2009.

Mkhize, Nhlanhla. "Ubuntu and Harmony: An African Approach to Morality and Ethics." In *Persons in Community: African Ethics in a Global Culture*. Edited by Ronald Nicolson. Scottsville: University of KwaZulu-Natal Press, 2008.

Mngxitama, Andile. "South Africa: Land Reform Blocked." *Green Left Weekly* 406. Accessed 1 November 2017. https://www.greenleft.org.au/node/22276.

Mnyaka, Mluleki, and Mokgethi Motlhabi. "Ubuntu and Its Socio-Moral Significance." In *African Ethics: An Anthology of Comparative and Applied Ethics*. Edited by Munyaradzi F. Murove. Scottsville: University of KwaZulu-Natal Press, 2009.

Moltmann, Jürgen. *God in Creation.* Translated by Margaret Kohl. Minneapolis: Fortress Press, 1993.

Monson, Tamlyn. "Everyday Politics and Collective Mobilisation against Foreigners in a South African Shack Settlement." *Africa: The Journal of the International African Institute* 85, no. 1 (2015), 131-52.

Mouffe, Chantal. *The Return of the Political.* London: Verso, 1993.

Müller, Julian C. "Postfoundational Practical Theology for a Time of Transition." *HTS Theological Studies* 67, no. 1 (2011), 1-5.

Nakayama, Thomas K., and Robert L. Krizek. "Whiteness: A Strategic Rhetoric." *Quarterly Journal of Speech* 81, no. 3 (1995), 291-309.

Nayak, Anoop. "After Race: Ethnography, Race, and Post-Race Theory." *Ethnic and Racial Studies* 29, no. 3 (2006), 411-30.

Nel, Marius. "Rather Spirit-filled than Learned! Pentecostalism's Tradition of Anti-intellectualism and Pentecostal Theological Scholarship." *Verbum et Ecclesia* 37, no.1 (2015).

Nelson, Leslie, and Colleen Warner Colaner. "Becoming a Transracial Family: Communicatively Negotiating Divergent Identities in Families Formed through Transracial Adoption." *Journal of Family Communication* 18 (2018).

Nelson, Leslie, and Haley Kranstuber Horstman. "Communicated Meaning-Making in Foster Families: Relationships between Foster Parents' Entrance Narratives and Foster Child Well-Being." *Communication Quarterly* 65 (2017).

Nelson, Leslie. "The Evolving Nature and Process of Foster Family Communication: An Application and Adaptation of the Family Adoption Communication Model." *Journal of Family Theory & Review* 9 (2017).

Neocosmos, Michael. "The Politics of Fear and the Fear of Politics: Reflections on Xenophobic Violence in South Africa." *Journal of Asian and African Studies* 43 (2008): 586-594.

———. *From Foreign Natives to Native Foreigners: Explaining Xenophobia in Post-Apartheid South Africa.* Dakar: CODESRIA, 2010.

Nepantlera: Exploring Boundaries, Edges and Borders. Blog description. Reviewed and translated by Elena Huegel, 5 October 2017. https://bettebooth.wordpress.com/about/.

Neville, Robert Cummings. *Ultimates: Philosophical Theology, Vol. 1.* Albany: SUNY Press, 2013.

Nieftagodien, Noor. "Xenophobia in Alexandra." In *Go Home or Die Here: Violence, Xenophobia and the Reinvention of Difference in South Africa.* Edited by Shireen Hassim, Eric Worby, and Tawana Kupe. Johannesburg: Wits University Press, 2008.

Onstot, Lynn Iliff. Public Information Office, Joplin, MO. http://www.joplinmo.org/DocumentCenter/View/1985.

Oswald, Sylvia, Katharina Heil, and Lutz Goldbeck. "History of Maltreatment and Mental Health Problems in Foster Children: A Review of the Literature." *Journal of Pediatric Psychology* 35 (2010).

Ouaknin, Marc-Alain. *The Burnt Book: Reading the Talmud.* Princeton, NJ: Princeton University Press, 1998.

Park, Nicholas, and Patricia Hill. "Is Adoption an Option? The Role of Importance of Motherhood and Fertility Help-Seeking in Considering Adoption." *Journal of Family Issues* 35 (2013).

Parker, Ian. "Discursive Psychology." In *Critical Psychology: An Introduction*. Edited by Dennis Fox and Isaac Prilleltensky. London: Sage Publications, 1997.

Patrick, Saint. "The Deer's Cry" (St Patrick's Breastplate). In *The Deer's Cry: A Treasury of Irish Religious Verse*. Edited by Patrick Murray. Blackrock, Co. Dublin: Four Courts Press, 1986.

Perry, Barbara, and D.R. Dyck. "'I Don't Know Where It Is Safe:' Trans Women's Experiences of Violence." *Critical Criminology*, Vol. 22: 49-63. Accessed 1 October 2018. https://www.deepdyve.com/lp//springer-journals/i-don-t-know-where-it-is-safe-trans-women-s-experiences-of-violence-ofirpn4eue.

Pertman, Adam. *Adoption Nation*. New York: Basic Books, 2000.

Peters, Ted. *God, the World's Future: Systematic Theology for a New Era*. Second edition. Minneapolis: Fortress Press, 2000.

Petzold, Andreas. *Romanesque Art*. New York: Harry N. Abrams, 1995.

Placek, Paul. "National Adoption Data." In *Adoption Factbook IV*. Edited by T.C. Atwood et al. Alexandria, VA: National Council for Adoption, 2007.

Plummer, Charles. *Bethada Náem Nérenn: Lives of Irish Saints*, Vol. 2. Oxford: Clarendon Press, 1922.

Posel, Deborah. "Races to Consume: Revisiting South Africa's History of Race, Consumption, and the Struggle for Freedom." *Ethnic and Racial Studies* 33, no. 2 (2010), 157-75.

Potter, Jonathan, Margaret Wetherell, Rosalind Gill, and Derek Edwards. "Discourse: Noun, Verb or Social Practice?" *Philosophical Psychology* 3, nos 2 and 3 (1990), 205-17.

Prestwood-Taylor, Beverly and Elena Huegel. Unpublished materials in Spanish. "*Manual de Retoños en las Ruinas: Esperanza en el Trauma, nivel 1 (curso básico)*," 33. Translated by Elena Huegel. Centro Shalom, Chile, 2013, *revisión 2017*.

Pryor, Adam. *Body of Christ Incarnate for You: Conceptualizing God's Desire for the Flesh*. Studies in Body and Religion Series. Lanham, MD: Lexington, 2016.

Rasmussen, Larry. *Earth-Honoring Faith: Religious Ethics in a New Key*. New York: Oxford University Press, 2014.

Reed, Amber R. "Nostalgia in the Post-Apartheid State." *Anthropology Southern Africa* 39, no. 2 (2016), 97-109.

Renner, Judith. "The Local Roots of the Global Politics of Reconciliation: The Articulation of 'Reconciliation' as an Empty Universal in the South African Transition to Democracy." *Millennium: Journal of International Studies* 42, no. 2 (2014), 263-85.

Richard, Lee. "The Transracial Adoption Paradox: History, Research, and Counseling Implications of Cultural Socialization." *The Counseling Psychologist* 31 (2003).

Riley, Matthew T., and Whitney Bauman. "Wicked Problems in a Warming World: Religion and Environmental Ethics." *Worldviews* 21 (2017), 1-5.

Rilke, Rainer Maria. *Duino Elegies*. New York: W.W. Norton & Co., 1978.

———. *Letters to a Young Poet*. Translated by M.D. Herter Norton. New York: W.W. Norton & Co., 1993.

Rittel, Horst, and Melvin Webber. "Dilemmas in a General Theory of Planning." *Policy Sciences* 4 (June 1973),155-69.

Robinson, Timothy. "Nurturing Hope in the Face of Ecotastrophe: Advent, Eschatology, and the Future of Creation." *Liturgical Ministry* 19 (Winter 2010), 9-20.

Rohr, Richard. *Falling Upwards*. San Francisco: Jossey-Bass, 2011.

Rowling, J. K. *Harry Potter and the Deathly Hallows*. London: Bloomsbury, 2008.

Rumi, Jalal al-Din. *Rumi: Selected Poems*. Translated by Coleman Barks with John Moynce, A. J. Arberry, and Reynold Nicholson. New York: Harper One Books, 2004.

Russell, Alec. *After Mandela: The Battle for the Soul of South Africa*. London: Hutchinson, 2009.

Russell, Robert John. *Time in Eternity: Pannenberg, Physics, and Eschatology in Creative Mutual Interaction*. Notre Dame, IN: University of Notre Dame Press, 2012.

Sacks, Jonathan. *Covenant and Conversation: A Weekly Reading of the Jewish Bible*. Volume 1. Jerusalem: Maggid Books & The Orthodox Union, 2009.

Saramago, José. *Blindness*. New York: Harcourt, 1997.

Savran, George, and Andrew Mein. *Encountering the Divine: Theophany in Biblical Narrative*. London: T. & T. Clark International, 2005.

Sayers, Dorothy. *The Comedy of Dante Alighieri: Cantica 1, Hell*. Baltimore: Penguin Books, 1949.

Schilt, Kristen, and Laurel Westbrook. "Bathroom Battlegrounds and Penis Panics." *Contexts* (20 August 2015).

Schneiders, Sandra. "The Study of Christian Spirituality: Contours and Dynamics of a Discipline." *Christian Spirituality Bulletin* 6 (Spring 1998), 1, 3-12.

Schrag, Calvin O. *The Resources of Rationality: A Response to the Postmodern Challenge*. Bloomington, IA: Indiana University Press, 1992.

Schwartz-Salant, Nathan, and Murray Stein, eds. *Liminality and Transitional Phenomena*. Wilmette, IL: Chiron Publications, 1991.

Scott, Claire. "*Die Antwoord* and a Delegitimized South African Whiteness: A Potential Counter-Narrative?" *Critical Arts* 26, no. 5 (2012), 745-61.

Scott, Sarah. "Martin Buber." Internet Encyclopedia of Philosophy. Accessed 3 February 2018. http://www.iep.utm.edu/buber/#SH2b.

Seekings, Jeremy. "Race, Discrimination and Diversity in South Africa." *CSSR Working Paper no. 194*. Cape Town: University of Cape Town, Centre for Social Science Research, 2007.

———. "Poverty and Inequality after Apartheid." *CSSR Working Paper no. 200*. Cape Town: University of Cape Town, Centre for Social Science Research, 2007.

Seidel, Linda. *Legends in Limestone: Lazarus, Gislebertus, and the Cathedral of Autun*. Chicago: University of Chicago Press, 1999.

Sheldrake, Philip. *Spaces for the Sacred: Place, Memory, and Identity*. Baltimore: Johns Hopkins University Press, 2001.

Shutte, Augustine. *Philosophy for Africa*. Cape Town: University of Cape Town Press, 1993.

"South Africa Coffin Case: White Farmers Convicted." BBC, 25 August 2017. Accessed 15 February 2018. http://www.bbc.com/news/world-africa-41052626.

Spaull, Nicholas. *South Africa's Education Crisis: The Quality of Education in South Africa 1994-2011*. Report Commissioned by the Centre for Development and Enterprise, October 2013.

Stein, Jan, and Murray Stein. "Psychotherapy, Initiation, and the Midlife Transition." In *Betwixt and Between*. Edited by Louise Cams Mahdi. La Salle, IL: Open Court Pub. Co., 1987.

Stenger, Mary Ann, and Ronald H. Stone. *Dialogues of Paul Tillich*. Macon, GA: Mercer University Press, 2002.

Stevens, Garth. "'Racialized' Discourses: Understanding Perceptions of Threat in Post-Apartheid South Africa." *South African Journal of Psychology* 28 (1998), 1-19.

Steyn, Melissa. *Whiteness Just Isn't What It Used to Be: White Identity in a Changing South Africa*. Albany: State University of New York Press, 2001.

———. "Rehabilitating a Whiteness Disgraced: Afrikaner White Talk in Post-Apartheid South Africa." *Communication Quarterly* 52 (2004), 143-69.

———. "As the Postcolonial Moment Deepens: A Response to Green, Sonn, and Matsebula." *South African Journal of Psychology* 37, no. 3 (2007), 420-24.

Steyn, Melissa, and Don Foster. "Repertoires for Talking White: Resistant Whiteness in Post-Apartheid South Africa." *Ethnic and Racial Studies* 31 (2008), 25-51.

Stifler, Kenneth, Joanne Greer, William Sneck, and Robert Dovenmuehle. "An Empirical Investigation of the Discriminability of Reported Mystical Experiences among Religious Contemplatives, Psychotic Inpatients, and Normal Adults." *Journal for the Scientific Study of Religion* 32, no. 4 (1993), 366-72.

Stone, Rabbi Ira. *A Responsible Life: The Spiritual Path of Mussar*. Eugene, OR: Wipf & Stock Pub., 2013.

Sumption, Jonathan. *Pilgrimage: An Image of Mediaeval Religion*. Totowa, NJ: Rowman & Littlefield, 1975.

Suter, Elizabeth, and Robert Ballard. "'How Much Did You Pay for Her?' Decision-making Criteria Underlying Adoptive Parents' Responses to Inappropriate Remarks." *Journal of Family Communication* 9 (2009).

Thomas, Kate Hendricks, and David Albright. *Bulletproofing the Psyche: Preventing Mental Health Problems in Our Service Members and Veterans*. Santa Barbara, CA: ABC-CLIO/Praeger, 2018.

Thomassen, Bjorn. "The Uses and Meanings of Liminality." *International Journal of Political Anthropology* 2, no. 1 (2009).

Thomassen, Lasse. "Antagonism, Hegemony, and Ideology after Heterogeneity." *Journal of Political Ideologies* 10, no. 3 (2005), 289-309.

Thweatt-Bates, Jeanine. *Cyborg Selves: A Theological Anthropology of the Posthuman*. Ashgate Science and Religion. Farnham, Surrey and Burlington, VT: Ashgate, 2012.

Tillich, Paul. *The Protestant Era*. Chicago: University of Chicago Press, 1948.

———. *Systematic Theology*, Vol. 3. Chicago: University of Chicago Press, 1963.

———. *Political Expectation*. Edited by James Luther Adams. Macon, GA: Mercer University Press, 1981.

Tomazin, Farrah. "I Am Profoundly Unsettled: Inside the Hidden World of Gay Conversion Therapy." https://www.smh.com.au/national/i-am-profoundly-unsettled-inside-the-hidden-world-of-gay-conversion-therapy-20180227-p4z1xn.html.

Torfing, Jacob. "Discourse Theory: Achievements, Arguments, and Challenges." In *Discourse Theory in European Politics: Identity, Policy and Governance*. Edited by David Howarth and Jacob Torfing. Hampshire: Palgrave Macmillan, 2005.

Tsabary, Shefali. *The Awakened Family*. New York: Penguin, 2016.

Tucker, Mary Evelyn. *Worldly Wonder: Religions Enter Their Ecological Phase*. Chicago: Open Court, 2003.

Turner, Victor. "Betwixt and Between: The Liminal Period in Rites of Passage." In *The Forest of Symbols*. Ithaca: Cornell University Press, 1967.

———. *The Ritual Process: Structure and Anti-Structure*. Chicago and New York: Aldine Publishing Company, 1969.

———. *From Ritual to Theatre: The Human Seriousness of Play*. New York: Performing Arts Journal Publications, 1982.

———. "Liminality, Kabbalah, and the Media." *Religion* 15 (1985), 205-17.

———. "Dewey, Dilthey, and the Drama: An Essay in the Anthropology of Experience." In *The Anthropology of Experience*. Edited by Victor Turner and Edward M. Bruner, with an epilogue by Clifford Geertz Turner. Urbana, IL: University of Illinois Press, 1986.

———. *The Ritual Process: Structure and Anti-Structure*. New Brunswick, NJ: Aldine Transaction Publishers, 2011.

Turner, Victor, and Edith L.B. Turner. *Image and Pilgrimage in Christian Culture: Anthropological Perspectives*. New York: Columbia University Press, 1978.

Tutu, Desmond M. *No Future without Forgiveness*. London: Rider, 1999.

United Nations High Commissioner for Refugees. *Global Trends 2012 – Displacement: The New 20th Century Challenge*. Geneva: UNHCR, 2012.

Veneranda Dies Sermon. In *The Miracles of Saint James: Translations from the Liber Sancti Jacobi*. Translated by Thomas F. Coffey, Linda Kay Davidson, and Maryjane Dunn. New York: Italica Press, 1996.

Verwey, Cornel, and Michael Quayle. "Whiteness, Racism, and Afrikaner Identity in Post-Apartheid South Africa." *African Affairs* 111, no. 445 (2012), 551-75.

Vivero, Veronica, and Sharon Jenkins. "Existential Hazards of the Multicultural Individual: Defining and Understanding 'Cultural Homelessness.'" *Cultural Diversity and Ethnic Minority Psychology 5*, no. 1(1999), 6-26.

Voight, Ellen Bryant. *Headwaters*. New York: W.W. Norton, 2013.

Vuuren, Hennie van. *South Africa: Democracy, Corruption and Conflict Management*. Centre for Development and Enterprise. Accessed 3 January 2018. http://democracy.cde.org.za/wp-content/uploads/2014/05/democracy-works-south-africa-conference-paper-democracy-corruption-and-conflict-management-by-hennie-van-vuuren-pdf-.pdf.

Waal, Esther de. "Introduction." In *Beasts and Saints*. Translated by Helen Waddell. Grand Rapids, MI: Eerdmans Publishing Co., 1996.

Waddell, Helen, trans. *Beasts and Saints*. Grand Rapids, MI: Eerdmans Publishing Co., 1996.

Wale, Kim, and Don Foster. "Investing in Discourses of Poverty and Development: How White Wealthy South Africans Mobilize Meaning to Maintain Privilege." *South African Review of Sociology* 38 (2007), 45-69.

Walsh, Brian. *Kicking at the Darkness: Bruce Cockburn and the Christian Imagination*. Grand Rapids, MI: Brazos Press, 2011.

Waters, Emily, Jindasurat, Chai, and Wolfe, Cecilia. "Lesbian, Gay, Bisexual, Transgender, Queer, and HIV-Affected Hate Violence in 2015. NY: National Coalition of Anti-Violence Programs." NCAVP Report 2015, 13-15. Accessed 1 October 2018, http://avp.org/wp-content/uploads/2017/04/ncavp_hvreport_2015_final.pdf.

Watson, Bernadette. "Intercultural and Cross-Cultural Communication." In *Inter/ Cultural Communication*. Edited by A. Kurylo. Thousand Oaks, CA: Sage, 2013.

Wenman, Mark A. "Laclau or Mouffe? Splitting the Difference." *Philosophy & Social Criticism* 29, no. 50 (2003), 581-606.

Werfel, Franz. *The Song of Bernadette*. London: Hamish Hamilton, 1942.

Wetherell, Margaret. "Positioning and Interpretative Repertoires: Conversation Analysis and Post-structuralism in Dialogue." *Discourse & Society* 9 (1998), 387-412.

White, Carolinne, trans. and ed. "Life of Paul of Thebes by Jerome." In *Early Christian Lives*. London: Penguin Books, 1998.

White, Lynn, Jr. "The Historical Roots of our Ecologic Crisis." *Science* 155, no. 3767 (10 March 1967).

White, Michael. *Narrative Practice and the Unpacking of Identity Conclusions*. Accessed on 3 Dec 2017. http://www.dulwichcentre.com.au./narrativepractice.htm.

"White Genocide Continues in South Africa." *Red Ice News*, 17 October 2017. Accessed at https://redice.tv/news/white-genocide-continues-in-south-africa.

"Whites Deserve to Be Hacked and Killed like Jews." *Politicsweb*, 6 January 2016. Accessed on 15 February 2018. http://www.politicsweb.co.za/news-and-analysis/ whites-deserve-to-be-hacked-and-killed-like-jews--.

Wildman, Wesley J. "Distributed Identity: Human Beings as Walking, Thinking, Ecologies in the Microbial World." In *Human Identity at the Intersection of Science, Technology and Religion*. Edited by Nancey Murphy and Christopher C. Knight. Burlington, VT: Ashgate, 2010.

Wood, Robert E. *Martin Buber's Ontology: An Analysis of I and Thou*. Northwestern University Studies in Phenomenology & Existential Philosophy. Evanston, IL: Northwestern University Press, 1969.

Wright, Lionel. "The Stonewall Riots." *Socialist Alternative*. https://www. socialistalternative.org/stonewall-riots-1969/. Originally appeared in*Socialism Today* 40 (July 1999).

Zola, Emile. *Lourdes*. Translated by Ernest A. Vizetelly. Reprint. Amherst, NY: Prometheus Books, 2000.

Zornberg, Avivah Gottlieb. *The Murmuring Deep: Reflections on the Biblical Unconscious*. New York: Shochen Books, 2009.

Index

You may also be interested in:

Liminal Reality and Transformational Power
Revised Edition: Transition, Renewal and Hope

by Timothy Carson

Liminal Reality and Transformational Power explores, draws together, and integrates the many facets of liminality, and informs our understanding of liminal phenomena in the world. Through anthropology, sociology, theology, neurology and psychology, Carson correlates exterior transitions with their corresponding intra-psychic movements and points toward useful methods that contribute to personal and social transformation.

In this revised edition, Carson has recognised the resurgence of liminality, and addresses the social transitions that are prevalent today in communities around the world. He examines the identity of the 'liminal' person and highlights the role of ritual leaders and religious professionals as they guide people through liminal time and space.

Carson's work greatly contributes to an expanded understanding of the complex dimensions of religious leadership and provides useful insight into our intra-psychic processes during the significant transitional stages in life.

Specifications: 234x156mm   110pp   Published 2016   PB ISBN 978 0 7188 9401 6
ePub ISBN 978 0 7188 4401 1 / Kindle ISBN 978 0 7188 4402 8 / PDF ISBN 978 0 7188 4400 4